Colombia Urbanization Review

Colombia Urbanization Review

Amplifying the Gains from the Urban Transition

Editors
Taimur Samad
Nancy Lozano-Gracia
Alexandra Panman

THE WORLD BANK
Washington, D.C.

Contents

Boxes

Figures

Maps

Tables

Foreword

Colombia Urbanization Review: Amplifying the Gains from the Urban Transition is part of a series of prototypes under a global product, called the Urbanization Review, being developed by the Finance, Economics, and Urban Development Department of the World Bank, in collaboration with regional urban units. The objective of this analytical program is to provide diagnostic tools to inform policy dialog and investment priorities on urbanization by operationalizing the framework for urban policy developed in the *World Development Report 2009—Reshaping Economic Geography* and the World Bank's new Urban and Local Government Strategy—System of Cities: Harnessing Urbanization for Growth and Poverty Reduction. To test the relevance and flexibility of the core diagnostic tools across countries at incipient, intermediate, and advanced stages of urbanization, prototype pilots are being initiated in several countries, including India (incipient); China, Indonesia, and Vietnam (intermediate); and Colombia (advanced).

At incipient stages of urbanization, policy focuses on common institutions that regulate factor markets (land in particular) and basic service delivery are the main priority. Fluid land markets (including property rights and land-use and transfer regulations) have a strong bearing on facilitating rural and urban transformations and the agglomeration of economic activities and people. Identifying regulatory barriers to changes in land use and the economic and fiscal implications of relaxing regulatory constraints should be part of core urbanization diagnostics. At the same time, identifying service gaps in the delivery of water, sanitation, and paved roads is important for improving local welfare.

As urbanization advances toward more-intermediate stages, connective extra-urban and intra-urban infrastructure become essential. Transport infrastructure that connects cities and the rural hinterlands can integrate product markets, enhance inter-regional trade, and facilitate economic specialization. Intra-urban transport infrastructure can also integrate labor markets and manage congestion. In intermediate-stage countries, the Urbanization Review aims to measure the symptoms and drivers of extra-urban and intra-urban connectivity and consider how differences in fiscal capacity and institutional arrangements contribute to these gaps.

For places in advanced stages of urbanization, targeted remedial and social interventions acquire significance because greenfield development is not possible, and urbanization may yield undesirable results, such as congestion or pollution. In many cities, government failures, such as over-regulated land markets, end up pushing households into slums. These urban systems are also characterized by large gaps between formal and informal settlements in the access to and quality of services and in the degree of vulnerability to hazards. In addition, market failures often generate negative results when individual firms and households do not consider the social costs of their location decisions, which can lock cities into emission streams and unsustainable urban forms. Remedial interventions can reduce these vulnerabilities and improve livability. Measuring the extent of these challenges and identifying alternative social interventions is likely to provide useful policy insights in countries with advanced stages of urbanization.

The Colombia Urbanization Review was implemented in two stages. The first stage, summarized in chapter 2, looked at the system of cities in Colombia and identified a series of bottlenecks that limit the efficiency of the system. Stage I identified five key topics that required further analysis to be carried out in a second stage of the Urbanization Review. These five topics were efficiency of land and housing markets, equality of opportunities across the urban portfolio (basic services), options for financing cities, interjurisdictional coordination, and connectivity between cities.

Stage II of the Urbanization Review focused only on the last three topics: connecting, coordinating, and financing. The choice of these topics was made in close discussion with the Department of National Planning, which requested that the work focus on the three topics where they felt the analytical gap was widest and the contribution of the Bank would be the greatest. This choice was made with the aim to do a policy analysis "deep dive" on core cross-cutting issues that are critical to the overall efficiency and productivity of Colombia's system of cities and across many sectors. For example, the ability to develop effective mechanisms for coordination at the regional and metropolitan levels is equally essential for the development of integrated mass transport systems, efficient land-use planning, and the provision of basic social, educational, and health services. Similarly, defining appropriate strategies to finance the enormous infrastructure gaps that Colombian cities face is applicable for structuring urban redevelopment, improving the quality of basic water and sanitation services in mid-sized and small cities, and upgrading informal urban settlements.

The choice of core themes for this report was also made with a sense of pragmatism. The range of urban challenges that Colombia faces—at an advanced stage of urbanization—are extremely broad. It is not possible to cover all these topics in an analytical report of this nature. Efficient and productive cities must also connect people to jobs and goods to consumers—through an efficient and affordable transport network. Equitable cities must also enable access to affordable land and housing through the efficient functioning of land markets and a smart housing policy. The challenges of urban environmental sustainability are also immense, requiring a range of innovative solutions, from improved energy-efficient building standards, to integrated carbon-mitigation strategies, to the effective planning and mitigation of hazard risks. Finally, larger cities in highly urbanized, middle-income countries, such as Colombia, will increasingly face the real challenge of renovating urban brownfield areas and underutilized urban spaces to maximize productive capacity. These challenges of congestion and urban transport, disaster risk management, urban environmental protection, and city redevelopment are also the subject of the World Bank's broader knowledge and lending services program of support to the government of Colombia.

This report and the associated knowledge agenda serve the critical and timely purpose of refocusing our attention on the opportunities and challenges of urbanization in Colombia. We hope the policy analysis and recommendations included herein will be of particular service to the government of Colombia in charting a path to creating more productive and sustainable cities.

Gloria M. Grandolini
Country Director, Mexico and Colombia
Latin America and the Caribbean Region

About the Editors and Contributors

Taimur Samad is a Senior Urban Specialist in the Latin America and the Caribbean Region at the World Bank. He works on public-private partnerships in land and housing development, urban redevelopment, and infrastructure finance in Brazil and Colombia. He holds a master's degree in city and regional planning from the Massachusetts Institute of Technology.

Nancy Lozano-Gracia is an economist working in the Urban and Local Government Unit of the Finance, Economics, and Urban Department. As a core team member of the Urbanization Review flagship study, she has worked in Brazil, Colombia, India, and Vietnam. She holds a Ph.D. in applied economics from the University of Illinois. Her areas of work include urban and regional economics, spatial economic analysis, spatial econometric applications, and environmental issues.

Alexandra Panman works on low-income housing, urban renovation, and integrated municipal development projects in the Latin America and the Caribbean Region at the World Bank, with a focus on Brazil and Colombia. She holds master's degrees from the University of Oxford and Johns Hopkins (SAIS).

Contributors
Chapter 2: Somik V. Lall, Nancy Lozano-Gracia, and Tito Yepes
Chapter 3: Hyoung Gun Wang and Bernadette Baird-Zars
Chapter 4: Nancy Lozano-Gracia, Alexandra Panman, and Alejandro Rodriguez
Chapter 5: Yoonhee Kim, Alexandra Panman, and Alejandro Rodriguez

Acknowledgments

This report has been prepared by a team led by Taimur Samad (task team leader [TTL]) and Nancy Lozano-Gracia (co-TTL), and consisting of Yoonhee Kim, Hyoung Gun Wang, Somik V. Lall, Alexandra Panman, Henry Jewell, Bernadette Baird-Zars, and Alejandro Rodriguez. The team also acknowledges the following consultants, whose reports served as inputs for this work: Pablo Roda, Francisco Perdomo, Francisco Rodriguez Vitta, Tito Yepes, Juan Benavides, Mauricio Olivera, Oscar Arboleda, Claudia Patricia Quintero (Fedesarollo), Robert Yaro, and Nicolas Ronderos (RPA). The team also benefited from early contributions from Fabio Sanchez Torres and Irina España Eljaiek (CEDE).

This report reflects several rounds of discussions with the National Planning Department (Departament Nacional de Planeación, DNP). We appreciate the support and helpful comments of Juan Mauricio Ramírez Cortes, José Alejandro Bayona Chaparro, José Antonio Pinzón Bermudez, Augusto Cesar Pinto Carrillo, and others. The continued support and guidance of DNP was critical for this analysis.

The team is grateful for peer review from Shomik Raj Mehndiratta, Thomas Kenyon, Songsu Choi, and Andres Cadena (McKinsey). Helpful comments and guidance were also provided by Ede Jorge Ijjasz-Vasquez,

Daniel Sellen, Geoffrey H. Bergen, Abha Joshi-Ghani, Paloma Anos Casero, Harold L. Bedoya, David Sislen, and Guang Zhe Chen.

This report was produced with support from the Swiss State Secretariat for Economic Affairs (SECO) and the Spanish Fund for Latin America and the Caribbean (SFLAC).

Abbreviations

AMVA	Metropolitan Area of Aburrá Valley (*Area Metropolitana del Valle de Aburrá*)
ANI (formerly INCO)	National Infrastructure Agency (*Agencia Nacional de Infraestructura*) (formerly *Instituto Nacional de Concesiones*)
BCOM	Egis BCEOM International (*Bureau Central d'Etudes pour les Equipments d'Outre-Mer*)
BRTS	Bus Rapid Transit System
CAF	Andean Finance Corporation (*Corporación Andina de Fomento*)
CAR	Regional Autonomous Corporation (*Corporación Autónoma Regional*)
CECM	Metropolitan Coordination Executive Committee (Mexico)
CEPAC	Certificates of Additional Building Potential
CIF	cost, insurance, and freight
CNC	National Competitiveness Commission (*Comision Nacional de Competitividad*)
CONFIS	National Fiscal Council (*Consejo Superior de Política Fiscal*)

CONPES	National Economic and Social Policy Council (*Consejo Nacional de Política Económica y Social*)
CPS	Country Partnership Strategy
CUA	*Communaute d'Aglomeration* (France)
DAK	*Dana Alokasi Khusus*
DANE	National Bureau of Statistics (*Departamento Administrativo Nacional de Estadística*)
DEA	Data Envelopment Analysis
DIAN	Directorate of Taxes
DNP	National Planning Department (*Departamento Nacional de Planeación*)
DP	Development Plan
EMT	Metropolitan Transit Organization (Spain)
EPM	*Empresas Públicas de Medellín*
ETESA	Territorial Company for Health (*Empresa Territorial para la Salud*)
FINDETER	Financial Support for Territorial Development S.A. (*Financiadora del Desarrollo Territorial*)
FIS	*Fondo de Cofinanciación para la Inversión Social*
FNA	National Savings Fund (*Fondo Nacional de Ahorros*)
FOB	free on board
FONPET	National Fund for Pensions of Territorial Entities (*Fondo Nacional de Pensiones de las Entidades Territoriales*)
FOSYGA	Guarantee and Solidarity Fund (*Fondo de Solidaridad y Garantía*)
FSI	floor space index
FUNDREM	Foundation for the Development of the Metropolitan Region (Brazil)
GDP	gross domestic product
GLA	Greater London Authority (United Kingdom)
GoC	government of Colombia
GRT	gross receipts tax
GTSB	Greater Toronto Services Board (Canada)
HDM-IV	Highway Development Management Model
HHI	Herfindahl-Hirschman Index
IDB	Inter-American Development Bank
IFC	International Finance Corporation

IGAC	Augustin Codazzi Geographic Institute (*Instituto Geográfico Augustín Codazzi*)
INCODER	*Instituto Colombiano para el Desarrollo Rural*
INVIAS	National Roads Institute (*Instituto Nacional de Vias*)
LOOT	Territorial Ordering Act (*Ley Orgánica de Ordenamiento Territorial*)
MAVDT	Ministry of Environment, Housing, and Territorial Development (*Ministerio del Ambiente, Vivienda y Desarollo Territorial*)
MDF	Municipal Development Fund
MLGFI	market-based local government financial intermediary
MPO	Metropolitan Planning Organization (United States)
MVCT	Ministry of Housing, Cities, and Territories (*Ministerio de Vivienda, Ciudad y Territorio*)
NBI	Unsatisfied Basic Needs (*Necesidades Básicas Insatisfechas*)
NDP	National Development Plan
NUTP	National Urban Transport Program
OECD	Organisation for Economic Co-operation and Development
PANYNJ	Port Authority of New York and New Jersey (United States)
PDR	purchase development rights
PDWP	Project Development Work Program (United States)
PISA	Programme for International Student Assessment (OECD)
PMIB	Program for Neighborhood Improvement (*Programa de Mejoramiento Integral de Barrios*)
PNL	National Logistics Policy (*Política Nacional Logística*)
POT	Territorial Ordering Plans (*Plan de Ordenamiento Territorial*)
PPIAF	Public-Private Infrastructure Advisory Facility
PPP	public-private partnership
PTP	Policy for Productivity Transformation (*La Política de Transformación Productiva*)

RPA	Regions for Planning and Administration
RPG	Regions for Planning and Management
RTP	Regional Transportation Plans (United States)
SGP	System of National Transfers (*Sistema General de Participaciones*)
SICEP	*Sistema de Información para Captura de la Ejecución Presupuestal*
SNC	National Competitiveness System (*Sistema Nacional de Competitividad*)
SNTA	Sub-National Technical Assistance
TDR	tradable development rights
TE	territorial entity
TFP	total factor productivity
TIDD	Tax Increment Development District
TIF	tax increment financing
TIP	Transportation Improvement Program (United States)
TTL	task team leader
UO	Urban Operations
VOC	vehicle operating cost
WB	World Bank
WDR	*World Development Report* (World Bank)
WSS	water supply and sanitation
ZEIS	Special Zones of Social Interest (*Zonas Especiales de Interes Social*)
ZMVM	Metropolitan Area for the Valley of Mexico (Mexico)

CHAPTER 1

Introduction

Setting the Table: Macroeconomics and Cities in Colombia

The efficiency and productivity of Colombia's urban system will be a key determinant in the ability of the country to transition from a middle-income to a higher-income economy. Colombia, as with most Latin American countries, has experienced positive growth rates in the past few years, mitigating the potential adverse impacts of the global financial crisis. High commodity prices as well as improvements in macroeconomic and financial management, diversification of trading partners (particularly through stronger links with China), and the safe integration into international financial markets are the main drivers for recent success in Colombia and the Latin American region (World Bank 2011).

The Colombian economy is highly dependent on commodities.[1] The mining sector represents more than 7 percent of Colombian gross domestic product (GDP), and manufacturing represents only 13 percent. Most importantly, while some countries in the region such as Argentina, Brazil, and Uruguay have diversified away from commodity exports, this diversification has not taken place in Colombia. Colombia is, consequently, as vulnerable to changes in commodity prices today as it was 50 years ago. If anything, this vulnerability might have increased because Colombia has shifted away from agricultural exports (from over

50 percent in the 1970s to less than 10 percent today) and toward energy (from less than 5 percent to over 50 percent in the same period), which is particularly vulnerable to a global slowdown. Despite the change in the composition of exports, in terms of value, Colombia's exports have remained stagnant for over 50 years. Per capita exports have barely doubled since the 1960s, compared to countries such as Brazil and Chile, where exports per capita have grown to nearly 10 times their 1960s level (Hausmann and Klinger 2008).

Urban activities are also an important factor in Colombia's growth. GDP growth in Colombia was 4.3 percent in 2010, up from a low 1.5 percent in 2009 in the aftermath of the global financial crisis. Approximately 11 percent of GDP growth can be attributed to mining industries. In addition, approximately 6 percent of GDP growth can be attributed to commerce, restaurants, hotels, and related services and 4.9 percent to manufacturing sectors. Conversely, the agricultural sector did not contribute to growth. Despite the large growth in commodities, urban activities[2] have contributed to more than 50 percent of the GDP's growth rate[3] in the last 4 decades.

Colombia is a highly urbanized country—75 percent of the population lives in cities. The country's economic landscape is dominated by the cities of Bogotá, Cali, Medellín, and Barranquilla. These cities account for 30 percent of the country's population and a high proportion of its jobs (map 1.1). There is also a growing number of small and midsized cities in the urban portfolio—the number of cities with more than 100,000 inhabitants grew from 9 in 1951 to 33 in 2006.

In this economic and demographic context, the urban system in Colombia will play a critical role in supporting growth in three principal forms. First, the contribution of urban activities to urban growth is not negligible when all urban activities are added. Second, strengthening the roles of cities might contribute to mitigating the risks inherent to commodity-intensive economies. Recent work by the World Bank points to the risks of commodity-led growth. While there is no evidence of a commodity curse in Colombia, the World Bank work identifies several commodity-related risks that, if not managed correctly, can adversely affect a country's prospects for economic and institutional development (World Bank 2010a). As Colombia aims for a higher income trajectory, an efficient urban system will be necessary to support the move from a commodity-driven economic system to a stronger resource-based manufacturing structure, and then to more knowledge-intensive industries, following the evolution of some of today's high-income countries

Map 1.1   Distribution and Concentration of Jobs in Colombia

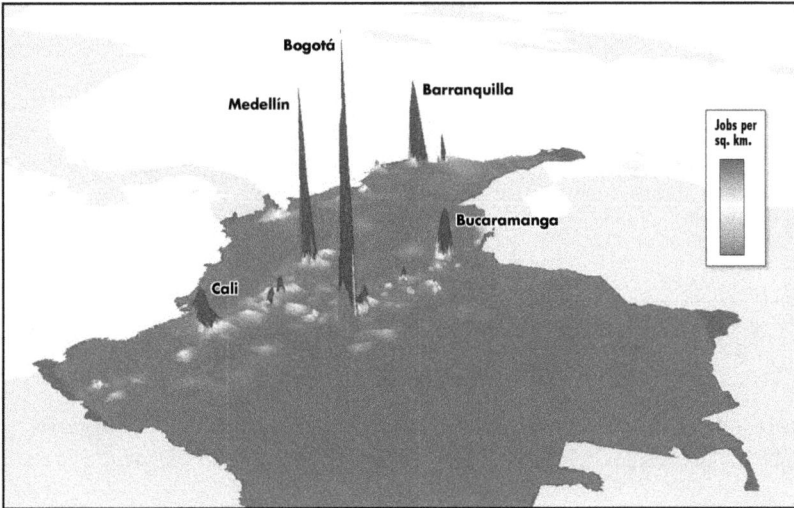

Source: World Bank 2010b; DANE Census 2005.
Note: sq km = square kilometer.

(Australia, Canada, Scandinavian countries, and the United States) (Blomström and Zejan 1991; de Ferranti et al. 2002). Third, today, more than three-quarters of Colombians live in urban areas, where unemployment rates are above 12 percent—among the highest in the region. Therefore, promoting a well-functioning urban system may foster growth and improve the quality of life of a largely urban population.

Efficient Cities Are Essential for Putting Colombia on an Inclusive Growth Path

The efficient management of cities and urban areas will be the key determinants of whether Colombia will be able to cash in on a potential growth dividend to reduce poverty and inequality. Historically, urbanization is highly correlated with reductions in poverty and inequality and improvements in access to basic services.[4] Colombia is no exception to this rule. Figure 1.1 shows that lower poverty rates are highly correlated with the levels of urbanization in a department.[5]

Urbanization has been inclusive—growth has been accompanied by improved living conditions across the country. In 1964, only 50 percent of people in today's largest cities had access to electricity, water, and sanitation. In smaller cities, the coverage rates approximated

Figure 1.1   Urbanization Contributes to Poverty Reduction

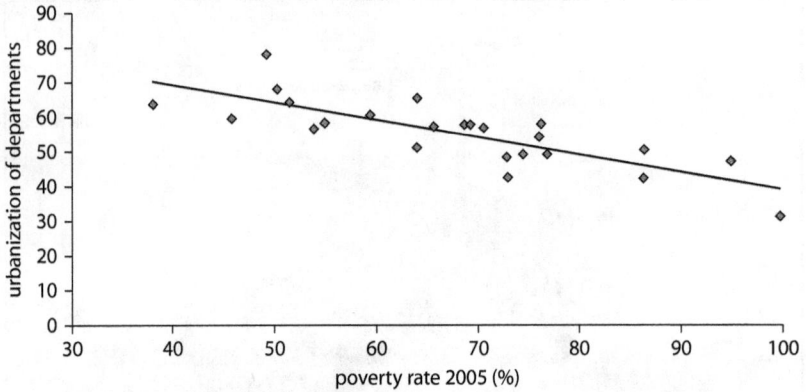

Sources: DANE (Departamento Administrativo Nacional de Estadística) census 2005, DNP (Departamento Nacional de Planeación).

Figure 1.2   Evolution of Access to Services Based on City Size

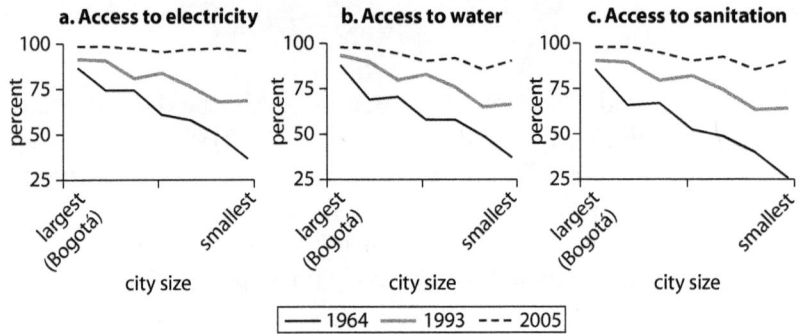

Sources: DANE census 1964, 1993, and 2005.
Note: The years in the graph reflect census years. Additional censuses were carried out in 1973 and 1985 but are not included in the graph because of space constraints.

40 percent for water and electricity and 20 percent for sanitation. Today, there is almost universal access to basic services in cities of all sizes (figure 1.2).

Decentralization has helped to reduce the gaps between urban and rural access to services, as well as in health and education (Sanchez 2006). However, differences persist, particularly in terms of access to secondary education, which remains at 55 percent in rural areas, compared to 75 percent in urban areas. Additional incentives are therefore needed to amplify and extend the benefits of urbanization to rural areas.

Colombia's Urban Challenge—Connecting, Coordinating, and Financing

What are the key drivers that will enable the urban system in Colombia to cash in on its growth dividend? This book focuses on three key priorities across the system of cities in Colombia—reinforcing the need to deepen economic connectivity, enhance coordination on a regional and metropolitan scale, and foster efficiency and innovativeness in how cities finance themselves. The fundamentals of connecting, coordinating, and financing are the factors that will, in large part, determine whether Colombian cities can drive an economic transition from high-risk commodity- and natural resource–driven growth to a more-balanced model characterized by increasingly more productive, innovative, and diversified manufacturing and service sectors.

The drivers of connecting, coordinating, and financing are by no means an exhaustive list of the challenges faced by Colombian cities. As outlined in chapter 2, Colombian cities confront a range of development challenges, including congestion, natural hazards, social inequality, and economic competitiveness. This study, however, chooses to focus on in-depth analysis of the three core issues identified previously. Additional development challenges omitted in the in-depth analysis are nonetheless being studied in parallel work by either the World Bank or the national government.[6] For example, the ability of cities to capture the benefits of agglomeration through knowledge spillovers, innovation, and productivity gains also depends on the quality of human capital and the educational and technological infrastructure across the public, private, and academic sectors. Efficient and productive cities must also connect people to jobs and goods to consumers—through an efficient and affordable transport network. Equitable cities must also enable access to affordable land and housing through the efficient functioning of land markets and a smart housing policy. The challenges of urban environmental sustainability are also immense, requiring a range of innovative solutions from improved energy-efficient building standards, to integrated carbon-mitigation strategies, to the effective planning and mitigation of hazard risks. In addition, larger cities in highly urbanized middle-income countries, such as Colombia, will increasingly face the challenge of renovating urban brownfield areas and underutilized urban spaces to maximize productive capacity.

The challenges of connecting, coordinating, and financing vary in intensity, scale, and nature across small, midsized, and large cities.

While connectivity is most typically a challenge for countries at intermediate stages of urbanization, Colombia lags behind in terms of connective infrastructure. Connectivity for smaller cities is critical to improve the potential for trade with midsized and large cities and reduce economic isolation. For midsized cities, improved economic linkages might encourage specialization and improved trade with both diversified urban agglomerations and external markets. Improved connectivity for large cities may enable them to move from a currently autarkic economic structure to regional networks of midsized and small cities, exploiting economic complementarities. Finally, connecting large cities to international markets is also a critical challenge in Colombia, given the increasing importance of external trade and the high logistics costs for primary inland cities.

In highly decentralized countries in Latin America—where a wide range of responsibilities for land use planning, social services, and infrastructure investment are vested in municipalities—the challenges of coordination are significant. Similarly, coordination challenges vary across the urban system. The efficiency and productivity of larger cities is strongly linked to their ability to coordinate land use and strategic and structural investment planning across these boundaries (for example, the development of logistics platforms to enable more-efficient movement of goods or regional investments for flood and hazard risk mitigation). Midsized cities have an opportunity to anticipate emerging coordination challenges associated with, for example, the development of integrated mass transit systems or the structuring of metropolitan-level water and sanitation utilities. Conversely, small municipalities face considerably fewer coordination challenges. Nonetheless, small towns and municipalities could benefit from a more-formal framework for interjurisdictional cooperation to address specific issues as they arise.

Urban infrastructure investment is vital for productive and inclusive cities, and the challenges of meeting infrastructure financing gaps vary by city size. Smaller municipalities are highly dependent on transfers from the national government and require technical assistance and a more-explicit incentive framework to improve the efficiency of transfers and to assemble "building blocks" for greater local revenue effort. Midsized cities also confront the challenges associated with increasing the efficiency of transfers. These municipalities—with a greater potential tax base than smaller cities—would greatly benefit from fiscal and sector performance-based incentives in the transfer system. Midsized cities also require support to develop a more-diversified and sophisticated framework for investment planning—building on the lessons of larger cities and relevant regional and international experience. Large cities perhaps face the most-complex financing challenges. Infrastructure gaps are monumental, in part caused by inefficient or reactive metropolitan land use and transport planning. Larger cities must continue to intensify tax effort and build capacity with a wide range of innovative and sophisticated financing instruments within the context of a coherent financing strategy.

This book takes a differentiated approach to diagnostic work and policy recommendations across this "system of cities" and focuses on the important role of the national government in structuring policies across sectors to increase the efficiency of the urban system. It also emphasizes the importance of learning from regional and international experience and includes "deep" case studies and reviews of international practice as a strategy to inform policy choices for Colombia.

This book is organized as follows: chapter 2 concentrates on establishing patterns and trends of the spatial and urban transformation in Colombia. Key policy issues for Colombia's urbanization process are highlighted and policy alternatives considered. It also attempts to identify areas where further in-depth analysis would be valuable. Three of these areas are further developed in chapters 3 through 5. The remainder of this chapter will highlight key messages from each of the three crosscutting themes of connectivity, coordination, and finance. The chapter will conclude with a discussion on the World Bank's strategic engagement strategy for sustainable cities.

Connecting Cities

Message 1: Colombian cities are poorly connected to internal and external markets. Colombia's geography poses serious challenges for interregional transport. Many studies have noted how the natural and economic geography poses a particular challenge for transport in Colombia, with references in the literature appearing as early as 1927 (Renner 1927; Stokes 1967). A relatively large number of cities are dispersed across mountainous terrain and far from coastal ports. Bogotá, the country's primary production center, is more than a day's drive from the Atlantic and Pacific coasts, where agricultural products for export, fossil fuels, and raw materials are concentrated. Many imports and exports are processed in maritime ports. Consequently, freight travels long distances in Colombia. A 2006 study showed that freight distances in Colombia were almost three times those in Brazil and Chile, five times those in Malaysia, and six times those in Argentina, China, and the Republic of Korea.

In Colombia, economic distances exacerbate physical distances (table 1.1). Inefficiencies in infrastructure and transportation, coupled with a difficult terrain, lead to high costs of moving goods across Colombia. A comparison of internal transport costs to international transport costs of goods can illustrate how expensive it can be to move goods between Colombian cities. It costs US$94 to move one ton from Bogotá to the Atlantic coast and US$88 to move one ton to Barranquilla. This compares to US$75 to ship goods from the coast to the United States or US$60 from Buenaventura to Shanghai. These high internal costs undermine the competitiveness of goods produced in Colombia's largest cities, when compared to other large cities of the world.

In Colombia, logistics costs represent, on average, 18.6 percent of the total value of company sales. While this is lower than the 21 percent observed in Mexico, logistics costs in Colombia are larger than the average in the Andean Region, Central America, and the United States (see figure 1.3) (World Bank 2005).

Message 2: High economic distances are a drag on growth and competitiveness. International experience confirms the critical linkage between competitiveness and connectivity. The success of local and regional economies, from an urban systems perspective, is closely linked to their connectivity with domestic and international markets. With Colombia's unique city locations, the connection between industrial competitiveness and inter-regional transport costs is especially strong.

Fragmentation and low inter-regional trade, as well as under-exploited trade and industrial potential, characterize Colombian cities and regional economies. Additionally, there is a high concentration of resources, human capital, and industrial bases in the area with the highest transport costs—

Table 1.1   Road Freight Costs, by Origin-Destination
US$ per ton

Origin-destination	Bogotá	Medellín	Cali	Other regions
Barranquilla	88	71	111	91
Cartagena	94	68	116	96
Santa Marta	83	79	106	88
Buenaventura	54	56	16	75
Cúcuta (to Venezuela, RB)	79	81	108	97
Ipiales (to Ecuador)	91	94	47	103

Source: Roda and Perdomo 2011.

Figure 1.3   Logistics Costs in Colombia

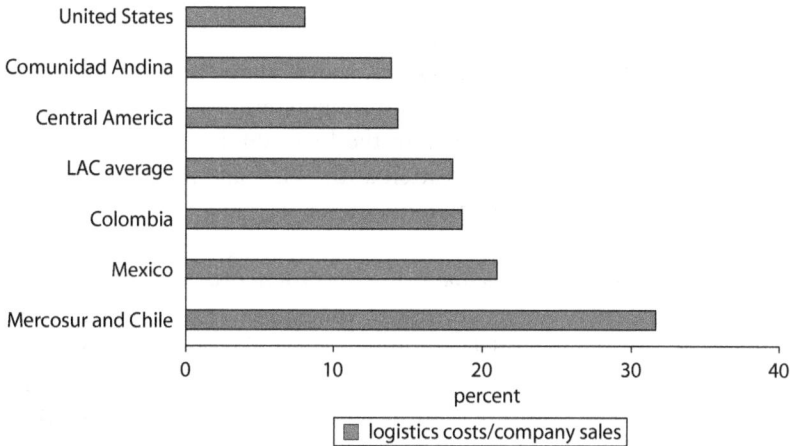

Source: World Bank 2005.
Note: LAC = Latin America and the Caribbean.

the Andes Corridor. Accordingly, recent economic indicators highlight shifts in growth and investment from the three largest Andean cities—Bogotá, Medellín, and Cali—to coastal areas characterized by lower transport costs. Lowering transport costs along key trade corridors is an important way of realizing the unexploited economic potential of the Colombian urban system. Further, lack of alternative transport modes and modal competition undermines the efficiency of inter-regional transportation.

Message 3: Connecting cities increases the economic efficiency of the urban system. Improving the international connectivity of large Andean cities is extremely important, because GDP growth and investment are gravitating toward the trade centers on the coasts or adjacent regions with easier access to international markets, with the Andean urban system increasingly being left out of the global economy. Improving connectivity between large Andean cities and coastal regions would be a win-win strategy for the national economy.

Lowering transport costs will catalyze growth and improve overall efficiency across the system of cities in Colombia. In addition to boosting local GDP growth, preliminary empirical analysis performed in this review suggests that reductions in transport costs would have a significant positive effect on inter-regional trade. Other studies have found similar results in terms of the impact of reduction in transport costs on exports.

Lowering transport costs may create new economic opportunities in local and regional economies that have not emerged yet—favoring specific economic regions over others. However, the overall benefit of reducing transport costs to Colombia's system of cities will be positive. The benefits of transport infrastructure improvements are not limited to direct savings in vehicle operating costs. In the long run, lower transport costs will facilitate industrial specialization at the local and regional levels and catalyze growth across the system of cities.

Message 4: Improved connective infrastructure across modes and in key corridors is critical to reduce transport costs. Improving the intermodality of transport in Colombia might lead to considerable transport costs reductions. The current lack of alternative transport modes to long-distance trucking on major trade corridors reduces competition and efficiency. Modal sharing may lead to considerable savings because the ton per kilometer costs of rail and river in Colombia are estimated to be about half of the ton per kilometer costs by truck. Furthermore, fostering intermodality might also lead to lower congestion and lower costs because of competition.

A preliminary simulation analyzing the competitiveness of three modes (truck, rail, and rivers) was conducted for this book. The simulation found that under the assumption of direct access to marine terminals (figure 1.4, panel a) rail is more competitive than river transport, and these two modes are more competitive than road transport.[7] The difference in transportation costs widens as the trip distance increases. If the simulation is modified

Figure 1.4   Simulation of Freight Transport Costs in Different Modes
US$ per ton-km

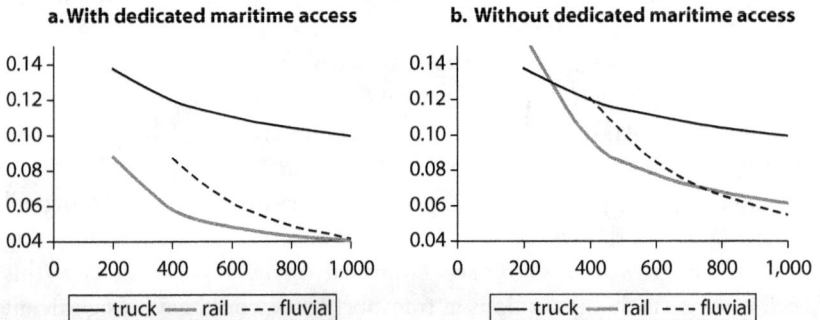

a. With dedicated maritime access

b. Without dedicated maritime access

— truck — rail - - - fluvial

Source: Roda and Perdomo 2011.
Note: km = kilometer.

to recognize the lack of direct access to marine terminals (as is the case for Barranquilla and Cartagena by rail and Santa Marta by river), the simulation suggests trucking is the most cost-effective mode for distances under 300 kilometers. However, for medium distances the most cost-effective mode is rail, while for distances beyond 700 kilometers, river transport is more cost-effective (figure 1.4, panel b). Distance from Bogotá to the Atlantic Coast is approximately 1,000 kilometers, suggesting a significant benefit from greater modal diversity.

This book also uses a demand-side approach to look at trade flows along five major corridors, with the objective of identifying potential, strategic connectivity investments. This demand-side approach indicates that there are two corridors that are medium-term investment priorities: the corridor along the eastern mountain chain, connecting Bogotá to the Atlantic Coast ports, and the route connecting the highlands to the Pacific ports (from Bogotá to Buenaventura). The demand models used in this assessment factor in existing pipeline investment (for example, Ruta del Sol along the Bogotá–Atlantic Coast Corridor). Even when these investments are factored in, demand growth projections suggest significant congestion on these critical routes as early as 2020. Further analyses to determine the feasibility and costs of each of the investment alternatives would be required to supplement this demand-side approach.

Reduction of transport costs because of intermodal competition and overall connectivity investment will probably alter the distribution of trade across the system of cities. It will also open new opportunities for products and places, which were constrained by the barrier of high costs. The book recommends that—rather than focusing on "picking winners and losers" in terms of places and products—national policy should aim at reducing market and government failures. In this case, market failures related to the provision of infrastructure act as barriers to trade among Colombian cities and between Colombian cities and the rest of the world.

Coordinating Cities

Message 1: Improved regional and metropolitan coordination positions cities to respond to the urban growth challenge. Colombia is one of the most-highly decentralized countries in Latin America. Over 1,000 municipal governments in Colombia have identical responsibilities for basic infrastructure service delivery, land use, economic development planning, and the provision of social services. However, natural economic forces—such as access to affordable land—drive firms and households outside of municipal boundaries, creating an urban footprint that is much larger than the administrative borders. The metropolitan area of Bogotá, for example, covers seven municipal jurisdictions (Bogotá, La Calera, Chía, Cota, Funza, Mosquera, and Soacha) and has a population of approximately 8.2 million inhabitants.

Coordination can foster economies of scale in service provision, and help mitigate the negative externalities associated with rapid urbanization. In large and midsized cities, water, sewerage, solid waste management, electricity, and transport networks frequently span several administrative boundaries in a metropolitan area. Organizing provision and management at a regional level can help harness efficiency gains. Coordination can also prevent the wasteful duplication of policies and jurisdictional competition. The benefits of coordination can range from preventing regional epidemics that might erupt out of limited access to treated water in one jurisdiction, to reducing congestion and pollution by developing integrated road transportation systems across jurisdictions. Efforts to improve the coordinated delivery of services across different levels of government and between jurisdictions could also have an important impact on the quality of service in intermediate and small urban areas.

Coordinated land use and investment planning on a regional or metropolitan scale is also critical for the productivity of urban systems. Metropolitan areas in Colombia currently face crippling inertia and bottle-necks in terms of planning land use and strategic investment. The benefits of coordinated land use include the development of productive and logistics infrastructure, structural drainage and flood protection infrastructure, and the efficient spatial organization of economic activities.

Despite the clear benefits that might arise from interjurisdictional coordination, strong political economy incentives discourage the delivery of coordinated services and planning across administrative boundaries. In decentralized systems, such as Colombia, local administrators and politicians face strong disincentives in facilitating coordinated regional action on these challenges. Strong resistance often emerges to aggregation or any "clawing back" of power and responsibility from the municipal level. The government has an important role in aligning incentives and fostering coordination among local governments.

Message 2: The role of the national government is to build a framework and create the right incentives for coordination. As highlighted in this review, international experience demonstrates that national governments and urban areas have successfully responded to changing conditions by reforming interjurisdictional coordination arrangements. The role of national governments in these cases has been to build a framework and create the right incentives for coordination. This role might include strengthening metropolitan governance structures through capacity building, expanding metropolitan competencies, regulating and promoting cooperation structures, and developing coordinated projects between the national and regional governments. Positive financial incentives can be a forceful instrument in promoting coordination in Colombia. This review outlines international experience from Germany and the United States, which used financial incentives to coordinate regional infrastructure investments.

Efforts to address interjurisdictional coordination are particularly timely in light of the new legal reforms. The new law regulating spatial planning—Ley Orgánica de Ordenamiento Territorial (LOOT)—responds to the need to develop a clear institutional framework to support the aggregation of municipal functions and coordination between territorial entities. The law opens new space for voluntary collaboration in institutional interjurisdictional arrangements and enables the formation of organizational entities (commissions) to collaborate on territorial planning issues. The law potentially resolves the legal uncertainty that had hindered the implementation of many previous coordination instruments. It does not, however, go as far as to establish clearly defined coordination responsibilities. The pending regulation of LOOT will serve as a critical opportunity for the government to ensure the new legal framework has the ability to "claw back" excessive decentralization.

Financing Cities
Message 1: Midsized and small cities must strengthen fiscal fundamentals. Municipal tax collection has increased with decentralization and administrative reforms across all categories of cities. However, midsized and small cities have not kept pace with larger cities in their ability to increase local revenues (see figure 1.5). The capacity of the municipality to raise real property taxes is closely connected to the efficiency of the cadastral system; there is a positive correlation between real tax revenue and the accuracy of the cadastral system. Large cities have more-comprehensive land cadastres. Bogotá, for example, has attained 100 percent registration of land. In comparison, only 43 percent of all rural area in Colombia is included in the system. Only three cities in Colombia (Bogotá, Medellín, and Cali) have independent cadastre offices and all others are handled at the national level.[8]

Figure 1.5   Per Capita Municipal Taxation, 1995–2009

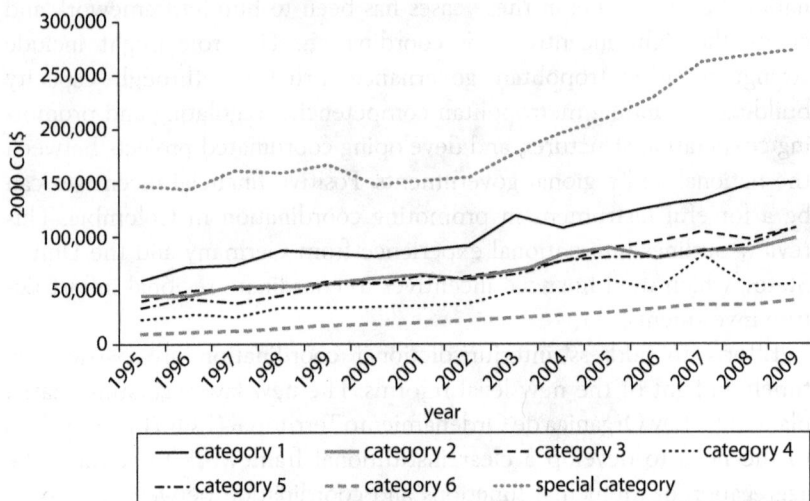

Source: SICEP.
Note: Law 617 of 2000 established seven categories of municipality in Colombia based on population and earnings. For a full description of this categorization, please see table 5.1 in chapter 5.

There is considerable variation in the main sources of funding for investment across the different municipal categories. Larger cities have greater resources for investment than cities in the other municipal categories, both in per capita and absolute terms—and these funds are predominantly self-generated. Approximately 70 percent of the revenues of small municipalities come from national transfers, compared to about 30 percent for the largest municipalities. Heavy reliance on transfers in smaller municipalities might weaken accountability as the political costs of raising the funds are born at national level and not directly where they are spent. This is important because quality of service remains a major challenge in Colombia. Earmarking transfers for spending on particular sectors might not be sufficient to ensure quality improvements, without mechanisms to measure the effectiveness of the investments. Excessive reliance on earmarking could also have the negative effect of encouraging "fiscal laziness," because municipalities lack the incentive to raise revenue and direct it to specific local needs. Additionally, evidence suggests that heavy reliance on transfers can lead to inefficient spending. Recent work by the National Planning Department (Departamento Nacional de Planeación, DNP) found evidence that funds from *regalias* (royalties) and transfers from departments to municipalities were correlated with less-efficient education and health expenditure (World Bank 2009)[9].

A strong push is required to strengthen the fiscal fundamentals for midsized and small cities. This might be done through increased capacity building in municipal fiscal management, strengthening local cadastral systems *and* the structuring of fiscal and performance incentives within the national transfer system.

Message 2: Midsized and large cities must continuously innovate with financial instruments. In the face of considerable infrastructure finance gaps, midsized and large cities must find new and innovative ways to finance urban infrastructure. Cities will require broad and diversified strategies to finance themselves, including increasing access to municipal bonds and credit markets, accessing municipal development funds and specialized financial intermediaries, and elaborating on existing land-based financing instruments. Colombia is a leader in land-based financing instruments in Latin America. However, these innovative land-based financing instruments have had limited "penetration" beyond Colombia's large cities—where they have also run into capacity and technical constraints. Midsized and large cities should aim to work through and collaborate on these methodological challenges, rather than discard the instruments.

Midsized and large cities should also innovate with new instruments for infrastructure financing, adapting international and regional experience to the Colombian context. This review provides a wide range of suggestions for possible instruments, including the analysis and application of instruments as diverse as tradable development rights (TDRs), land sales and leases, tax increment financing (TIF), and the structuring of public-private partnerships (PPPs) for urban redevelopment and renovation. These recommendations are not exhaustive of all potential innovations. This review strongly recommends that large and midsized cities foster and renew a culture of innovation in infrastructure finance to find solutions appropriate for their development challenges.

Message 3: The national government has a broad role—strengthen core local government capacity, link transfer systems to performance and strategic investments, and incubate innovation. There is a clear need for increased monitoring and evaluation of the efficiency of municipal investment. Improving the efficiency of investment is vital for addressing the significant challenge posed by the low access to and low quality of services experienced in Colombia, outside of the largest cities. More-systematic data recording of expenditures could facilitate the measurement of investment and provide more-concrete evidence on what institutional strengthening efforts could be beneficial to improve the quality of investments. Monitoring and evaluation would also clarify what the impacts of specific conditions, such as earmarking, are on the efficiency of investment.

The government may also consider developing and deepening efforts to support fiscal capacity at the municipal level—targeting assistance strategically within the "system-of-cities" approach. Efforts might include programs to develop municipal cadastres in midsized cities, targeting technical assistance across the system of cities in investment planning and fiscal management, and working with midsized cities on municipal creditworthiness.

The government may choose to analyze and develop greater performance-based incentives within the System of National Transfers (*Sistema General de Participaciones*, SGP) framework. Output- and performance-based incentive systems that focus on sector outcomes can potentially improve the efficiency and effectiveness of SGP transfers and overall municipal investment. Performance-based systems have been implemented in a wide range of developed and developing countries and—when appropriately designed—can create real incentives for subnational governments to improve performance in targeted sectors or in response to strategic priorities within sectors. The government might also consider developing fiscal and management performance incentives for the SGP framework. Linking a portion of the transfer system to improved municipal fiscal or fiscal management performance (for example, updating cadastral systems, increasing property tax revenues, or improving effective tax effort) can mitigate the negative externalities that the transfer system may cause.

The government also has a unique opportunity to structure the regional development fund within the context of the Royalties Law (*Ley de Regalias*) to create the right incentives for strategic investment planning and development. Allowing this fund to be a formula-driven transfer to departments would only reproduce past errors in the royalties system. The royalties fund for regional development should be designed with strong performance-based criteria, filter investment priorities through a strong "system-of-cities" technical framework, and create incentives for effective cooperation across municipalities and between departments.

This book makes a strong case for enhancing innovation in the financing of urban infrastructure. The government could play a critical role in fostering innovation in how cities finance themselves. The government may consider providing greater assistance to the piloting and application of the innovative financing instruments discussed above. Specifically, the government could provide support to large and midsized cities to "fine-tune" and replicate land-based financing instruments, such as *plus-valía* (capital gains) and *valorización* (valorization). The government might also support efforts to regulate the methodological aspects of existing instruments to provide clarity for municipalities. Additionally, the government could consider analyzing the regulatory aspects of innovative financial instruments, such as transferable development rights (for example, the Brazilian Certificates of Additional Building Potential [CEPACs]) or TIF, and supporting the piloting of such instruments in larger cities.

Colombian Policy Response and the Bank's Programmatic Engagement Framework for Sustainable and Productive Cities

The Government of Colombia (GoC) has outlined a comprehensive platform to address identified urban challenges. Two successive National Development Plans (NDPs) have established clear priorities for urban development. These priorities are contextualized within the 2005 "Livable Cities" strategy, which focused on creating access to affordable urban land and housing, improving water and sanitation service delivery, and increasing the affordability and availability of urban transport.

In response to the global financial crisis, the GoC has implemented an aggressive, countercyclical public investment program to stimulate growth, increase employment, and improve access to infrastructure and services. Investments to stimulate the low- and middle-income residential real estate sector were a key component of this strategy. The construction, residential rental, and real estate service sectors constituted a combined 15.5 percent of GDP in 2007. It has been noted that the countercyclical investment program reinforced growth and employment in these sectors.

To address the housing deficit in Colombian cities, the GoC has committed to enabling the construction of 1 million houses in the 2010–14 NDP period. Toward this objective, the Ministry of Housing, Cities, and Territories (MVCT) has developed an ambitious package of policy reforms, programs, and incentives, both on the demand and the supply side of the housing equation. These initiatives include a substantial demand subsidy program, interest rate subsidies for mortgage lending to low-income households, and targeted housing subsidies for internally displaced populations. Additionally, the government continues to support the growth of the savings-linked low-income mortgage lending product through the Fondo Nacional de Ahorros (National Savings

Fund, FNA), which to date, has over 350,000 participating clients. Finally, the MVCT has outlined an ambitious reform agenda to be implemented in 2011/12 to further deepen support and incentives for the low-income housing sector. These include the development of rental housing subsidies and the regulation of the new Macroproyectos Program law passed in 2011.

More broadly, the Santos Administration has passed, or has under development, a series of important structural reforms that will potentially have a significant impact on the productivity and efficiency of Colombia's system of cities. In 2011, the government passed the *Ley Orgánica de Ordenamiento Territorial*, which creates a legal framework for voluntary collaboration across subnational jurisdictions to collaborate on regional planning and investment programs. Also in 2011, the government passed the *Ley de Regalías*, which reforms the national royalties program, including the creation of a dedicated fund to finance strategic regional investment priorities. The government also created the National Infrastructure Agency (ANI)—formerly the Instituto Nacional de Concesiones (INCO)—with expanded responsibilities and a targeted capacity-building program to manage the government's concessions program across a range of sectors in the logistics network, for example, airports, ports, and toll roads.

A range of additional critical reforms are also underway, including the development of a legal framework on PPPs, which will regulate PPPs in infrastructure and social sectors, and a law on metropolitan areas, which will aim to strengthen the fiscal and planning functions of metropolitan agencies. The effective development and regulation of this broad reform program has been a major focus of the GoC in 2011 and 2012.

The World Bank's strategic and programmatic engagement aims to support the creation of sustainable and productive cities through integrated interventions in housing, land, and transport. The Country Partnership Strategy (CPS) for the period 2012–16 sets out a results-focused package of support, grouped under three strategic themes: (1) expanding opportunities for social prosperity (including enhanced social promotion, improved citizens' security, improved opportunities in education, and improved performance of social services); (2) sustainable growth with enhanced climate change resilience (including improved sustainable urban development, enhanced disaster risk management and improved environmental management and climate change resilience); and (3) inclusive growth with enhanced productivity (including improved fiscal, financial and social risk management, improved public sector management and equity and efficiency of economic policies, and improved productivity and innovation). The CPS supports the NDP through a portfolio of financial, knowledge, and convening services.

The Sustainable and Productive Cities engagement of the urban sector is anchored in the Bank's CPS and is well positioned to support the government strategic objectives. The main pillars of this thematic engagement are: (1) land and housing markets; (2) interjurisdictional coordination; (3) improved competitiveness and connectivity across the urban system; (4) innovative infrastructure finance; and (5) extending of access to quality services.

Notes

1. South America is the most commodity-dependent subregion in Latin America.
2. Commerce, restaurants, hotels, manufacture, financing, and other services to support, among others.
3. Urbanization review calculations based on a moving average of the component of the economy's growth rate contributed by purely urban activities.
4. See World Bank (2009).
5. Colombia has 32 regions or *departamentos*. These are referred to as *departments* throughout the book. A full description of the roles and responsibilities of departments is provided in chapter 4.
6. For further details on the process of choosing these three topics, see the Foreword.
7. It was assumed that trucks carry the load directly from the factory gate to the seaport. In the first graph, a truck transports a load to a hypothetical railway station located in the metropolitan area. The railroad in this scenario directly downloads the product on the marine terminal. Loads are assumed to be transported 200 kilometers by truck, for fluvial transport because none of the major Colombian cities are located on the banks of the rivers. Fluvial loads are assumed to transfer directly to the seaport, without a further modal shift.
8. The department of Antioquia has an independent cadastre, for a total of four entities that are independent from the national cadastre.
9. See discussion in chapter 5 and World Bank 2009.

Bibliography

Blomström, M., and M. Zejan. 1991. "Why Do Multinational Firms Seek Out Joint Ventures?" *Journal of International Development* 3 (1): 53–63.

de Ferranti, D., G. Perry, D. Lederman, and W. Maloney. 2002. *From Natural Resources to the Knowledge Economy*. Washington, DC: World Bank.

Hausmann, R., and B. Klinger. 2008. "Achieving Export-led Growth in Colombia." Center for International Development and HKS Faculty Research Working Paper Series (182 and RWP08-063), John F. Kennedy School of Government, Harvard University, Cambridge, MA.

IMF (International Monetary Fund). 2011. *Regional Economic Outlook: Western Hemisphere, Shifting Winds, New Policy Challenges.* Washington, DC: International Monetary Fund.

Renner, G. T. 1927. "Colombia's Internal Development." *Economic Geography* 3 (2): 259–64.

Roda, P., and F. Perdomo. 2011. "Costos de transporte y eficiencia económica en Colombia: Revisión del proceso de urbanización en Colombia. Fase II." Background study for chapter 3 of this volume, "Competitiveness and Connectivity across the Colombian Urban System" by Hyoung Gun Wang and Bernadette Baird-Zars.

Sanchez, F. 2006. "Descentralización y Progreso en el Acceso a los Servicios Sociales de Educación, Salud y Agua y Alcantarillado." Documentos CEDE 002287, Universidad de los Andes–CEDE, Bogotá.

Stokes, C. J. 1967. "The Freight Transport System of Colombia, 1959." *Economic Geography* 43 (1): 71–90.

World Bank. 2005. *Infraestructura Logística y de Calidad para la Competitividad de Colombia.* Washington, DC: World Bank Group.

———. 2009. "Colombia Decentralization: Options and Incentives for Efficiency." World Bank, Washington, DC.

———. 2010a. *Natural Resources in Latin America and the Caribbean Beyond Booms and Busts?* Washington, DC: World Bank.

———. 2010b. *Reshaping Colombia's Economic Geography through Local Institutions.* Washington, DC: World Bank.

———. 2011. *LAC Success Put to Test.* Washington, DC: World Bank.

CHAPTER 2

Amplifying the Gains from Urbanization

Somik V. Lall, Nancy Lozano-Gracia, and Tito Yepes

Taking Stock

Seventy-five percent of Colombians live in urban areas, up from 31 percent in 1938. Thirty percent of the national population is concentrated in Bogotá, Cali, Medellín, and Barranquilla. Thirty-three additional cities have populations of more than 100,000 people (see box 2.1). However, the portfolio of cities also includes many areas at an incipient stage of urbanization; almost 30 percent of the country's municipalities have urbanization rates below 25 percent.

By 2005, Colombia reached an advanced level of urbanization. Bogotá is currently home to more than 20 percent of the country's urban population—16 percent of the total population—and more than 10 times its population in 1951. Medium and large cities continue to expand throughout Colombia's urban system. By 2005, four cities boasted over 1 million inhabitants, three cities had populations between 500,000 and 1 million, and 33 cities had between 100,000 and 500,000 inhabitants. These 40 cities consist of more than 68 percent of the urban population (figure 2.1).

This chapter summarizes the results from Phase One of the *Colombia Urbanization Review*. The *Colombia Urbanization Review* is part of a series of prototypes for the Urbanization Review, a global product being developed by the Department of Finance, Economics, and Urban Development of the World Bank.

Box 2.1

City Class Definition and Distribution

This chapter categorizes municipalities into seven classes, according to their urban population figures (derived from the 2005 Census). Under this categorization, the city of Bogotá constitutes a class of its own, with over 7 million inhabitants. The remaining six classes are as follows:

1. Urban population ≥ 1 million and < 4 million
2. Urban population ≥ 500,000 and < 1 million
3. Urban population ≥ 100,000 and < 500,000
4. Urban population ≥ 50,000 and < 100,000
5. Urban population ≥ 20,000 and < 50,000
6. Urban population < 20,000

The absolute size of Colombian cities has increased across the urban portfolio. Since the 1950s, the relative rank of Colombia's largest cities has remained stable. Bogotá and Class 1 cities, such as Medellín, Barranquilla, and Cali continue to be the country's most-populous cities. However, the number of cities with populations over 100,000 has increased substantially. As the figure 2B.1 shows, the number of cities with more than 100,000 inhabitants rose from 9 in 1951 to 33 in 2006. The growing number of cities and the fact that approximately 75 percent of Colombia's population lives in cities render an urban lens that is essential for policy analysis.

Figure 2B.1   The Evolution of Cities with More Than 100,000 Inhabitants

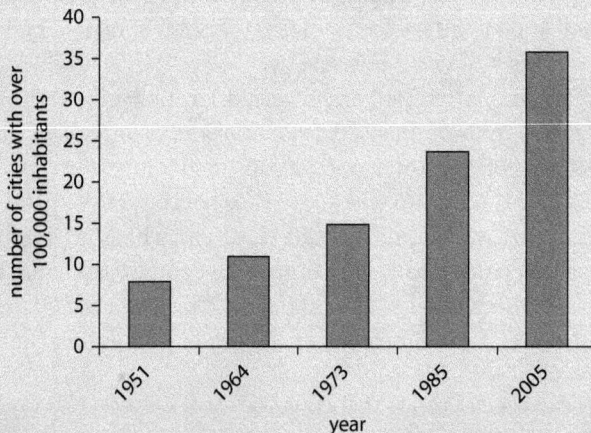

Source: DANE Census.

Figure 2.1   Urban Population Is Highly Concentrated in Few of the Largest Cities

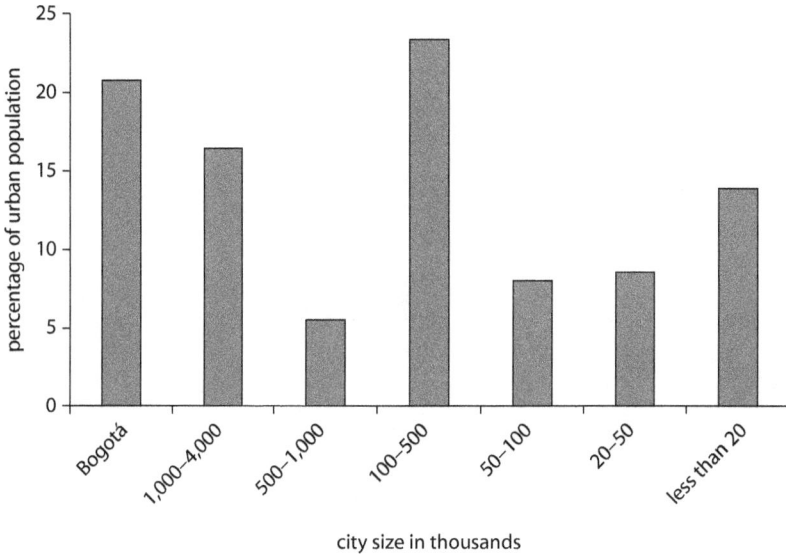

city size in thousands

Source: DANE Census 2005.

Bogotá, Cali, and Medellín, located in the Andean region, are Colombia's major economic hubs. Seventy-five percent of the national gross domestic product (GDP), excluding mining-related activities, are concentrated in the departments where these cities are located. Map 2.1 further illustrates the dominance of these three cities in terms of economic density. The map shows jobs for square kilometer, using jobs reported in Departamento Administrativo Nacional de Estadística (DANE) 2005 census, divided by land area. It is expected that the effect noted would be accentuated if other components of economic value added were included.

Colombian cities have high population densities and are centers of growth. Bogotá, Medellín, and Bucaramanga rank among the world's 50 most-densely populated cities. Decades of sustained urbanization gradually increased the concentration of people and jobs, consolidating economies of scale and agglomeration (figure 2.2). The urban economy has made major contributions to Colombia's economic progress. Building on industry and services, the urban sector has contributed to more than 50 percent of the GDP growth over the past 40 years.

However, high population densities have not been matched by commensurately high economic densities. For instance, a comparison of actual building densities with legally permitted densities in cities such as Bogotá

Map 2.1   Jobs Are Concentrated in the Largest Cities

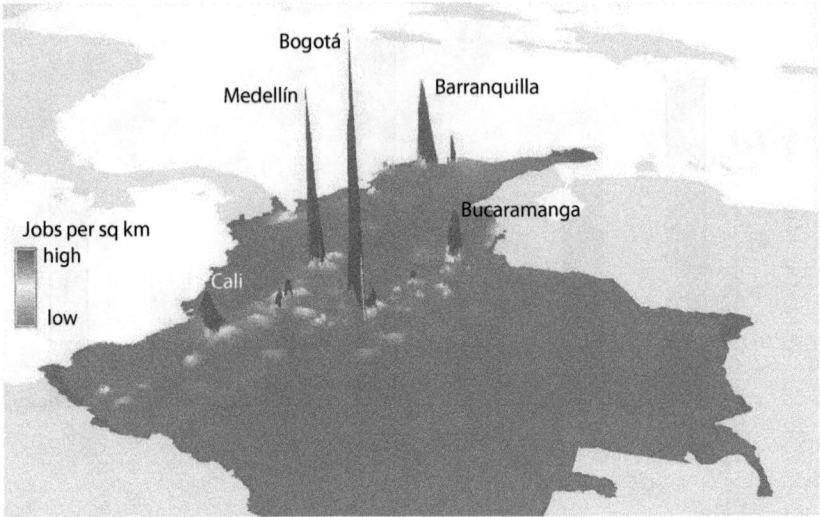

Sources: World Bank 2010a; DANE Census 2005.

Figure 2.2   Urban Population Density and Growth

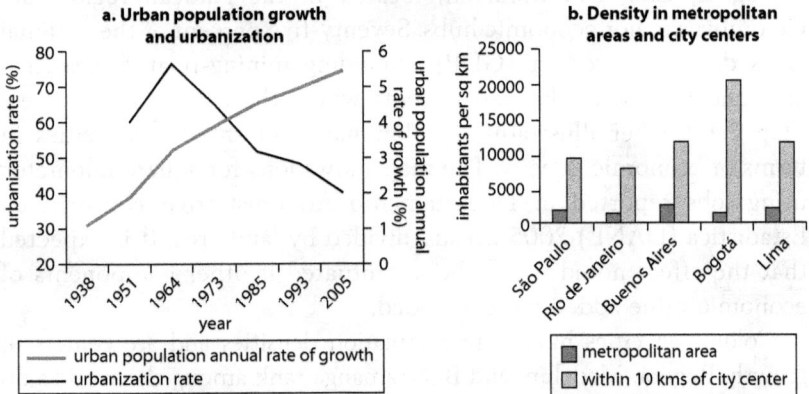

Sources: DANE; Urban Age 2009.
Note: km = kilometer; sq km = square kilometer.

shows considerable underuse of available land. In 2010, 63 percent of commercial space, 53 percent of residential space, and 54 percent of industrial space in Bogotá were underused.

When organized by economic specialization, the urban portfolio falls into two distinct groups: large cities with highly diversified economies and a few moderately specialized, medium-sized cities. Lack of specialization results in cities that do not perform their intended function in the system. While there is a strong correlation between specialization and city size, Colombian cities have low specialization rates overall. This can be seen in figure 2.3, which measures the importance of a sector in a city's economy using Herfindahl indices. When there is only one sector in a city, the Herfindahl index equals 1; if no single sector dominates the economy, it approaches 0. More specifically, an index greater than 0.1 is considered moderately specialized, while indices of 0.8 and above are highly special-ized. As the figure demonstrates, medium-sized Colombian cities are considered to be specialized, with Herfindahl indices above 0.1, while the four largest Colombian cities are more diversified, with Herfindahl indices below 0.1. The city of Cúcuta appears to be a special case, with an index that suggests high specialization. The figure also includes Cundinamarca to illustrate the differences between the municipality of Bogotá proper and its surrounding, urbanized areas. In addition, the figure shows that all cities became further specialized between 1997 and 2008. Given the his-torically low production of complementary goods and services in Colombia's cities, increased specialization is a positive sign.

Colombian cities find it difficult to transform their productive bases, slowing the dynamic development of new hubs of production. Data from González (2007) and manufacturing surveys suggest that patterns

Figure 2.3   City Diversity and Specialization

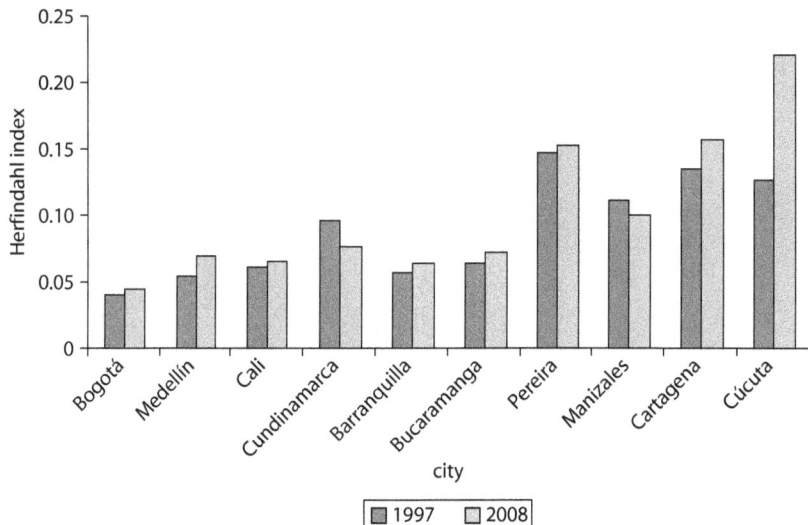

Source: Calculated Herfindahl indices using data from DANE's Manufacturing Survey.

of specialization are more than three decades old. In fact, no substantial changes have been observed in specialization patterns since 1977 (figure 2.4).

Compared to other Latin American countries, Colombia's urban system enjoys a relatively balanced concentration of economic activity across its largest cities. Figure 2.5 shows the national GDP share attributable to 29 main cities in the region. Each of these cities accounts for at least 1 percent of the national GDP. Argentina and Chile's national GDP is concentrated in specific cities. The economy of Buenos Aires constitutes 46 percent of the national GDP, making it more than five times larger than that of Rosario, the second-largest city in Argentina. Likewise, the economy of Santiago, at 31 percent of the national GDP, is more than five times the economy of Chile's second-largest city, Concepción. Colombian concentration patterns are similar to those seen in Brazil and Mexico. Mexico City's share of the national GDP is 3.1 times larger than that of Monterrey's, while São Paulo's share is 2.3 times larger than that of Rio de Janeiro's. Similarly, Bogotá's share of the Colombian GDP is only 2.5 times larger than that of Medellín's. To

Figure 2.4   Localization Index

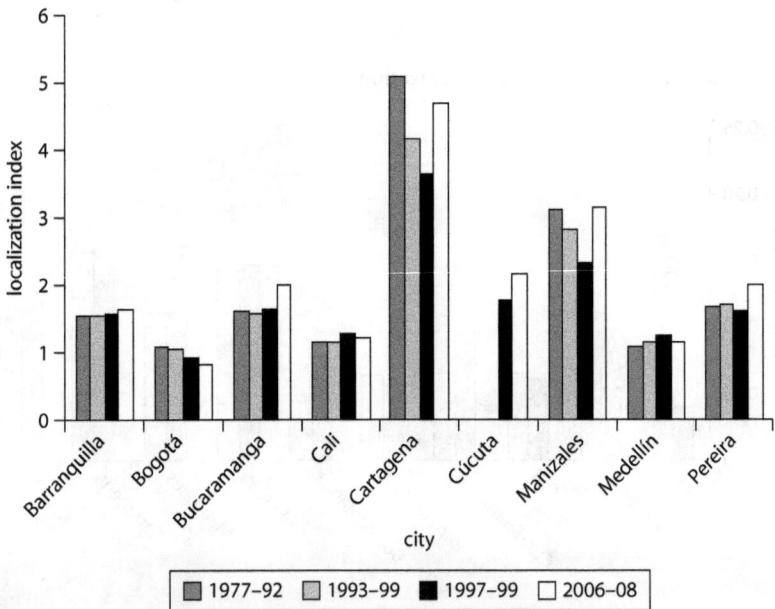

Sources: Based on data from DANE and indicators calculated by González 2007.

Figure 2.5   Share of GDP in the Main Cities of Selected Countries

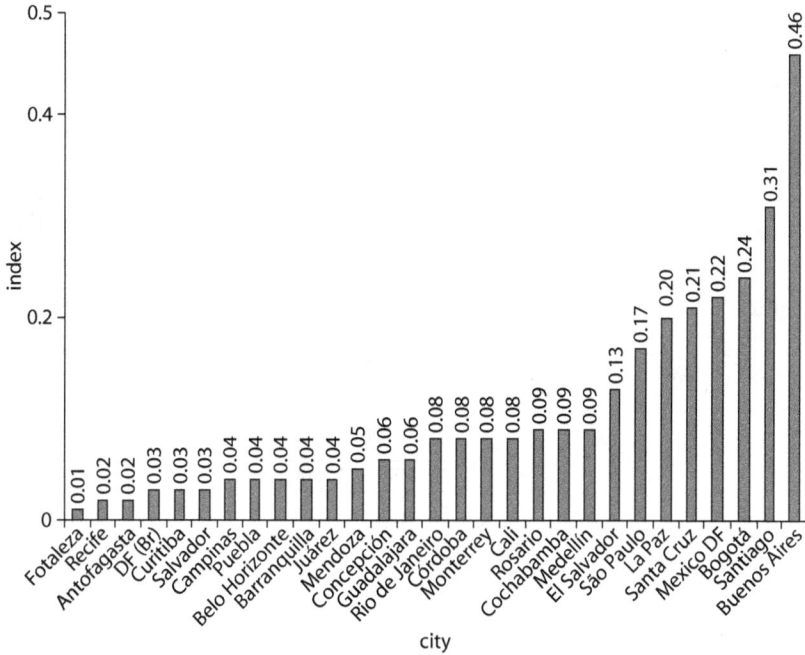

Sources: Instituto Nacional de Estadística Geografía e Informática de México 2000, 2004; Instituto Nacional de Estadísticas y Censos de Argentina 1993, 2001; Instituto Brasileiro de Geografia e Estatística 2004; Instituto Alexander Von Humboldt 2003 y Departamento Administrativo Nacional de Estadística de Colombia 2003; and Sistema Nacional de Información Municipal de Chile 2006.
Note: DF = *Distrito Federal* (Federal District); GDP = gross domestic product.

summarize, Colombia's economic production and population are relatively dispersed compared to Argentina and Chile's.

The economies of large cities mirror Bogotá's economy; smaller cities are more specialized in manufacturing. An index of symmetry was calculated using the Annual Manufacturing Survey. The index compares each sector's share in the total manufacturing value added between two cities. If the share of a given sector is the same in both cities, they are said to have similar productive bases. The index consists of the sum of the squared differences between shares. When cities have very similar productive bases, their index is close to zero. Cities with entirely different bases have an index closer to one. Figure 2.6 compares some of the productive structures of the main cities with those of Bogotá. While larger cities tend to be very similar, smaller cities have more-specialized manufacturing bases. More importantly, between

Figure 2.6   Index of Symmetry between Bogotá and Other Colombian Cities

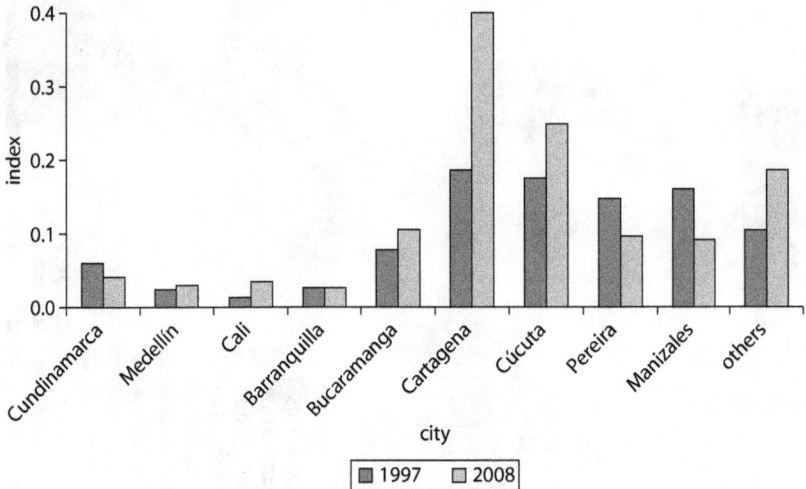

Source: Based on DANE's Manufacturing Survey 1997, 2008.

1997 and 2008, most cities had become less similar to Bogotá. This indicates the possibility of increased specialization, which would be a movement in the desired direction. Exceptions to this trend include the cities in the coffee-growing highlands and Cundinamarca, which attracted some of Bogotá's firms.

The lack of inter-regional trade in the urban system affects exports. Instead of engaging in complementary economic activities, cities compete with one another. An analysis of regional economic interaction in Colombia's seven subregions suggests that the competition between cities results in negative relationships between regional economies, as indicated in table 2.1. Consequently, the growth in one subregion leads to a decrease in the shares of trade of other subregions. In terms of external trade, export-oriented firms are driven toward the Atlantic Coast and smaller agglomerations, where they have better access to the import of inputs.

Cities have been the engines of Colombia's economic growth, but they have been slow to increase productivity. Over the past 40 years, cities have contributed more than 50 percent to GDP growth. Figure 2.7, panel b, shows the moving average of the contribution of urban activities to the rate of economic growth. Between 2000 and 2004, GDP growth in large and mid-sized cities has been 1 percent higher than national growth, contrary to trends in countries such as Brazil and Mexico, where nonurban

Table 2.1   Competitive and Complementary Relationships between Colombia's Subregions

	North-Central	South-Central	Caribbean	Pacific	New Departments	Bogotá	West-Central
Caribbean	+	+	+	+	−	−	−
North-Central	+	−	−	−	−	−	−
New Departments	−	−	−	−	+	−	−
West-Central	−	−	−	−	−	−	−
South-Central	−	−	−	−	−	−	−
Pacific	−	−	−	−	−	−	+

Source: Bonet 2003.
Note: A positive sign indicates a complementary relationship; a negative sign indicates a competitive relationship.

Figure 2.7   Economic Contributions by Cities

a. Contribution to growth from medium-sized and large cities

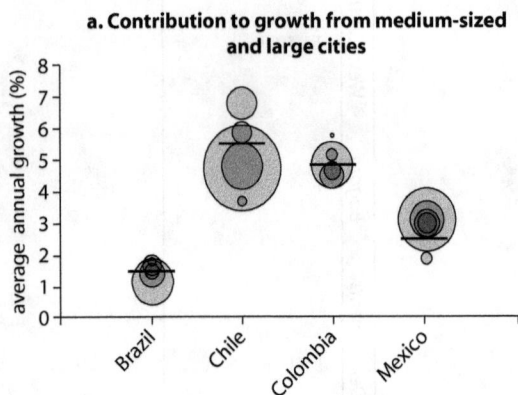

Source: Based on data from the National Statistical Offices and the Humboldt Institute, Colombia.

b. Urban sector service GDP per capita

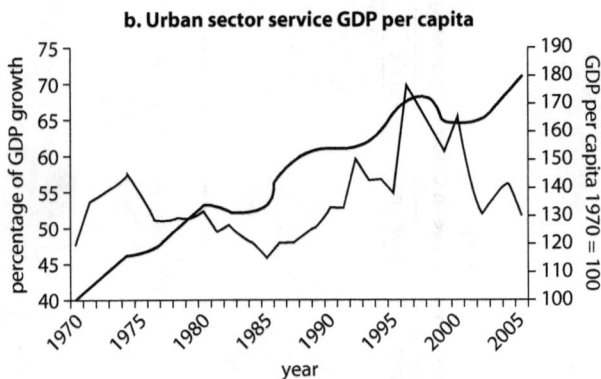

Source: Based on data from DANE.
Note: GDP = gross domestic product.

sectors are more dominant. This trend is visible in figure 2.7, panel a, in which circle size represents city size; the center of the circle indicates a growth rate between 2000 and 2004, and the lines highlight national GDP growth. The growth rates suggest that urban sectors, such as nontraditional manufacturing, contribute significantly to the economy, while the influence of small cities remains limited.

Total factor productivity (TFP) growth rates are relatively low. Between 1971 and 2005, TFP growth rates averaged 1.5 percent per year. As figure 2.8, panel b, indicates, this growth rate compares poorly to other countries in Latin America. A 1.5 percent average is comparable to TFP growth rates seen in Sub-Saharan Africa and is considerably lower

Figure 2.8   Comparative Productivity of Colombian Cities

a. TFP by city: average and growth, 1992–2002

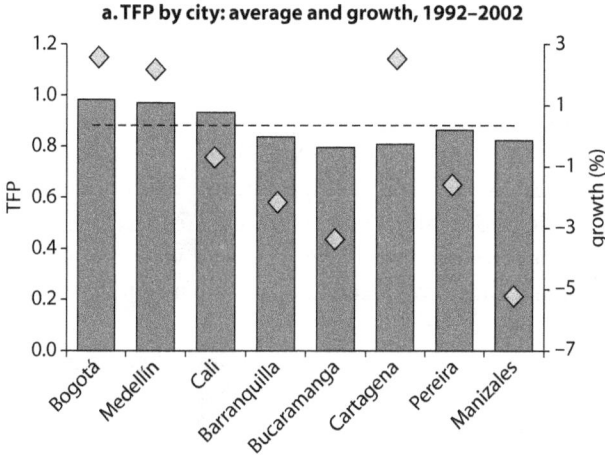

Source: World Bank 2008.
Note: TFP = total factor productivity.

b. Percentage change in TFP for selected Latin America and the Caribbean Countries, 2001–05

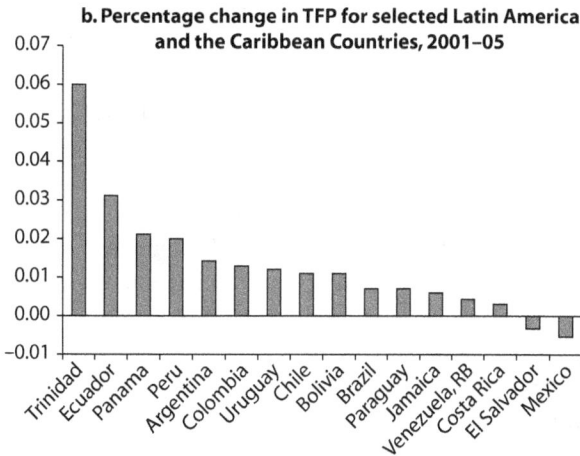

Source: Lopez and Guasch 2007.
Note: TFP = total factor productivity.

than East Asian (3.8 percent) and Organisation for Economic Co-operation and Development (OECD) (92.8 percent) rates. Bogotá has the highest productivity of Colombian cities, and the wages and value-added shares of other cities have decreased in comparison with the capital. The relative productivity of Colombian cities can be seen in figure 2.8, panel a, where the TFP for each city is divided by the TFP for Bogotá. The diamonds represent growth rates between 1992 and 2002.

Constraints Facing the Colombian System of Cities

After taking stock of Colombia's urban portfolio, it is important to understand the constraints that Colombian cities face. The key constraints in delivering gains from urbanization often stem from: (1) regulations that negatively impact land markets and impose barriers to rural-urban transformation or urban expansion; (2) government investments in health, education, water, sanitation, transport, and communication; and (3) planning decisions by government agencies that can bias resource allocation both across the urban portfolio as well as within individual cities. Identifying these constraints is the first step toward defining a set of policy priorities for urbanization.

The sections that follow will first examine whether institutions that regulate factor markets and deliver basic services have laid the foundations for high-quality urbanization. Then, the chapter will investigate if extra- and intra-urban infrastructures are amplifying localization economies. Finally, it will identify remedial and social interventions that could enhance livability and sustainability by offsetting government and market failures.

Land Use Planning and Coordination Could Amplify Economic Density and Productivity in Colombian Cities

Land use planning problems limit the capacity of large cities to exploit their economic density. In particular, limited coordination—between Territorial Ordering Plans (*Planes de Ordenamiento Territorial*, POTs), which are spatial planning instruments, and development plans, which are sectoral planning instruments—slows down Colombia's economic transformation. While POTs are designed to guide medium- to long-term investments and land regulations, development plans focus on the near term and reflect the preferences of elected officials. As a result, higher densities permitted by zoning regulations often do not translate into development permits because the departments determining the location of supporting infrastructure might have different priorities. Indeed, in Bogotá, it takes about four years to acquire approvals to consolidate land for business projects.

Lack of coordinated land use planning also exacerbates qualitative and quantitative housing deficits, particularly in poorer areas. In Cali, for example, the qualitative housing deficit was 6.8 percent in the three poorest *comunas*, contrasting with only 2.5 percent in the three richest *comunas*. In the poor areas on the periphery of Barranquilla, over 16 percent of households lack access to adequate shelter compared to 7 percent of households in the inner city. In the poorest area of Bogotá, Ciudad Bolívar, 11 percent of households experience a qualitative housing deficit compared to 2.9 percent in the wealthy neighborhood of Usaquén.

Improved administrative and interjurisdictional organization is key to enhance coordination between spatial and sectoral planning. Improving coordination between spatial and sectoral planning could include the operationalizing multilayer planning already articulated in POT Law 388/97. POTs are to serve as macro plans for the entire city, with a focus on urban function and form. POTs could also guide neighborhood development, defining land use regulations as well as giving priority to areas and functions identified in the development plans.

Effective coordination would improve the quality of basic services and livability across the urban portfolio. In Colombia, urbanization has been inclusive; growth has been accompanied by improved living conditions across the country. In 1964, only 50 percent of people living in today's largest cities had access to electricity, water, and sanitation. In smaller cities, the coverage rates were lower, at approximately 40 percent for water and electricity and 20 percent for sanitation. Today, cities of all sizes have nearly universal access to basic services (see figure 2.9). The index for Unsatisfied Basic Needs (NBI) has declined continuously across cities of all sizes, and departmental-level data points to a negative relationship between poverty and urbanization. As figure 2.10 indicates, more urbanized departments, where larger portions of the total population live, also have lower poverty rates.

Figure 2.9   Evolution of Access to Services Based on City Size

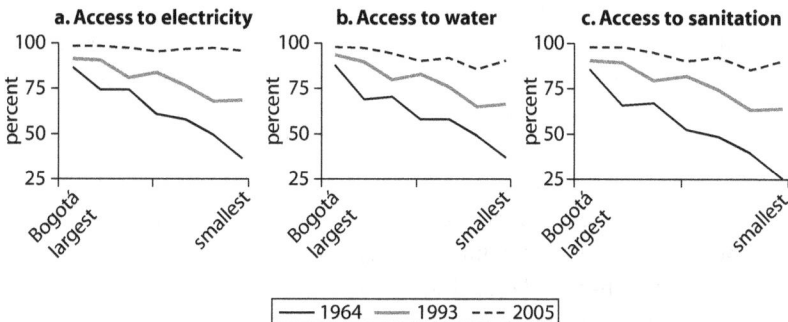

Sources: DANE Census 1964, 1993, and 2005; World Bank data.
Note: The years on the graph reflect Census years. Additional Censuses were carried out in 1973 and 1985 but are not included in the graph because of space restrictions.

Figure 2.10   Urbanization's Contribution to Poverty Reduction

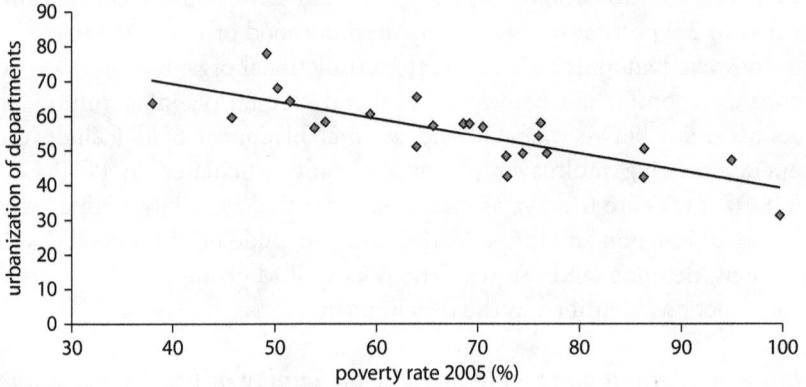

Source: DANE Census 2005, DNP.

Policies, particularly decentralization, have brought about major improvements that go beyond basic services. Sanchez (2006) suggests that decentralization has led to improved access to both health and education. While the gap between urban and rural areas in terms of access to primary education has decreased, differences persist between access to secondary education in urban areas (75 percent) and in rural areas (55 percent).

Colombian cities have nearly universal access to primary education, but access to high school remains low, even in the largest cities. Looking at the gross coverage rate of high school education, the high school deficit in Colombian cities appears to be below 20 percent on average. Cartagena and Medellín stand out as good examples, with deficits of less than 5 percent, a level comparable to the Republic of Korea. Bucaramanga is the only city in Colombia where supply exceeds demand (figure 2.11).[1] Low access to high school might be a powerful factor that prevents household growth into upper-middle-income bracket. Lack of access is a barrier to an educated workforce and limits the availability of the qualified labor required for productive activities with higher returns.

However, high levels of access to basic services do not necessarily translate into quality services, which still lags behind international standards. Water quality is high in large cities, with just a few exceptions. The index of risk for human consumption is quite low for the largest cities. For cities such as Santa Marta Pereira, Villavicencio, and Pasto, risk levels are above 15 percent (Consejo Privado de Competitividad 2008). Nonetheless,

Figure 2.11   High School Education Coverage

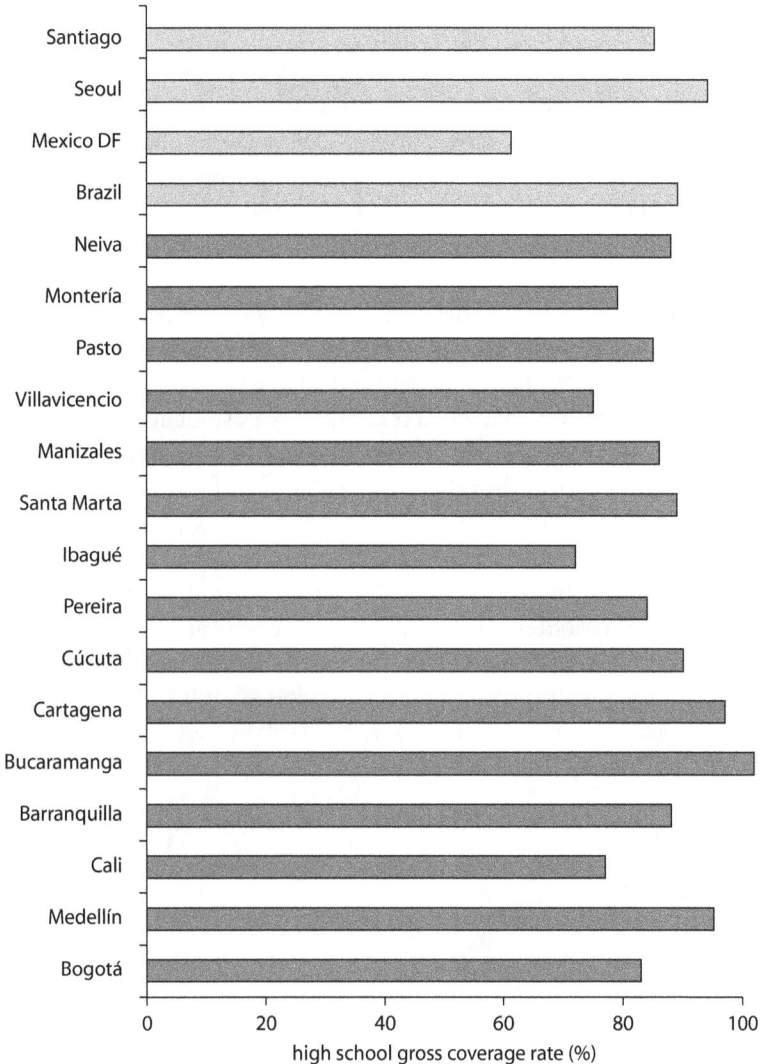

Source: Consejo Privado de Competitividad 2008.
Note: The lighter bars are not cities in Colombia.

challenges are particularly acute in intermediate and small urban areas,[2] where small utility companies face strong financial constraints and cannot exploit economies of scale. Quality of service remains a major challenge in rural areas; a recent study found that almost 60 percent of the drinking water samples taken outside the largest cities failed to meet minimum quality standards. Furthermore, education and health indicators, such as infant mortality rates, also rise considerably outside the three largest Colombian cities (World Bank-REDI 2004).

Quality of education should be a service priority as Colombia moves to being a higher-income nation. Colombia achieved almost universal access to basic services in the move to a middle-income country. Today, as Colombia moves to a higher-income status, the country should raise its standards and find ways to improve the quality of education and health services. Low-quality education imposes strong constraints on the availability of labor, which in turn affects productivity. In Colombia, the quality of education is considerably below the quality levels in comparable countries. For example, there is a stark difference in the exam results measured in the Programme for International Student Assessment (PISA) between Colombia and the Republic of Korea: Colombia's students achieve only 7 to 9 percent of the scores that Korean students attain (figure 2.12). The situation is no better for health indicators. While infant mortality levels in the Republic of Korea are around 5 percent, mortality rates in Colombian cities are above 15 percent. Larger cities, such as Bogotá, Medellín, and Cali have considerably lower rates (17, 18, and 15 percent, respectively) than Santa Marta and Montería, where the mortality rates are above 30 percent. The quality of health in Colombia seems to be low, even when compared with Colombia's Latin American peers. Chile has an infant mortality rate of only 8 percent; while Argentina's is higher at 14 percent.

Figure 2.12   Colombia's Position Relative to the Republic of Korea in PISA Exams

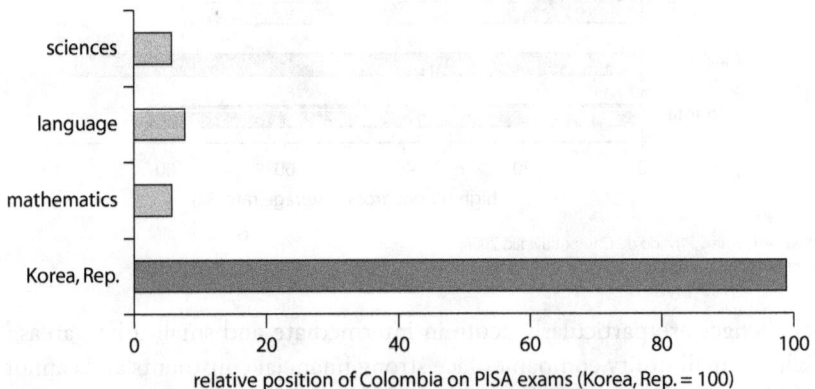

Source: Consejo Privado de Competitividad 2008.
Note: PISA = Organisation for Economic Co-operation and Development Programme for International Student Assessment.

Recent work by the World Bank suggests that municipal health and education performance is weakly related to the fiscal capacity of the municipality. Some poor jurisdictions perform well; conversely, some of the richer municipalities and departments could improve. Further, a municipality or department providing relatively efficient education services does not necessarily provide efficient health services, and vice versa. Reasons for the contrasting levels of performance are rooted in both structural factors (geographic location and population size) and institutional factors (such as local capacity). In terms of health, fiscal capacity seems to be weakly related to output efficiency but this is not so for education (World Bank 2009).

While urban areas have achieved almost-universal service coverage, rural areas have been left behind. Comparing rural and urban areas reveals the most-dramatic differences in access to services. As figure 2.13, panel b, indicates, while 90 percent of the urban population has access to services, on average, only about 50 percent of the rural population has comparable access. Lack of drinking water is another major concern.

Urban development is beneficial for rural development. Colombian cities have contributed to improving social indicators. Looking at access to basic services in rural areas by the urbanization level of the municipality (see figure 2.13, panel b) it is clear that on average, rural areas in municipalities with higher levels of urbanization have better access to services. Furthermore, the NBI index for rural areas in municipalities at advanced stages of urbanization is, on average, lower than the NBI index for rural areas in municipalities at an earlier stage in the urbanization process. Additionally, on average, rural areas in the municipalities with large cities are better off than rural areas sharing a jurisdiction with smaller cities. While the NBI is below 20 percent for rural areas surrounding cities with between 1 and 3 million inhabitants, the NBI goes up to 40 percent for areas surrounding cities with between 50,000 and 1 million inhabitants and increases to nearly 50 percent for rural areas surrounding cities with less than 50,000 inhabitants. Urban areas are extending their benefits to neighboring rural areas; this effect and contribute to narrowing the improved coordination could amplify urban-rural gap.

Reducing Transportation and Connectivity Costs Could Promote Mutually Beneficial Trade between Cities

Significant physical and economic distances separate Colombian cities. To move goods from one city to another often requires transport over the Andes and includes navigating altitude differences in excess of 2,000 meters. To reach major ports, goods coming from cities must, on average,

Figure 2.13   Unequal Distribution of Living Conditions in Colombia

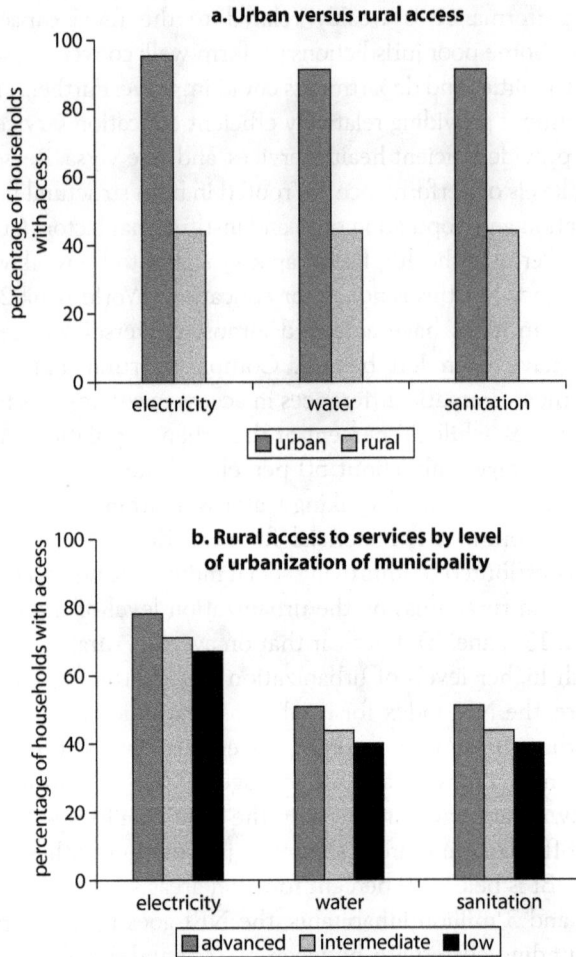

a. Urban versus rural access

b. Rural access to services by level of urbanization of municipality

Sources: DANE 2005; World Bank 2010b.

be transported about three times further than in Brazil and Chile, and six times further than in Argentina, the Republic of Korea, and China. Unlike many vibrant cities across the globe that benefit from proximity to coasts, waterways, and large home markets, Colombian cities are at a distance from ports and other cities in the urban portfolio. Bogotá and Medellín are more than 500 kilometers from a port. Contrast this with Shenzhen, Mumbai, and Bangkok—port cities that connect their countries to world markets.

Freight transport costs in Colombia are high. For long distances, transport costs are around US$0.09 per ton-kilometer. This is about three times the cost of freight transport in the United States. For shorter routes, the costs go up to US$0.16 per ton-kilometer. Further, for the main transport corridors, such as Bogotá-Barranquilla, road transport costs are higher than the costs of shipping goods from Cartagena to Rotterdam (US$60 per ton) (see chapter 3 for further details). Higher transport costs reduce export competitiveness and increase the costs of imported capital goods. Adverse physical topography, coupled with rising transport costs, has created a de facto internal trade barrier, undermining the formation of internal networks that allow trade and complementary specialization across cities (see map 2.2).

A World Bank (2006) report—based on a supply-side analysis and a survey of user viewpoints—found that, though some relevant infrastructure bottlenecks do exist, the freight logistics system has other critical problems. However, weaknesses in Colombia's freight logistics system are not limited to infrastructure; regulation and government-managed processes also impose restrictions. Colombia's logistics weaknesses are usually associated with inadequate infrastructure. Three main areas were detected as particularly critical: the trucking industry, public-use ports, and inspections of international gateways. With 81 percent of internal and regional freight moved by trucks, the trucking industry's

Map 2.2   Transport Flows in Trucks, 2005

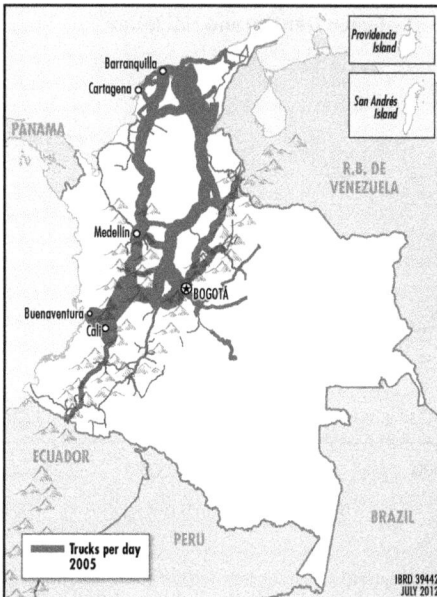

Source: Pablo, Roda for USAID 2007.

poor performance has pushed up transport costs. On average, trucks travel around 50,000 kilometers per year—half the efficient level. In addition, the industry is fragmented with multiple small operators, the vehicle fleet is aging, and only a few companies have evolved into logistic operators. As such, productivity is lower, costs are higher, and service quality has suffered. Moreover, the regulation of freight rates has lowered truckers' incentives to improve performance.

Further, the modal composition of Colombia's freight transport is imbalanced, with almost all freight transport depending exclusively on roads. In 2010, out of a total of 276.0 tons transported within the country, 177 were transported by road. Today, the use of rail and river infrastructure for freight movement is limited and ineffective. The expanding multimodality of freight transport might improve efficiency. However, it is of primary importance to understand which options are feasible and which options are likely to reduce transport costs while increasing efficiency gains.

Congestion and Wide Gaps within Cities Reduce Quality of Life

Looking at cities with more than 100,000 inhabitants suggests a negative correlation between the NBI index and a city's density; as density increases, the percentage of deprived households decreases (figure 2.14). Although denser cities deliver more to their citizens, increased density

Figure 2.14   Correlation between Density and NBI Index

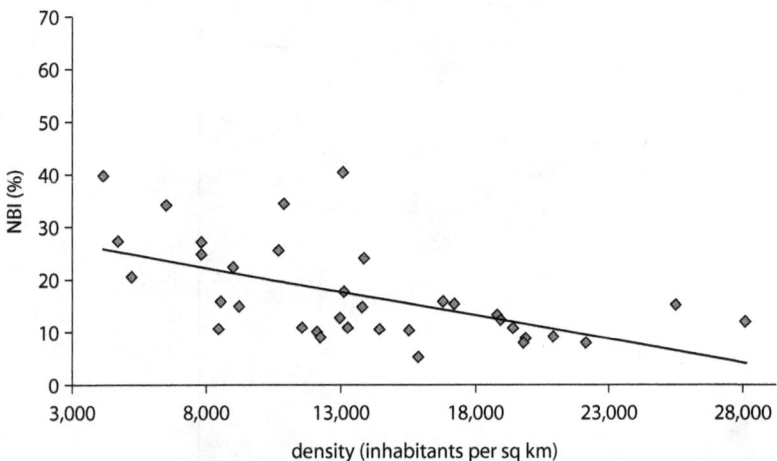

Source: DANE Census 2005, DNP.
Note: NBI = Unsatisfied basic needs. Quibdó is excluded from this sample because it appears to be an outlier in terms of NBI.

may bring unintended consequences. As the country moves to higher leaves of income, state governments should find ways to reap benefits from economic growth and improvements in the social indicators associated with urbanization, while mitigating the negative externalities of urbanization. Traffic congestion, increased pollution, housing and land shortages, and decreasing public resources are among the common byproducts of urbanization.

While Colombian cities have high population densities, business densities remain low. A recent World Bank study (World Bank 2010b) found that business density was roughly 149 businesses per square kilometer for selected areas in Bogotá,[3] which is much lower than business density in U.S. cities such as Miami, FL (207 per square kilometers), San Francisco, CA (276 per square kilometers), and Washington, DC (216 per square kilometers). Improving connective infrastructure might also contribute to increasing urban business density and act as a development strategy. Additionally, this study (World Bank 2010b) suggests that limited access to financial services in several neighborhoods might act as a barrier to wealth creation.

As cities become denser, congestion will increase, further underscoring the importance of efficient transport. A city that wants to grow denser must recognize that a dense center is feasible only when workers can be transported efficiently to their work places. It is essential to connect people to labor markets. An integrated mass transport system is key. Colombian cities have been progressing in this direction; TransMilenio in Bogotá is an ideal example. With average increases of more than 100,000 passengers per year since 2002, TransMilenio's Bus Rapid Transit System (BRTS) has managed to reduce the average commuting time by more than 10 minutes (Yepes 2008). TransMilenio's ridership is increasing at an average annual rate of 12 percent. The benefits of the TransMilenio BRTS have also been capitalized in the housing market. A recent study suggests that the positive impact on residential prices varies between 5.8 and 17.0 percent (Yepes and Lall 2008).

Similar to other Colombian cities, Bogotá faces serious congestion problems despite the recent improvements brought about by TransMilenio. The vehicle fleet has increased disproportionately to the change in population. In addition, by 2006, the large investments in the BRTS system corresponded to a decline in the quality of the city's road network, recovering only partially by 2008. Increases in the number of vehicles, lower road quality, and an almost constant number of kilometers of arterial roads have all led to average speeds that are almost half the average speeds found in Santiago, Chile. In addition, average travel time in Bogotá has increased by about 5 percent from 2005 to 2008 (figure 2.15). While congestion is a natural byproduct of urbanization and higher population densities, it is important that these associated costs do not become as high as to offset the benefits derived from urbanization. In 2010, the total cost of congestion in urban areas in the United States was estimated at US$101 billion (Schrank, Lomax, and Eisele 2011).

Compared to other cities of the world, Bogotá does not currently provide sufficient incentives to reduce the use of private cars and reduce congestion. Car taxes are 10 times lower in Bogotá than they are in Singapore and about 3 times lower than in New York (figure 2.16). While the surcharge on gasoline and the cost of cars taken together appear to be pointing incentives in the right direction and are well above the values in New York, they are still only about half the levels in Hong Kong SAR, China.

Apart from mobility, the social exclusion of poor people has become a pressing problem in the largest cities. In addition to the inequalities in

Figure 2.15   Congestion in Bogotá

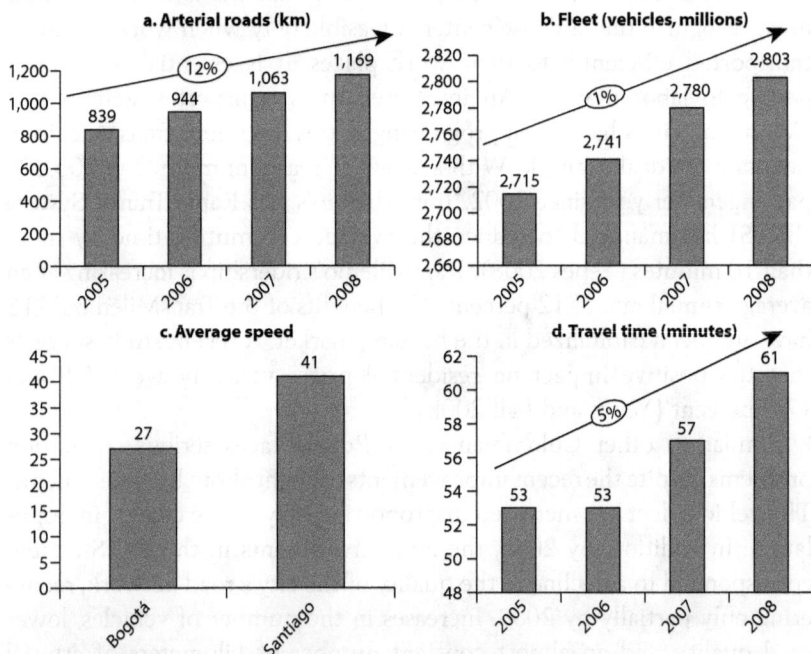

Source: Secretaria Distrital de Planeación de Bogotá.

Figure 2.16 Bogotá: Insufficient Incentives to Reduce Private Car Use

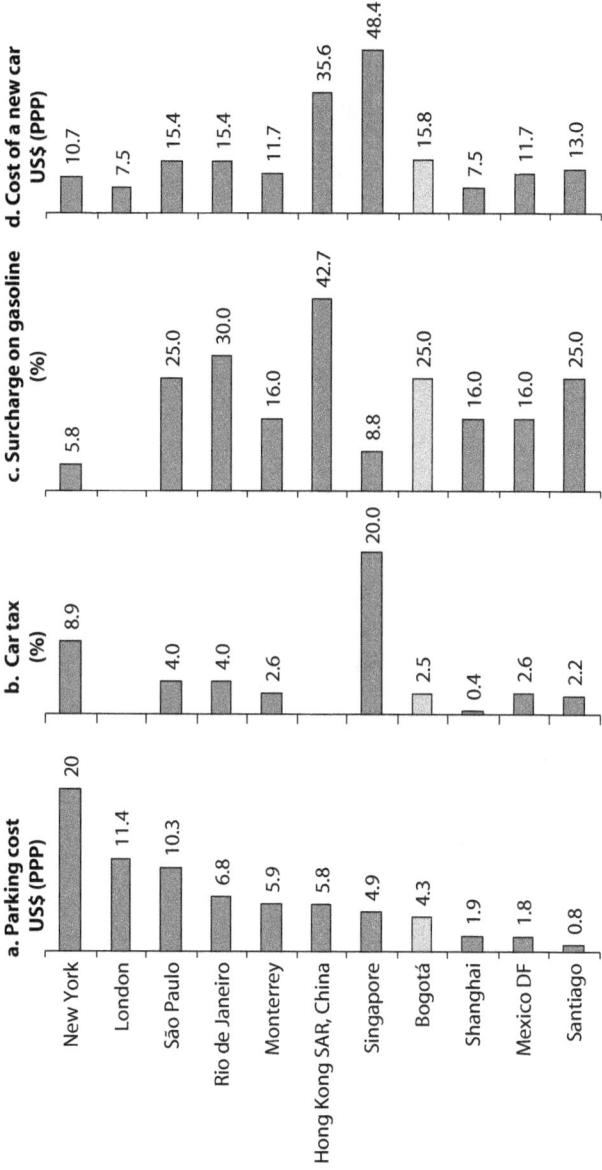

	a. Parking cost US$ (PPP)	b. Car tax (%)	c. Surcharge on gasoline (%)	d. Cost of a new car US$ (PPP)
New York	20	8.9	5.8	10.7
London	11.4			7.5
São Paulo	10.3	4.0	25.0	15.4
Rio de Janeiro	6.8	4.0	30.0	15.4
Monterrey	5.9	2.6	16.0	11.7
Hong Kong SAR, China	5.8		42.7	35.6
Singapore	4.9	20.0	8.8	48.4
Bogotá	4.3	2.5	25.0	15.8
Shanghai	1.9	0.4	16.0	7.5
Mexico DF	1.8	2.6	16.0	11.7
Santiago	0.8	2.2	25.0	13.0

Source: Secretaria Distrital de Planeación de Bogotá.
Note: PPP = purchasing power parity.

the qualitative housing deficit described above, the under-supply of units is especially critical in poor areas.

The diagnostics presented in this section identify specific challenges that Colombian cities face. How can these conclusions inform policy priorities? Which public policies and investments will help amplify the contribution of the urbanization process and the urban economy and lead to economic progress and poverty reduction? How can policies be prioritized and sequenced to effectively address pressing challenges at different stages of urbanization? What are appropriate responsibilities for local and national governments in translating priorities into action? To address these questions, the Urbanization Review has developed a policy framework and provided a sequencing of options for policy and investments. The following section describes the policy framework and sequencing.

Prioritizing and Sequencing Urbanization Policies

The Urbanization Review Framework

The core premise of the Urbanization Review Framework is that the complexity of policy efforts increases with urbanization (see figure 2.17). The challenges of incomplete markets and under-provision of public goods are dominant in early stages of urbanization. These challenges are amplified as congestion diseconomies kick in for places that rapidly take off, and remedial measures to correct for externalities and retrofit the built environment dominate as the urban system or a city matures. Why does this prove to be the case?

At incipient stages of urbanization, common institutions that regulate factor markets (land in particular) and deliver basic services are the main priority. Fluid land markets (including property rights and land use and transfer regulations) have a strong bearing on facilitating rural and urban transformations and the agglomeration of economic activities and people. When urbanization is low, agricultural economic activities prevail and economic densities are low. Because it is not clear which areas the market will pick, providing flexibility in land markets and universal access to basic services will allow firms and people to locate where it is most efficient. Because markets are incipient, the government must step in to address market failures. For example, incomplete or asymmetric information on land prices might prevent land markets from flourishing. Efforts to provide an independent institution for land valuation would help minimize the effects of this market failure. From

Figure 2.17   Prioritizing and Sequencing Policies and Investments for Urbanization

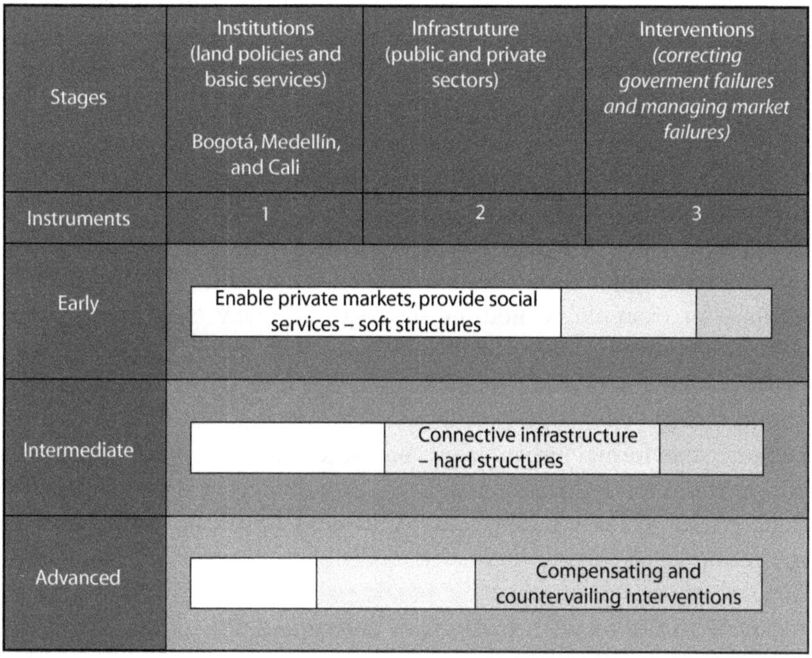

Stages	Institutions (land policies and basic services) Bogotá, Medellín, and Cali	Infrastruture (public and private sectors)	Interventions (correcting goverment failures and managing market failures)
Instruments	1	2	3
Early	Enable private markets, provide social services – soft structures		
Intermediate		Connective infrastructure – hard structures	
Advanced			Compensating and countervailing interventions

Source: World Bank Urbanization Review Team.

the perspective of a firm, providing basic services and enabling land markets to become more fluid are efforts that will allow it to exploit internal economies.

As urbanization advances toward more-intermediate stages and markets grow stronger, connective extra-urban and intra-urban infrastructure become essential. Transport infrastructure connecting cities and rural hinterlands can integrate product markets, enhance inter-regional trade, and facilitate economic specialization. If cities are not connected, they will be forced to behave as autarkies, instead of specializing in the activity in which they are more productive. Improvements in connectivity will allow firms to access product and input markets that are farther away, allowing them to exploit internal, local, and urban economies of scale, both within the region as well as in places at some distance. This is not to say that land markets and basic services will lose importance. On the contrary, as firms and people start locating in urban centers to exploit localization economies, flexibility in land markets will be of increased importance. Land assembly is a key element of infrastructure provision.

The institutions that guarantee the fluidity of land markets will also facilitate infrastructure expansion. Further, government failures in the provision of public services could lead to inefficient rural-to-urban migration. This migration may lead to increased congestion rather than higher productivity.

At advanced stages of urbanization, green-field development is not possible and urbanization might yield undesirable results. Externalities from urbanization may lead to under-pricing private actions, resulting, for example, in congestion or pollution. Institutional bottlenecks and government failures might also impose barriers on the fluidity of factor markets, leading, for example, to housing shortages. In many cities, government failures at previous stages of urbanization, such as over-regulated land markets, end up pushing many households into slums. Consequently, within a single city, large gaps in access to services continue to expand between the formal urban fabric and informal settlements. Remedial interventions can reduce these differences and improve livability. In addition, market failures might cause individual firms and households to ignore the social costs of their location decisions, locking cities into emission streams and unsustainable urban forms.

The maturity of the urban system determines the complexity of the policies required. At high urbanization rates, green-field development is not possible and regions are bound into patterns that will prevail for several years. As discussed in the framework provided above, for countries at early stages of urbanization,[4] much of the policy effort is likely to involve establishing basic institutions for land use transformation and delivering basic services. A sequence of policies that starts by developing "soft structures" or common institutions, followed by the development of "hard structures," focusing on connective infrastructure, would be ideal to generate win-win results for spatial efficiency and equity. Even in countries at early stages of urbanization, a few large cities will dominate the economic landscape. As a result, infrastructure will be needed to connect these poles with international markets, other national cities, and rural areas. Mobility needs to be maintained within these economic engines. In addition, remedial interventions may be needed to correct government failures, where institutions related to land use and service delivery were not put in place, or when market failures from urban externalities were not managed as the largest cities grew. However, these interventions will only constitute a small part of the overall policy effort for urbanization, with most of the attention focused on the building of "soft structures."

As urbanization takes off, large cities dominate a bigger share of a country's landscape and connective infrastructure becomes a more important component of the policy portfolio. The pace of urbanization often outstrips the capacity of policies and investments to build soft and hard structures. As a result, at advanced stages, when most people and economic activities are concentrated in cities, targeted interventions gain greater importance. Compensating and countervailing interventions aid in catching up.

Because Colombia is at an advanced stage of urbanization, policy efforts are likely to have a stronger component of targeted intervention than in a country such as India, where the government's attention focuses on establishing the right institutions. High urbanization rates rule out specific policy options because starting cities based on ideal plans is not feasible. Targeted interventions become an important policy instrument because they may be directed at fixing previous policy mistakes. In addition, given fiscal constraints, high demands for soft and hard structures might be met more efficiently through the definition of priorities.

How can public policies improve prosperity and livability across Colombia's urban landscape? How can they improve the lives of people in rural areas? To address these questions, the Urbanization Review assesses the health of Colombia's urban economy and the process of urbanization through a series of indicators, highlighting specific policy challenges for places across the urban portfolio. By identifying the main constraints to the urbanization process, the Urbanization Review aims at shedding light on this priority-setting process.

This book identifies several key bottlenecks in Colombia's portfolio of cities. First, interjurisdictional coordination can extend the benefits beyond the core city. Colombia has laid out the institutions required for successful urbanization. For example, access to basic services has moved rapidly toward universal access in urban areas. However, rural areas are still lagging behind and the quality of service provision is still low. Interjurisdictional coordination in such areas as land policy might help spread the benefits from cities to their neighboring rural areas and improve the quality of services. Second, the portfolio of cities is not well articulated; cities do not perform complementary roles and compete in a way that might negatively affect productivity. Accordingly, Colombia must find ways to connect cities efficiently. Finally, for its largest cities, Colombia must envisage tools that will allow cities to mitigate the negative externalities of urbanization and address government and market failures that were not addressed at early stages.

Sequencing Spatial and Sectoral Priorities Using the Urbanization Review Framework

Using the Urbanization Review Framework, Colombia's urban system is organized into three categories and differentiated urbanization policy priorities have been defined for each stage, ranging from incipient to high urbanization. The diagnostics outlined above suggest different challenges for small, medium, and large cities. Incipient urbanization could be defined as cities with urban populations below 20,000 individuals. This would represent about 30 percent of Colombian municipalities. Large cities—defined as those with urban populations above 100,000—make up almost 70 percent of Colombia's urban population (see map 2.3). The following paragraphs provide policy priorities for each of these categories.

For isolated areas with incipient urbanization, institutions that regulate land use and deliver basic services should be the mainstay of policy efforts. Coordination and integration is crucial to boosting growth and quality of life in lagging areas. Institutional and legal frameworks need to be aligned to support spatial transformations through planned development. Efforts to improve the coordinated delivery of services across different levels of government and between jurisdictions could have an important impact on the quality of service in intermediate and small urban areas.

Traditional urban and regional planning assumes that local governments have the capacity to correctly plan the distribution of businesses and people within a territory. It also assumes that the local governments have the enforcement capabilities to compel markets to follow their regulations. Several examples illustrate how this vision of planning can be ineffective and distort information. However, it is also true that a complete lack of regulation will result in chaotic urban growth—for example, the formation of slums. Achieving the right balance to direct land markets, without distorting their efficient allocation while achieving order, is one of the main tradeoffs of urbanization. Alternatives include zoning, allowing for lower housing sizes in central areas, and easing migration across economic activities in business districts. Land policy institutions and access to basic services should be the focus for small areas.

The complexity of challenges increases for medium-sized cities (where urbanization approaches intermediate levels). In these areas, the policy challenge is to encourage productivity and economic specialization by connecting these areas to local and regional markets.

Map 2.3   Colombia's Portfolio of Places for Urban Policies

a. Urban population by municipality

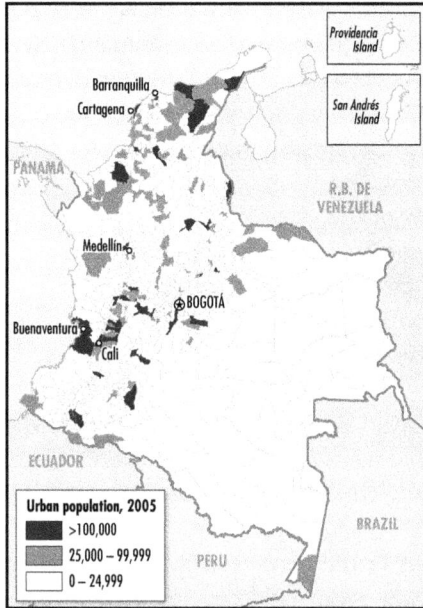

Providencia Island

San Andrés Island

Barranquilla
Cartagena

PANAMA

R.B. DE VENEZUELA

Medellín

BOGOTÁ

Buenaventura
Cali

ECUADOR

Urban population, 2005	
■	>100,000
■	25,000 – 99,999
□	0 – 24,999

BRAZIL

PERU

b. Density by municipality

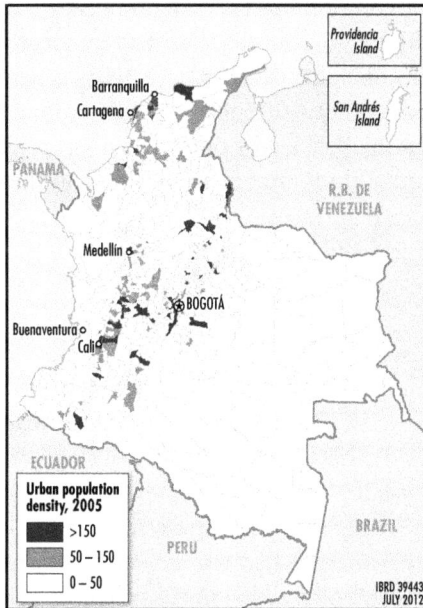

Providencia Island

San Andrés Island

Barranquilla
Cartagena

PANAMA

R.B. DE VENEZUELA

Medellín

BOGOTÁ

Buenaventura
Cali

ECUADOR

Urban population density, 2005	
■	>150
■	50 – 150
□	0 – 50

BRAZIL

PERU

IBRD 39443
JULY 2012

Sources: DANE Census 2005.

Efforts in connective infrastructure, which include investments in both hard and soft infrastructures, are key to support continuous growth. Because high transportation costs limit mutually beneficial trade, Colombian subregions are predominantly self-sufficient. High transportation costs act as an internal trade barrier within the country. The system of cities has evolved to be largely autarchic; because trade is limited between cities, the largest cities have grown based on self-sufficient production.

The connectivity of the urban portfolio must improve to capitalize on the value of Colombian cities and to promote growth. Reducing interregional transport costs can help cities exploit the gains from trade and economic specialization. It can also have a significant impact on spatial equity. This is a particularly pressing priority for medium-sized cities in the Colombian portfolio. Transportation investments to connect these cities to local and regional markets can help reverse declining productivity trends and encourage economic specialization. Getting the most value out of its cities and reducing economic distance are among Colombia's main challenges.

The largest cities in the urban portfolio face the most-complex challenges. In these cities, green-field development is increasingly infeasible. Attending to market and government failures not previously addressed becomes increasingly important. Remedial interventions can reduce vulnerabilities and improve livability in the most-marginalized areas. Interventions might include disincentives to use private vehicles and improve urban connectivity through a combination of investments to enhance public transit. Policies to promote urban renewal and increase housing supply though slum improvement and housing finance programs are also a priority.

Progressive zoning policies can reduce housing shortages for the poor. Special Zones of Social Interest (ZEIS) reduce the legally permitted minimum plot size for development and allow squatters to regularize their housing conditions without the twin pressures of speculation and eviction. Colombian programs, such as Bogotá's *Programa de Mejoramiento Integral de Barrios* (Program for Neighborhood Improvement, PMIB), have also improved living conditions in slums; they have gone beyond in situ upgrades by first providing secure property rights and improving infrastructure to connect slum dwellers to the rest of the urban economy. Land policy institutions and connective infrastructure preceded targeted slum improvements in this case, contributing to the success of this initiative.

There is scope to improve service delivery and enhance economic density through better interjurisdictional coordination. Effective mechanisms for coordination across municipalities in the delivery of services could significantly improve livability across the urban portfolio. Coordination is especially important for services that cross regional boundaries, such as transportation, planning, water, and sewage. Strengthening and leveraging links between a city and its neighbors proves to be a significant development strategy. As observed in some Colombian cities, benefits from the cities spill over their boundaries. Focusing on the largest cities in Colombia, we find that Bogotá, Medellín, and Cali have been more successful in spreading their benefits than Barranquilla has, as measured by the respective social indicators. On average, neighbors of Bogotá and Medellín saw reductions of 14 percentage points in the number of deprived households between 1993 and 2005, and Cali's neighbors experienced a similar reduction of nearly 10 percentage points. Barranquilla's neighbors, on the other hand, have not received benefits from the city because they only experienced reductions of 4 percentage points in the NBI index during the same period. Looking beyond city boundaries suggests that the neighbors of larger cities in Colombia have managed to observe increases in their access to social services more than the neighbors of smaller municipalities have. The question then is: how to extend the benefits of urbanization beyond city boundaries?

For large and rapidly growing cities, as densities of people and businesses increase, congestion will also increase. Consequently, connecting people to jobs will become more important. Supply-side efforts to add and upgrade infrastructure can be critical when paired with demand management policies. The main challenge is to align policies so that all incentives are directed toward the use of public transport. Gasoline taxes, car taxes, parking permits, and fees can influence individual behavior away from private transportation and complement supply-side investment policies. In recent years, cities such as London, Oslo, and Singapore have implemented different forms of demand management policies.

Efforts to improve the governance of metropolitan areas might positively affect the financing and delivery of services, as well as the ability to coordinate service provision across municipal boundaries (box 2.2). Effective systems of governance for metropolitan areas are needed to ensure the efficient delivery of services. Colombia is one of the most-highly decentralized countries in the Latin American region. Almost

Box 2.2

The Jury Is Still Out on Appropriate Models for Managing Expanding Metropolitan Areas

Debates exist on how to manage expanding cities and who should be responsible. How cities are managed and governed is a critical question because cities are the motors of Colombia's economic prosperity. Urban governance structures matter; they shape the quantity, quality, and efficiency of services and determine whether costs are shared throughout the metropolitan areas in a fair and efficient way.

Metropolitan-wide coordination in service delivery matters for transportation (coordination across municipal boundaries), water (determining where treatment facilities will be located), solid waste (determining where garbage disposal sites will be located), policing (crime spills across municipal boundaries), social services, health, and education (decisions on levels of expenditures and cost sharing). Several metropolitan governance models have been established around the world to address coordination:

- One-tier government model (fragmented local government)
- One-tier government model (consolidated local governments through annexation or amalgamation)
- Two-tier government model
- Voluntary cooperation (including special-purpose districts)

Researchers have identified several criteria to evaluate alternate models of governance: (1) efficiency—ability to achieve economies of scale and to reduce negative spillovers (externalities) across local boundaries; (2) equity—ability to share the costs and benefits of services fairly across the metropolitan area; (3) accessibility and accountability for decision-making; and (4) local responsiveness/competition. Studies across metropolitan areas highlight that governance models evolve over time (Toronto, Cape Town, Abidjan) and consolidation does not necessarily reduce costs (as in Toronto). However, neither theory nor practice tells us clearly which model of governance is the most effective for large metropolitan areas.

Source: Enid Slack 2007.

45 percent of current central government revenue is transferred to subnational governments through the *Sistema General de Participaciones* (System of National Transfers, SGP). Under this system, local governments are responsible for the execution of basic service provision expenditures. Both the local capacity and the particularities of each service sector have influenced the quality of service delivery across the country. For example, while the electricity sector was privatized in the 1990s, there remain key political initiatives to ensure national electrification. The water sector, on the other hand, is fully decentralized and managed by local governments and utilities.

Colombia may explore alternative models of governance, which have been used successfully around the world, to enhance coordination in service delivery (box 2.3). Interjurisdictional coordination can provide options to exploit economies of scale in service provision, consequently

---

Box 2.3

The Key to Successful Regional Integration

Institutionalizing long-, medium-, and short-term planning activities is a key factor for achieving successful regional integration. Planning does not rely exclusively on government initiatives; it can also be encouraged by civilians. Although private organizations need to put more effort into positioning and funding their projects, they could also promote an impartial regional development plan. The Regional Plan Association in the United States is one example of how civic groups can serve as planning agencies. Since 1919, the Regional Plan Association has been providing advice in regional development for the Connecticut, New Jersey, and New York areas. The association has positioned itself as an independent organization with an impartial perspective and a representative of public interests.

Structure, scale, and strategies are the three main components in the planning of regional integration and development. Structure points out the dynamics and components to take into account; scale proposes the levels at which the structure should be analyzed; and strategies point to criteria for prioritizing investment.

(continued next page)

Box 2.3 *(continued)*

Structure: Productivity, connectivity, and sustainability are key elements in transforming the economic space to spur development. Productivity should be stimulated in the densest economic spots to take advantage of scale economies; the success of the region depends on the success of the central city. However, peripherals should not be neglected; they must be connected to the core of the metropolitan area so that they can benefit from its spillovers. Connectivity is crucial for competitiveness on all scales. Good infrastructure systems that reduce distance also reduce transport cost, stimulating domestic trade and increasing the competitiveness of local products in foreign markets. International experience includes high-speed rail lines linking Tokyo and Niigata in Japan, reducing a seven-hour trip to one hour.

Scale: Development patterns should be analyzed on three scales, each of which prioritizes productivity and connectivity differently. On a national scale, strategic policies should aim at making the country competitive at a global level and at promoting connectivity with foreign markets. At a mega-regional level, policies should seek to boost productivity and growth, connecting the biggest regions and promoting the specialization of their productive structure. Finally, on a metropolitan scale, spatial transformations at the economic and social levels should be the main concerns.

- *Connectivity at the national scale.* Planning at the national level seeks to prioritize investments that promote national competitiveness. National efforts using national funds must be focused on connecting the main production centers of the country. In Colombia, shortening distances among the main cities—Bogotá, Cali, and Medellín—will promote greater economies of scale. This, in turn, will strengthen the country's trade position abroad and strengthen the spillovers to neighboring regions.

- *Connectivity and densification at the mega-regional scale.* Encouraging specialization and connection between and within mega-regions will position them as strong economic centers. Connection and specialization create synergies that will result in greater economic growth.

- *Connectivity, densification, and redistribution at the metropolitan scale.* Metropolitan areas can benefit from agglomeration and connectivity, promoting synergies at a lower scale. However, redistribution is a key element of metropolitan area consolidation. Density must be accompanied with redistribution,

(continued next page)

Box 2.3 *(continued)*

so that the benefits of concentration reach neighboring areas, and agglomeration can be further promoted. The metropolitan area, Valle de Aburrá, where Medellín is located, is an example of how coordination and association between municipalities can result in a win-win situation through a planning structure that encourages spatial transformation. The Metro Area Plan has a shared fund with a hybrid investment plan. Through this financial mechanism, Medellín, the biggest city, transfers to neighboring municipalities about 12 percent of the land tax it collects. Medellín contributes with 85 percent of the metropolitan budget but only receives 25 percent of it back.

Reshaping the Colombian metropolitan economic space should aim at strengthening the core city's "shadow," taking advantage of agglomeration at the different levels. Efforts should point at concentrating jobs, producers, and consumers in the core and not dissipating them. Keeping jobs inside the central city and connecting poor neighboring municipalities with the center will lead to larger overall gains. Taking jobs and production out of the city will not only weaken agglomeration economies, but in the absence of connective infrastructure, it will pose a barrier to growth in neighboring municipalities.

Strategy: The strategy for prioritizing investments should focus on the three components mentioned in the structure, by looking at them on different scales. To achieve high growth and successful urbanization, it is important to finely adjust the major decisions to strategically target key bottlenecks. Sorting the ways to achieve productivity in the biggest metropolitan centers, connectivity with the surroundings areas, and protection of the environmental hot spots will provide a framework for successful spatial transformation.

Source: Robert Yaro, Regional Plan Association, Presentation to Metropolitan Area Governments, Bogotá, Colombia, October 2010.

translating into higher quality of services. A better understanding of successful international examples and how they could apply to the Colombian context will be of use as the country searches for new mechanisms to foster coordination across municipalities in large metropolitan areas.

To finance these interventions without placing undue stress on municipal finances, cities may explore the possibility of adapting and applying value-capture instruments and other innovative financing tools. Colombia's National Development Plan for 2010–14 identified the development of context-appropriate financing mechanisms as a policy priority. In particular, there is considerable scope to capitalize on the fact that infrastructure investment is often associated with property value gains. "Land-value-capture" instruments have been utilized to leverage these gains to help extensively finance infrastructure investments for brown-field development and urban redevelopment, with mixed results. There is clear scope to identify gaps in the regulatory framework governing the successful application of innovative financing tools in Colombia.

Notes

1. The gross coverage rate is an indicator of the ratio of available spots for a target population. In that sense, an indicator of 70 would suggest a 30 percent deficit in the supply of education while an indicator of 130 would suggest a surplus of 30 percent.
2. Colombia has 927 municipalities with fewer than 20,000 inhabitants.
3. This study includes only five neighborhoods in Bogotá. These neighborhoods are 20 de Julio, Calandaima, Patio Bonito, San Jose, and Sosiego.
4. According to the *World Development Report 2009* classification, incipient urbanization includes regions with urban shares around 25 percent; intermediate refers to those with urban shares around 50 percent; and advanced refers to areas with urban shares more than 75 percent.

Bibliography

Bonet, J. 2003. "Colombian Regions: Competitive or Complementary?" *Revista de Economía del Rosario* 6 (I): 53–70.

Consejo Privado de Competitividad. 2008. *Ruta a la Prosperidad Colectiva.* Bogotá, Colombia: Gráficas Gilpor Ltda.

González, Daniel Toro. 2007. "Localización de la Industria Manufacturera en Colombia 1990–1999." Working paper 004299, Universidad Tecnológica de Bolívar, Cartagena de Indias, Colombia.

Lopez, H. P. F., and J. Luis Guasch. 2007. "Economic Performance in Latin America and the Caribbean: A Microeconomic Perspective." Report 40717-LAC Private and Finance Sector and Chief Economist Office, Latin America and the Caribbean Region, World Bank, Washington, DC.

Sanchez, F. 2006. "Descentralización y Progreso en el Acceso a los Servicios Sociales de Educación, Salud y Agua y Alcantarillado." Documentos CEDE 002287, Universidad de los Andes-CEDE, Bogotá, Colombia.

Schrank, David, Tim Lomax, and Bill Eisele. 2011. "Annual Urban Mobility Report." Texas Transportation Institute, Texas A&M University, College Station, Texas.

Slack, E. 2007. "Managing the Coordination of Service Delivery in Metropolitan Cities: The Role of Metropolitan Governance." Policy Research Working Paper WPS4317, World Bank, Washington, DC.

Urban Age. 2009. "Cities and Social Equity. Inequality, Territory and Urban Form." Report Urban Age Programme, The London School of Economics and Political Sciences, London, U.K.

World Bank. 2004. *Colombia: Recent Economic Developments in Infrastructure (REDI). Balancing Social and Productive Needs for Infrastructure.* Washington, DC: World Bank.

———. 2006. "Infraestructura Logística y de Calidad para la Competitividad de Colombia." Report 3506 1-CO, World Bank, Washington, DC.

———. 2009. *World Development Report–Reshaping Economic Geography.* Washington, DC: World Bank.

———. 2010a. *Reshaping Colombia's Economic Geography through Local Institutions.* Washington, DC: World Bank.

———. 2010b. *Bogotá Inner-City Market Assessment.* Washington, DC: World Bank.

Yaro, R. 2010. Presentation to Metropolitan Area Governments, Bogotá, October 2010.

Yepes, T. 2008. "Un Modelo de Ciudad con Economías Externas en el Consumo." Ph. D. in Economics Dissertation, Universidad Nacional de Colombia.

Yepes, T., and S. V. Lall. 2008. "Evaluating the Impacts of Urban Upgrading: Evidence from Bogotá." Paper, World Bank, Washington, DC.

CHAPTER 3

Competitiveness and Connectivity across the Colombian Urban System

Hyoung Gun Wang and Bernadette Baird-Zars

Introduction

Competitiveness has become a national priority for Colombia. Prompted by stagnant productivity growth since the mid-1990s, the current administration and the one preceding it have placed a premium on increasing domestic competitiveness. In 2006, the national government established a National Competitiveness System (SNC) and a National Competitiveness Commission (CNC),[1] and it has been assertively pursuing international commercial integration through free trade agreements. Specifically, the CNC supports the "Internal Agenda," a domestic process charged with identifying key bottlenecks to growth. The current National Plan (2010–14) expands this agenda, linking "growth and competitiveness," one of the three core pillars of the plan,[2] to economic development in a "system-of-cities" framework (*el sistema urbano regional*).

This chapter was based on a 2011 background study, "Costos de transporte y eficiencia económica en Colombia: Revisión del proceso de urbanización en Colombia. Fase II," by Pablo Roda and Francisco Perdomo. The full report is available on the World Bank's Urbanization Review website (http://www.urbanknowledge.org/ur.html). Henry Jewell (FEUUR) helped with map visualization.

The national government considers logistics and transport as the core elements of a competitiveness strategy. Since the mid-2000s, the National Planning Department (DNP) has identified and prioritized the most-effective policy approaches to catalyze competitiveness. The series of DNP studies employed in that process emphasize the role of inter-regional freight transport and logistics in robust economic development across the urban system.[3] Reflecting these findings, the current National Plan identifies improvements to transport infrastructure as a priority for every region in the country. One of the first actions of the CNC was the creation of a technical committee—Committee for Trade and Transport Facilitation, or Comifmal—focused on transport. The committee draws its members from key ministries and industries in the private sector.

International experience confirms the critical linkage between competitiveness and connectivity. The success of local and regional economies, from an urban systems perspective, is closely linked to their connectivity with domestic and international markets. Colombia's three major cities are located high in the Andes, and the distance between them (and to the coast) is significant. Given this economic geography landscape, the connection between industrial competitiveness and inter-regional transport costs is especially strong. However, reducing transport costs alone will not increase competitiveness. Improvements in connectivity would have to be accompanied by a proactive development policy for the private sector to drive specialization and competitiveness.

Recent joint work by the World Bank and the Inter-American Development Bank (IDB) stresses the link between connectivity and poverty reduction in Latin America and the Caribbean, through connectivity's impact on food prices. Transport and logistics costs make up a large part of the delivered cost of food products in Latin America and the Caribbean. The international maritime and road haulage components alone can total about 20 percent of the free on board (FOB) value of goods, if combined. On the other hand, national average logistics costs represent a share of product value of between 18 and 32 percent, compared to the OECD (Organisation for Economic Co-operation and Development) benchmarks of around 9 percent. Further, despite the sharp increase in commodity prices, transport costs as a percentage of the value of food products have hardly changed in the past years. The study finds that reduced logistics costs would in fact translate into a 5–25 percent reduction in the price of food products. Given that food expenditures make up a large part of the disposable income of the region's poor,[4] reductions in transport costs are likely to contribute to poverty reduction.

High transport costs are associated with fragmented regional economies. These costs contribute to underexploited interregional and international trade in Colombia. For instance, resources, human capital, and the industrial bases of the country are concentrated in the Andes. However, these areas also face the highest transport costs in the country. As a result, recent economic indicators highlight shifts in growth and investment from the three largest Andean cities (Bogotá, Medellín, and Cali) to coastal areas boasting lower transport costs. The Andean urban system may increasingly be left out of the global economy as gross domestic product (GDP) and investment gravitate toward trade centers on the coasts or in adjacent regions with easier access to international markets.

Therefore, improving the international connectivity of the largest Andean cities is extremely important. This phenomenon opens up a key policy question on whether to focus on strengthening existing industrial centers in the Andean highlands or to take proactive measures to develop key coastal regions with strong logistical advantages. Either way, improving connectivity between large Andean cities and coastal regions would be a win-win strategy for the national economy.

Lowering transport costs along key trade corridors will not only catalyze growth and improve the overall efficiency across the system of cities in Colombia; it will also help to realize the unexploited economic potential of the Colombian urban system. High domestic transport costs undermine the competitiveness of goods produced in Colombia's largest cities, especially when compared to other large cities of the world. Domestic road freight transport from Bogotá to the Atlantic Coast costs about US$94 per ton, compared to the lower international maritime transport cost from the Colombian coast to China of about US$60 per ton. Lowering transport costs could boost local GDP growth and increase trade. A recent study by Blyde and Martincus (2011) suggests that a reduction of 12 percent in internal transport costs resulting from the improvement of existing roads would lead to an increase of about 9 percent in average exports (Blyde and Volpe Martincus 2011). In addition, preliminary empirical analysis performed in this study suggests that a decrease of 10 percent in transport costs would lead to a comparable increase in inter-regional trade.

Lowering transport costs might also unlock new economic opportunities in local and regional economies because it will not only lead to direct savings in vehicle operating costs but also, in the long run, facilitate industrial specialization at local and regional levels. Inadequate infrastructure is a barrier to trade between cities within Colombia as well as between Colombian cities and the rest of the world. Lifting these barriers might open the door to rapid growth and more-efficient production and might change the current structure of the portfolio of cities and products. National policy should aim to reduce market and government failures rather than trying to pick "winners" among places and products.

This chapter identifies connectivity challenges by taking a demand-side approach and examining trade flows. Five major corridors and the Atlantic ports are identified as key areas that require transport infrastructure investments. Further analysis to determine the feasibility and cost of investing in each of these alternatives would be required to be able to prioritize the investments. This is beyond the scope of this chapter and should be considered for future work. From a demand perspective, this study recommends targeting investment along two corridors: the route connecting Bogotá to the Atlantic ports, and the route connecting the highlands to the Pacific ports, from Bogotá to Buenaventura.

This study further suggests that improving the intermodality of transport in Colombia might considerably reduce transport costs. Today, main corridors are dominated by truck transport, and the lack of alternative transport modes on major trade corridors reduces competition and efficiency. Modal sharing may lead to considerable savings as the ton-kilometer costs of transport by rail and river in Colombia are estimated to be about half of that for transport by truck. Fostering intermodality might also reduce congestion.

The chapter is organized into five sections. Following this introduction, the first section examines the economic geography of Colombia from a system-of-cities perspective. This section provides an overview of the role of cities by looking at the distribution of economic activities across cities. It also looks at the magnitude of national and international trade flows involving Colombian cities. The second section builds on the first by looking at the possible causes of bottlenecks in the system. The discussion is centered on high transport costs observed in Colombia, with particular attention paid to road freight transport. The discussion also covers logistic constraints and lack of intermodal options. The third section uses a newly developed transport model to identify five priority corridors that can be focused on to improve connectivity in Colombia's system of cities. It discusses each of these corridors in detail. Finally, the chapter concludes with recommendations for a policy agenda to improve connectivity, discussing both strategies for spatial planning and integration and key areas where institutional and regulatory reform will contribute to support integration.

Economic Geography in a System of Cities—Identifying Problems

Cities within a country are not isolated entities but rather components of a system, and if well articulated, can enhance development and growth of the system. The success of the local economy and the health of the system as a whole increasingly depend on these cities' connectivity with domestic and international markets. Low inter-regional transport costs are critical to foster industrial competitiveness, particularly in the context of challenging national economic geographies. This section aims to identify problems impeding the overall efficiency of the system by examining the functions of cities and trade flows connecting them to both domestic and international markets.

Colombia's system of cities does not appear to be well articulated. Cities and regional economies in Colombia suffer from fragmentation, low inter-regional trade, and underexploited trade and industrial potential. Colombia's financial resources, human capital, and industrial base are extremely concentrated in the Andean highlands, the area subject to highest transport costs. Recent economic trends highlight that growth and investments are increasingly shifting away from the three largest Andean cities (Bogotá, Medellín, and Cali) to areas with lower transport costs.

The Function of Cities and Specialization: A Fragmented Economic System

Colombia's local and regional economic systems are relatively isolated. This fragmentation has discouraged industrial specialization and economies of scale and weakened the overall competitiveness and productivity of the Colombian economy.

Industries in Colombia experience a low level of regional specialization. Except for cities with refineries, very few urban areas have significant concentrations of a single sector or a cluster of sectors. This lack of specialization can be explained by the relative isolation of each city given topographical constraints and high transportation costs. It also helps explain the low level of industrial linkages between specific local economies, such as those of Bogotá and Medellín, where cargo flows and inter-regional trade fall well below expectations given their proximity and size. The low level of industrial specialization has significant bearing on local and regional economies because it sacrifices economies of scale and the development of clusters, which has the effect of significantly constraining regional economic competitiveness (Box 3.1). Table 3.1 provides a measure of local industrial specialization at the departmental level.

To compare the industrial structures of any two regions, the Herfindahl-Hirschman Index (HHI) measures the sum of the squared difference between the shares of a particular industrial sector in the two regions. The indicator provides a quantitative measure, which is useful to determine the degree of complementarity or substitutability between the regions' industrial structures.

Box 3.1

Connecting Major Cities in the Andean Highlands: Historical Overview

The three major cities in the Andean highlands—Bogotá, Medellín, and Cali—face significant connectivity challenges. The two main urban centers of Bogotá and Medellín are located high in the Andes. This location, far from the ports, also has limited transport infrastructure. As a result, the dynamics of these cities have relied more on the domestic market than on the international market. Improving connectivity between Colombian cities will improve both domestic and foreign competitiveness of cities.

Historically, town settlements followed the banks of the Magdalena and Cauca Rivers and then traced along the eastern range (Cordillera). Later, in the mid-nineteenth century, towns were colonized in the central mountains around the cities of the coffee-growing highlands (*el eje cafetero*) and Medellín. Even well into the twentieth century, the major urban centers remained isolated. In 1914, according to maps of the Augustin Codazzi Geographic Institute (IGAC), the only fully functioning road network in the country was located in the eastern range, connecting the municipalities of the Boyaca highlands and Cundinamarca with Cambao in the Magdalena and Capitanejo on the road to Cúcuta.

(continued next page)

Box 3.1 *(continued)*

In 1938, it was possible to travel by road between Bogotá, Medellín, and Cali, but access to the maritime ports from the highlands remained a challenge. At this time, there were four relatively isolated road networks: one on the eastern range, the second along the Cauca River in the west, the third in the Upper Magdalena, and the fourth along the Atlantic Coast. The only connection between these networks was the Bogotá–Manizales road. In the 1950s, it was possible to go from Bogotá to the Atlantic Coast, but only along the Eastern Cordillera to Cúcuta and Ocaña, and then through Cali to access the Pacific Ocean. The direct connection between Bogotá and the coast through the Magdalena valley and the route linking Bogotá and Medellín, bypassing Manizales, were only finalized in the mid-1990s.

Table 3.1   Industrial Diversity, Herfindahl–Hirschman Index (HHI)

Department	HHI
Caqueta	1.0000
La Guajira	1.0000
Vichada	1.0000
Narino	0.8697
Huila	0.8660
Cesar	0.8563
Meta	0.8489
Magdalena	0.6883
Santander	0.6394
Sucre	0.6180
Córdoba	0.6110
Quindio	0.5447
Tolima	0.4335
Boyaca	0.3950
Norte de Santander	0.3116
Bolívar	0.3112
Cauca	0.2442
Risaralda	0.2327
Caldas	0.2255
Valle del Cauca	0.2228
Cundinamarca	0.2191
Atlántico	0.2052
Bogotá	0.1201
Antioquia	0.1192

Source: Annual Manufacturing Survey (EAM).
Note: HHI is a measure of local industrial specialization. A smaller value implies that a city has a more diversified industrial structure. The analysis was conducted at the two-digit level.

As highlighted in chapter 1, Colombia's two major cities, Bogotá and Medellín, have remarkably similar industrial structures. Table 3.2 extends the analysis by providing comparisons of industrial structure for most Colombian regions. Industrial production in Bogotá and the surrounding

Table 3.2   Difference in Regional Industrial Structure

Industrial relationship	Difference in industrial structure
Bogotá-Antioquia	0.0226
Bogotá-Valle del Cauca	0.0479
Bogotá-Atlántico	0.0564
Bogotá-Santander	0.6524
Bogotá-C/marca	0.0501
Bogotá-Bolívar	0.2780
Bogotá-Caldas	0.0818
Average Bogotá	**0.1699**
Antioquia-Valle del Cauca	0.0481
Antioquia-Atlántico	0.0489
Antioquia-Santander	0.6672
Antioquia-C/marca	0.0452
Antioquia-Bolívar	0.3002
Antioquia-Caldas	0.0721
Average Antioquia	**0.1720**
Valle del Cauca-Atlántico	0.0242
Valle del Cauca-Santander	0.7257
Valle del Cauca-C/marca	0.0200
Valle del Cauca-Bolívar	0.3250
Valle del Cauca-Caldas	0.0623
Average Valle del Cauca	**0.1790**
Atlántico-Santander	0.7279
Atlántico-C/marca	0.0277
Atlántico-Bolívar	0.2704
Atlántico-Caldas	0.0756
Average Atlántico	**0.1759**
Santander-C/marca	0.7078
Santander-Bolívar	0.2500
Santander-Caldas	0.7262
Average Santander	**0.6367**
C/marca-Bolívar	0.3396
C/marca-Caldas	0.0438
Average C/marca	**0.1763**
Bolívar-Caldas	0.4160
Average Bolívar	**0.3113**
National Average	**0.2111**

Source: Annual Manufacturing Survey (EAM) 2008.

Note: C/marca = Cundinamarca. Sum of squared industrial share differences between two regions. If the sum is low (high), the two regions have similar (different) industrial structures.

area of Cundinamarca is very similar to that of Medellín and the Antioquia region, and not substantially different from those of Cali and the Valle del Cauca. Bogotá and Medellín are the least-specialized industrial cities. The regions of Valle del Cauca, Atlántico, Cundinamarca, and Caldas show an industrial structure with close-to-average specialization. Santander and Bolívar, in contrast, have highly specialized industrial structures, predominantly in oil and petrochemicals, because of the Barrancabermeja and Cartagena refineries. For many of the less-developed regions, manufacturing and industrial production are minimal and limited to foods and beverages.

The country's GDP is heavily concentrated in three cities: Bogotá, Medellín, and Cali. Spatial concentration of industrial production in these cities is even more pronounced; industrial GDP in Bogotá is 50 percent greater than that of Medellín or Cali (maps 3.1 and 3.2; figures 3.1 and 3.2). Secondary clusters of production are along the Atlantic Coast and in Santander. Tertiary urban centers have the lowest contributions to GDP and trade flows. These include Ibagué and Neiva in the Upper Magdalena River region, Villavicencio and Yopal in the Llanos foothills, and the southern cities of the Caribbean region.

The difference in industrial GDP among these cities is largely accounted for by the production of high value added goods in Bogotá. These high value added goods dominate production in Bogotá because they are the only goods that can be priced competitively against competitors benefiting from lower transport costs. In addition, for Bogotá—where there is a concentration of public administration bodies, major universities, and leading firms in the financial and real estate sectors—the value added from the service sector is more than double that of Medellín or Cali. Medellín and Cali's share of value added from the service sector, in turn, is double that of the other major regions, such as the Atlantic coast or Santander.

Colombia's large inland urban centers lead production in almost every sector, yet they have lower levels of trade than other cities. This is the result of underexploitation of economic opportunities to export a wide range of industrial goods within and outside the country. The three major cities are net receivers of domestic and international freight. Bogotá and Medellín ship less than they receive, while Cali is closer to a net trade balance. In port cities, the largest registered shipment of origin is presumably associated with foreign trade. Because of their heavy weight and relatively low value, nonmetallic minerals are often processed in industrial areas close to local markets. In a large

Map 3.1   GDP, by Department, 2008

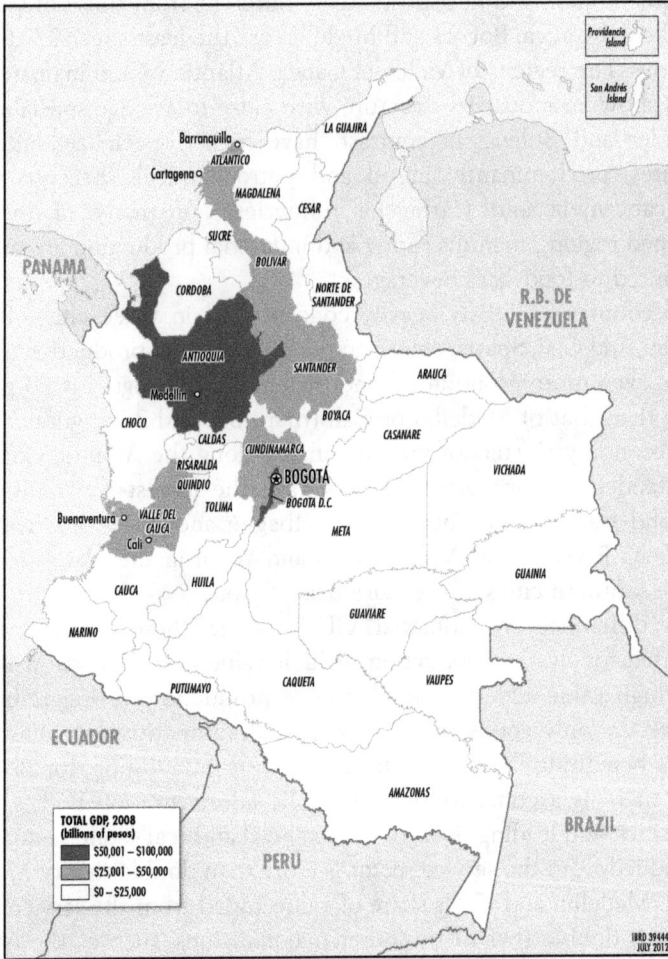

Providencia
Island

San Andrés
Island

Barranquilla

ATLANTICO

Cartagena

MAGDALENA

LA GUAJIRA

CESAR

SUCRE

BOLIVAR

PANAMA

CORDOBA

NORTE DE
SANTANDER

R.B. DE
VENEZUELA

ANTIOQUIA

SANTANDER

ARAUCA

Medellín

CHOCO

CALDAS

BOYACA

CASANARE

RISARALDA

CUNDINAMARCA

QUINDIO

BOGOTÁ

VICHADA

Buenaventura

VALLE DEL
CAUCA

TOLIMA

BOGOTA D.C.

Cali

META

CAUCA

HUILA

GUAINIA

NARINO

GUAVIARE

PUTUMAYO

CAQUETA

VAUPES

ECUADOR

AMAZONAS

BRAZIL

PERU

TOTAL GDP, 2008
(billions of pesos)

$50,001 – $100,000

$25,001 – $50,000

$0 – $25,000

IBRD 39444
JULY 2012

Source: DANE (Departamento Administrativo Nacional de Estadísticas) Regional Accounts.
Note: GDP = gross domestic product.

number of cities production exceeds consumption, but the extra production is consumed by neighboring localities rather than traded over long distances.[5] The spatial distribution of economic activity is consistent with freight trade flows.

Private investment is moving away from the large city core to neighboring municipalities (table 3.3). This is particularly the case for Bogotá and its neighboring municipalities in the state of Cundinamarca.

Map 3.2   Industrial GDP, by Department, 2008

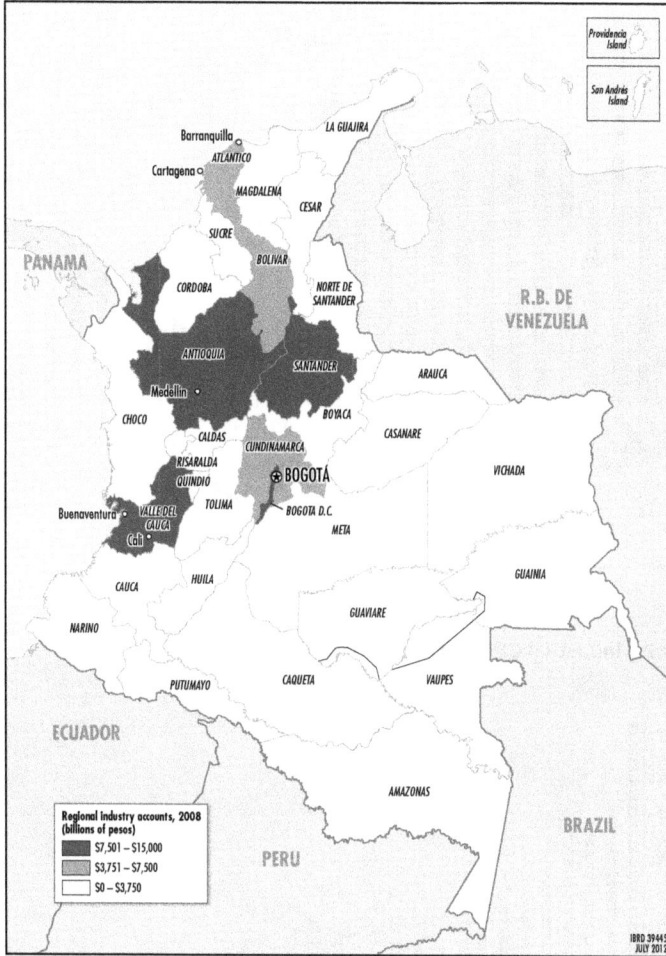

Source: DANE Regional Accounts.
Note: GDP = gross domestic product.

The shift in the spatial allocation of investments might be because of a mix of factors, including land availability and preferential tax agreements. In 2008, the municipalities neighboring Bogotá received an investment flow five times larger than that of Bogotá. Antioquia also received substantial investments, as well as the cities of the Atlantic Coast, Boyaca, and the Coffee Region. However, in a number of regions,

Figure 3.1   Per Capita GDP, by Department, 2008

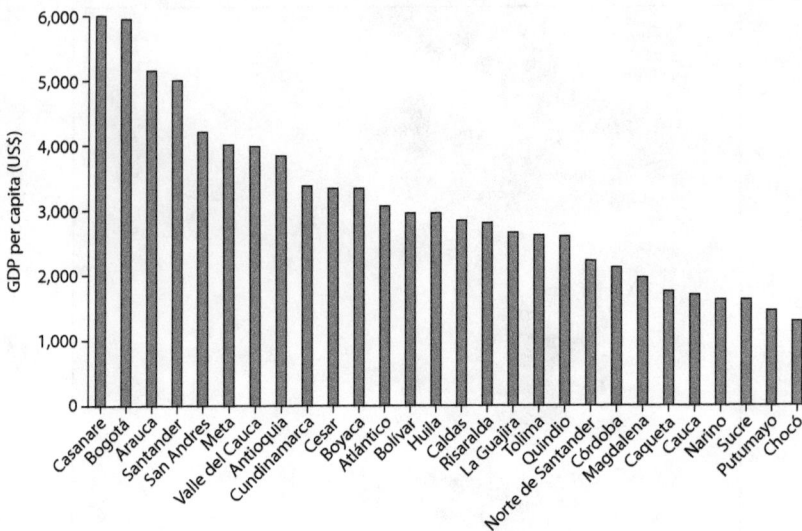

Source: DANE Regional Accounts.
Note: GDP = gross domestic product.

Figure 3.2   Industrial GDP, by Department, 2008

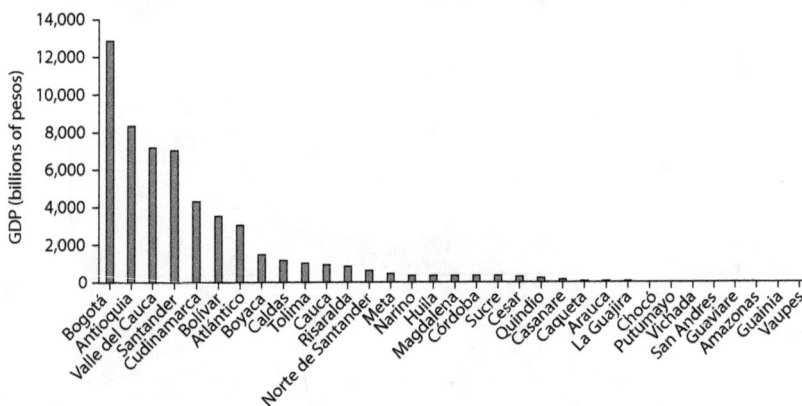

Source: DANE Regional Accounts.
Note: GDP = gross domestic product.

investment was almost zero or negative (the purchase of assets was not able to compensate for depreciation).

Larger firms have moved away from the city core in Bogotá and toward neighboring municipalities in Cundinamarca, a process

Table 3.3 Industrial Production and Investment, by Department

Department	Gross industrial production (1,000 million)	Percent	Value added (1,000 million)	Intermediate input (1,000 million)	Employment	Net investment (1,000 million)	Number of establishments
Bogotá	32,565	21.8	14,610	17,947	208,629	36	3,128
Antioquia	23,487	15.7	10,058	13,453	145,451	238	1,407
Santander	18,265	12.2	8,712	9,542	18,295	–26	344
Valle del Cauca	20,071	13.4	8,469	11,600	94,167	–126	1,111
Cundinamarca	13,558	9.1	6,278	7,295	56,880	188	404
Bolívar	11,840	7.9	4,306	7,539	14,179	577	122
Atlántico	8,893	5.9	3,886	5,009	36,394	140	331
Boyacá	2,528	1.7	1,329	1,198	6,254	124	59
Cauca	3,257	2.2	1,301	1,957	10,921	224	99
Córdoba	2,012	1.3	1,264	746	3,566	126	28
Caldas	2,638	1.8	932	1,702	14,279	134	150
Risaralda	2,439	1.6	919	1,525	15,882	–41	176
Tolima	2,267	1.5	802	1,471	6,547	–67	115
Meta	1,328	0.9	435	898	3,404	109	50
Norte de Santander	732	0.5	346	386	5,383	16	131
Cesar	1,010	0.7	294	716	2,807	5	34
Magdalena	654	0.4	230	425	2,266	2	47
Huila	796	0.5	202	594	1,804	8	51
Sucre	207	0.1	169	39	574	–1	14
Vichada	412	0.3	160	252	535	0	13
Quindío	452	0.3	125	328	2,727	4	56
Nariño	286	0.2	96	190	1,594	1	56
Caquetá	25	0.0	15	10	186	0	5
La Guajira	1	0.0	1	1	31	0	4
Total	149,721	100.0	64,939	84,822	652,755	1,671	7,935

Source: Annual Manufacturing Survey (EAM).

observed in other countries as well. Bogotá is the city with the highest number of companies, but most are relatively small. On average, Bogotá firms generate an output of Col$10,400 million and hire 66 employees. On the other hand, in Cundinamarca, which includes all suburban municipalities surrounding Bogotá, companies are on average three times greater than the size of Bogotá companies, with more than twice as many employees per establishment. Similarly, in Antioquia, the average facility has an output of Col$16,700 million and hires 103 employees. This phenomenon, where larger firms move out of the core city because of increased land costs and more-stringent regulations, has also been observed in other countries.[6] Outside the four major manufacturing centers—Bogotá, Antioquia, Valle del Cauca, and Santander—regional and local economies have an industrial structure characterized by a small number of large firms. Increasing firm size is a way of overcoming geographical remoteness, as observed in many international cases.

While GDP is concentrated in large cities, GDP growth in the last decade was significantly lower in large Andean cities, a pattern more prominent in the manufacturing sector. Economic and industrial activities, measured by total GDP and manufacturing GDP, are highly concentrated in the three largest cities of Bogotá, Medellín, and Cali, and their neighboring areas, as highlighted in map 3.3. However, their growth rates over the period of 2000–09 show quite different spatial patterns. As large urban clusters in the Andean highlands failed to accelerate productivity growth and capital investment, local industrial growth became stagnant compared to the national average.

Colombia's large urban centers no longer dominate growth in terms of investment received. Despite the concentration of value-added industrial production in the highlands, investment in the two coastal regions in 2008 was far greater. The three Andean highland regions[7] in and around Bogotá and Medellín produced nearly half of the value added to industrial production in Colombia, but received less than 27 percent of net (private) investment. In contrast, the three regions on the northern coast with port cities[8] produced less than 13 percent of value-added industrial production but received more than 43 percent of the total investment. Finally, the survey shows that investment in 2008 was concentrated in the main centers of development (Antioquia, the Coffee Region, Atlantic Coast, and Boyaca). Specifically, rapid economic growth is concentrated (1) along the main trade corridors to the Atlantic and Pacific Coasts; (2) in the outskirts of large urban centers; and (3) in the Andean highlands.

Map 3.3   Spatial Distribution of Economic and Industrial Activities and Their Growth

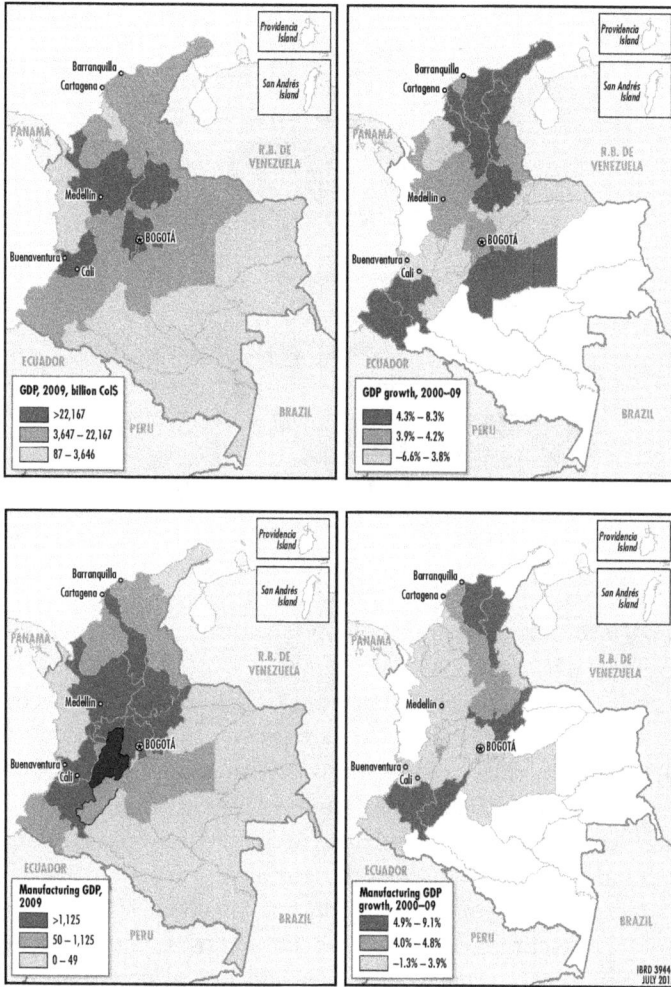

Source: DANE Regional Accounts 2009.
Note: The growth rate maps drop several sparsely populated departments in the southeast regions.

The recent mining boom has attracted private investment to these high-growth localities. This highlights some of the structural inefficiencies of the country's urban network because newer private investment cannot optimally utilize the large industrial infrastructure in major Andean cities. Other cities, in contrast, are simply too small to maximize the economic benefits of agglomeration.

Figure 3.3   Freight Flows in Colombia

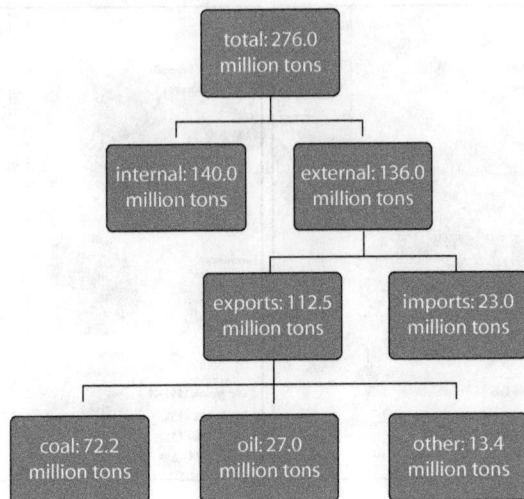

Source: DANE Regional Accounts 2010.

Structural Imbalances in Freight Flows: Another Hint at Inefficiencies in the System of Cities

Freight flows are structurally imbalanced.[9] There is significant geographic fragmentation in the national production chain. Industry and consumption are concentrated in cities in the Andean highlands, import/export ports are located along the coast, and extractive industries are based in a few areas with large natural resources. Underuse occurs because routes and, consequently, modes of transport along those routes are typically only used to transport one type of commodity in only one direction. With the exception of fossil fuels, freight transport also depends almost exclusively on roads.

Lack of alternative transport modes and modal competition undermines the efficiency of inter-regional transportation. Considering particular cargo characteristics, different types of freight need to be transported by different transport modes. Railways or inland waterways transport low-value, heavy raw materials more efficiently and cheaply than would other forms of transport. High-value cargo is shipped more efficiently by airplanes or container trucks, depending on the route. Having options for transport modes enables producers to choose the best and most efficient means of delivering goods to customers. Expanding transport modal choice options and competition among different transport modes will improve the efficiency of inter-regional transportation.

International trade flows.[10] International trade is important to the Colombian economy. The 2010 trade balance showed a surplus of US$1.4 billion, with an estimated value of US$39.8 billion in exports and US$38.4 billion in imports (each side representing more than 13 percent of the total economy). While current trade flows may seem high, it is important to consider, on a per capita basis, that Colombia's exports have barely doubled from levels in the 1960s. Other Latin American countries, such as Brazil and Chile, have exports per capita that are about 10 times their 1960s levels (Haussman and Klinger 2008).

In Colombia, export volume (tonnage) is concentrated on the coast, while export value is concentrated in the Andean highlands (tables 3.4 and 3.5). As a general rule, the greater the distance between an urban center and the coast, the higher the value added and the lower the tonnage of exports. Exports from inland cities, especially Bogotá, average between 6 and 10 times the value per ton as the heavy and low-value goods exported from coastal cities. In contrast, the tonnage of exports from Antioquia is double that of the Bogotá region and is surpassed by the tonnage exported from Buenaventura and the Caribbean cities. This trend reflects connectivity challenges: the high transport costs associated with exporting goods from Andean cities favors high-value goods and limits the opportunities for export diversification in inland cities.

The trend is visible across the three main categories of export flows: fossil fuels, manufactured products, and agricultural products. Fossil fuels account for the vast majority of export tonnage, but less than 50 percent of export value. They typically flow on dedicated infrastructure near the coast directly to maritime ports (box 3.2). Manufactured products of

Table 3.4   Implied Per Ton Customs Value (Excluding Coal and Oil)

Ports	Exports (US$/ton)	Imports (US$/ton)
Barranquilla	1,445	765
Bogotá	6,645	20,946
Buenaventura	1,786	948
Cartagena	1,013	1,676
Cúcuta	8,666	1,011
Ipiales	2,291	1,347
Maicao	1,755	350
Santa Marta	653	763
Turbo Port	415	964
Otros	5,310	3,336
Total	1,527	1,627

Source: External Commerce DANE-DIAN Database 2010.

Table 3.5　Trade Flows by Department, 2010

Department	Export			Import		
	Volume (million ton)	Value (million US$)	Unit value (US$/ton)	Volume (million ton)	Value (million US$)	Unit value (US$/ton)
Antioquia	**2.09**	**4,707.00**	**2,257.00**	**4.14**	**4,495.00**	**1,085.00**
Medellín	2.09	4,707.00	2,257.00	4.14	4,495.00	1,085.00
Barrancabermeja	**3.05**	**1,324.00**	**435.00**	**—**	**—**	**—**
Cafetera	**0.36**	**1,308.00**	**3,637.00**	**0.37**	**564.00**	**1,534.00**
Cundiboyacense	**1.08**	**4,556.00**	**4,236.00**	**6.62**	**20,806.00**	**3,143.00**
Bogotá D.C.	1.07	4,441.00	4,141.00	6.53	20,660.00	3,163.00
Tunja	0.00	115.00	39,962.00	0.09	146.00	1,669.00
Norte	**4.69**	**5,017.00**	**1,069.00**	**7.17**	**6,868.00**	**958.00**
Barranquilla	0.60	1,045.00	1,739.00	2.18	1,939.00	891.00
Cartagena	3.12	2,420.00	776.00	2.51	2,363.00	943.00
Santa Marta	0.57	318.00	558.00	1.69	1,353.00	801.00
Orinoquia	**0.00**	**2.00**	**1,732.00**	**0.06**	**224.00**	**3,518.00**
Santanderes	**0.38**	**546.00**	**1,423.00**	**1.10**	**721.00**	**656.00**
Bucaramanga	0.26	436.00	1,698.00	0.98	595.00	605.00
Cúcuta	0.13	110.00	868.00	0.12	126.00	1,092.00
Suroccidente	**1.58**	**2,486.00**	**1,571.00**	**4.00**	**4,562.00**	**1,141.00**
Cali	1.32	2,129.00	1,608.00	3.36	3,884.00	1,156.00
Suroriente	**0.11**	**439.00**	**4,096.00**	**0.11**	**98.00**	**901.00**
Others	**0.02**	**12.00**	**664.00**	**0.00**	**1.00**	**4,087.00**
Total	**13.35**	**20,397.07**	**21,120.94**	**23.58**	**38,339.74**	**17,022.16**

Source: DANE-DIAN 2010.

Note: — = Not available; D.C. = *distrito del capital* (capital district).

Box 3.2

Export of Fossil Fuels Is Significant in Terms of Both Tonnage and Value

Fossil fuels account for nearly 90 percent of exports by tonnage and 51 percent of exports by value. Fossil fuels are overwhelmingly transported by dedicated infrastructure. Nearly 90 percent of export freight occurs on privately owned or operated corridors. A relatively marginal amount of coal is moved by road and embarks from port facilities for public use; most coal and oil transport occurs on dedicated railways and port. These two products totaled nearly 100 million tons in 2010.

Coal is extracted near the coast and flows to regional markets in the Americas. The average value is about US$83.2 per ton, which is only 5.4 percent of the average tonnage value of exports (excluding fossil fuels). Coal exports are divided into coking (feedstock for steel) and heat. The first is listed on the international market at a price of approximately US$200 per ton, while the latter is approximately US$70 per ton. Under this price structure it is profitable to export coking coal from the northern region by road transport, while transferring through port facilities. It is not viable to export thermal coal from the hinterlands without developing dedicated transport infrastructure (map B3.1).

The average price of coal exports in Barranquilla, Cartagena, and Buenaventura (public port), is relatively high, implying a large share of coking coal transport. However, these three terminals have channeled just 3.2 million tons, or 4.5 percent, of the coal exported in 2010. Thermal coal accounts for 87 percent of the tonnage exported, which is handled by the private port of Puerto Bolívar in La Guajira (Cerrejón) and the port area of Ciénaga (ports of Drummond and Glencore) and Santa Marta. These ports have rail access systems operated by the owners of the cargo, and the mines are located a short distance—approximately 200 kilometers—from the sea. Of the 35.4 million tons exported by Santa Marta and Ciénaga, only 4.1 million tons correspond to the Regional Port Authority of Santa Marta (*Sociedad Portuaria Regional de Santa Marta*) and the rest went through private ports like those operated close to the mines by exporters such as Drummond and Glencore.

Oil is extracted in the Llanos and transported through pipelines. It has an implied value per ton of approximately US$500, which is more than six times the value of thermal coal and two times that of coking coal. Ninety-five percent of the 25 million tons exported in 2010 was collected from the eastern plains (Arauca's Caño Limón and Cusiana in Casanare) and the Magdalena Medio, transported through pipelines and then transferred to ships through a facility at Covenas. Oil from Putumayo is exported from the port of Tumaco on the Pacific coast.

(continued next page)

Box 3.2 *(continued)*

Map B3.1   Freight Flows of Coal

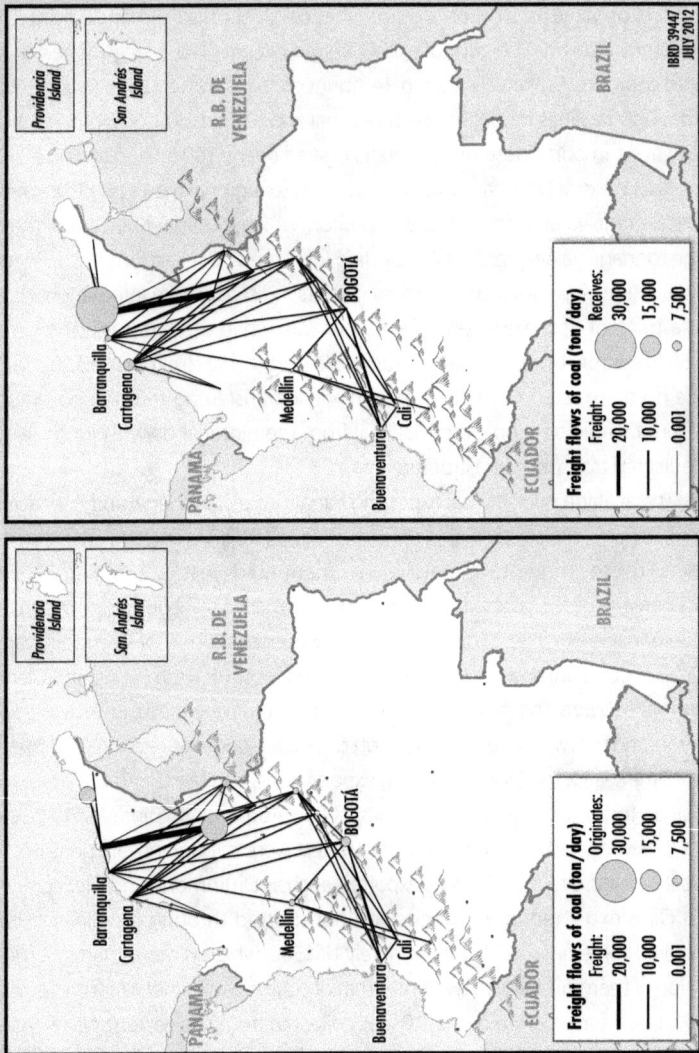

Source: National Survey of Cargo 2008, Ministry of Transport.

medium-to-high added value are typically produced in larger cities of the Andean highlands and then transported to maritime ports or to neighboring countries. These industrial exports include petroleum (which has a relatively low value per ton) and chemicals and metals, both of which have a relatively high value per ton. Agricultural exports make up about one-quarter of both the tonnage and the value of all exports. In keeping with the trend noted, the highest value agricultural goods such as flowers are typically transported by air from Bogotá,[11] while bananas are produced primarily on the northern coast and are transported relatively small distances to the Atlantic ports. However, some agricultural export products appear to go against this trend—such as coffee[12]—because they originate in areas where transport is not an important export factor, and they are exported largely by isolated transport means.

Import flows follow a similar pattern to exports, as coastal city imports tend to be lower value and larger tonnage. High-value imports are concentrated in the Andean cities, where freight is relatively specialized in industrial products, along with some cereals. Bogotá accounts for more than half of the value of imports to Colombia and a large portion of the 38 percent of imports that arrive by air (the large number of flights for the export of flowers has created opportunities for relatively low airfreight costs for imports). Seaports receive the greatest portion of imports in terms of tonnage, including inputs for fertilizers and other industrial processing. Buenaventura is the busiest seaport for imports, with one-third of the national import load. In general, in all regions, the volume of cargo imported exceeds that of cargo exported. The only exception is in the Coffee Region, precisely because of the high volume of coffee exports.

Domestic freight flows. Domestic freight flows encounter three marked bottlenecks: (1) heavy reliance on highways, where freight is predominantly shipped in relatively large semi-trailers; (2) structural imbalance in freight flows, with the coastal cities as net shippers and the large Andean highlands cities as net receivers; and (3) high logistics costs permeating all transport modes because of limited logistics and intermodal infrastructure.[13] Each of these bottlenecks is discussed in detail in the following sections.

Domestic freight transport is very reliant on highways. Survey data from a governmental 2008 freight study indicate that 70,601 tons were moved per kilometer of road and that every ton was transported 399 kilometers on average.[14] It is possible to infer that the average load per truck for 13.8 million trips was 12.8 tons (including empty trips).

Nearly three-quarters of the tonnage moved by road is transported using tractor-trailers for longer trips. Additionally, on average, this type of vehicle travels longer distances per trip, usually more than 400 kilometers, and carries an average load of 20 tons.

There are structural imbalances in domestic freight flows and the largest cities. With the caveat of separating purely domestic trade flows from international ones, map 3.4 shows domestic trade flows by origin-destination.[15] This indicates that trade flows among the three largest cities are low and that the most important flows of domestic freight are between the big cities and ports. Two important north-south trade corridors are identified in terms of domestic freight flows: the eastern corridor (Bogotá to Atlantic Coast) and the western corridor (Cali and Medellín to Atlantic Coast).

Identifying the Source of Inefficiencies: Transport Costs and Logistic Deficiencies

It is widely known, and has been documented in numerous studies, that the country's natural and economic geography poses challenges for inter-regional freight transport. References to these challenges appeared in the literature as early as 1927 (Renner 1927; Stokes 1967). Some of Colombia's largest and most important cities—Bogotá and other traditional centers of production—are dispersed across mountainous terrain, more than a day's drive from the Atlantic or Pacific coasts. For this reason, many imports and exports are processed in the maritime ports rather than the industrial cities in the highlands, including agricultural products for export, fossil fuels, and raw materials. As a result, freight travels a relatively long distance in Colombia. A 2006 study showed that freight distances in Colombia were almost three times those in Brazil and Chile; five times those in Malaysia; and six times those in Argentina, China, and the Republic of Korea (World Bank 2006). These comparisons are especially remarkable because some of these countries have similar geographical transport obstacles.

In the past 15 years, the national policy on transport and logistics has taken important steps forward. In 2008, the national government launched its National Logistics Policy (PNL) under National Economic and Social Policy Council (CONPES) 3547 to modernize and streamline processes and information tracking on freight. The policy also emphasized that investments in logistics development should be done strategically and coordinated with better distribution of products to their destinations

Map 3.4   Domestic Freight Flows by Origin-Destination

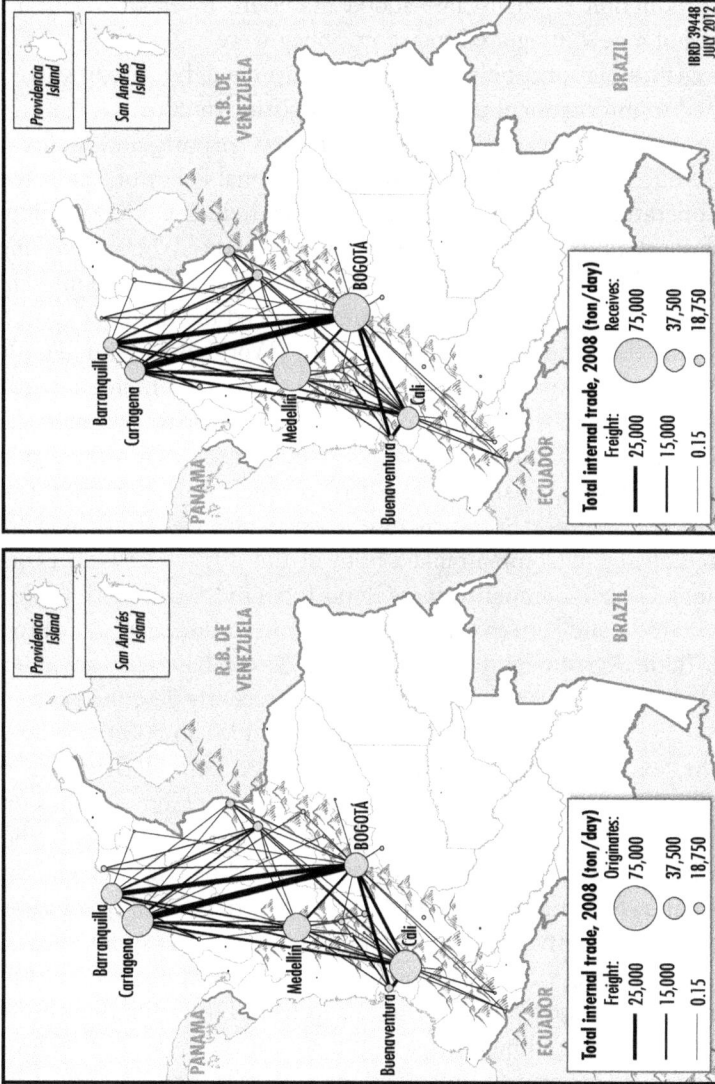

Source: National Survey of Cargo 2008, Ministry of Transport.

(IDB 2011). Assessment of the core needs of the transport and logistics sectors was prioritized in the plan, resulting in the 2008 design and implementation of the National Logistics Survey. In 2010, CONPES put forward a national Policy for Productivity Transformation (PTP) to promote the production of high-value-added materials. In early 2011, the first phases of a new integrated transport policy were initiated.[16]

Logistics platform policies have also improved, but progress has been limited to international trade and port logistics. In 2007, CONPES 3469 set simultaneous inspection policies for ports, airports, and border crossings, while CONPES 3489 initiated the National Policy of Public Freight. Port operating hours were extended in 2008, reducing port handling time by three days. Trading across borders was expedited; better banking services and the implementation of e-payments, electronic data interchange, and coordinated inspections in customs reduced the time to export by 10 days and the time to import by 5 days (World Bank and IFC 2011). Finally, single online customs declarations were implemented in 2010.

Still, Colombia's logistics and transport efficiency indicators lag far behind those of Latin American peer countries. Despite the significant policy and institutional reforms, there is much room for improvement. Colombia's transport infrastructure in particular lags far behind that of regional peers; Colombia ranked 68th in the 2011–12 World Economic Forum's Global Competitiveness Report, behind Brazil (53), Chile (31), Mexico (57), and Peru (67) (World Economic Forum 2011). The proposed Free Trade Agreement with the United States has been an important development, but transport costs have been recently described as a greater barrier to U.S. exporters than tariffs (Salin and Mello 2009).

The excessive freight time is systematic, and deficiencies occur across all modes of transport. Addressing the problem also has proven to be a challenge, as shown by the fact that Colombia lags far behind all other competitors in Latin America in road paving and road density per capita. Total rail kilometers dropped significantly in past years, with many lines inactive and abandoned. However, this rail shortage is quickly changing with the mining-driven railway boom.[17] Export by rail from Cerrejón started in the 1980s, and from Drummond in the 1990s. Colombia's four public ports, and the port authorities themselves, were concessioned to private organizations in 1993; tonnage moved by the ports more than doubled between 2000 and 2008. However, additional investment in port infrastructure did not keep pace during the same period, and Colombia's port infrastructure quality has been surpassed by that of neighboring countries, such as Ecuador.

However, constraints go beyond logistics. High transport costs from the unique economic geography of Colombia's cities has led to the low specialization and trade imbalance evidenced in previous sections.

Transport costs for road freight transport in Colombia are extremely high (table 3.6). According to simulations conducted by Roda and Perdomo (2011), the cost of moving 1 ton from Bogotá to the Atlantic Coast is about US$94; shipping the same ton from Cartagena to the United States costs only about US$75.[18] Further, the cost of transporting 1 ton from Bogotá to Barranquilla is US$88, and from Bogotá to Buenaventura is US$54. In other words, transporting freight from Bogotá to Cartagena costs US$6 per ton more than to Barranquilla. Despite this cost differential, Cartagena is still the main port used to export cargo from Bogotá, followed by Buenaventura and Barranquilla. This is because of the preference for shipping through the port of Cartagena, which has the best rates and most frequent service. Cartagena also is the most convenient port for shipping to Colombia's main trade partners.

Costs to carry cargo by sea from Cartagena or Buenaventura to Rotterdam or Shanghai (about US$60 per ton) are also lower than the transport costs from Bogotá to the ports on the Atlantic and slightly higher in the case of the Pacific.[19] Accessing inland borders, according to this simulation, would cost US$79 per ton in the case of República Bolivariana de Venezuela (Cúcuta) and US$91 per ton in the case of Ecuador (Ipiales).

Per-kilometer unit costs are highest for short trips (133 kilometers), are relatively similar for trips between 230 and 850 kilometers, and decrease significantly for routes longer than 850 kilometers (table 3.7). For short distances, logistics represent up to 28 percent of the total costs of transport. For longer routes, logistics amount to only 7 percent. On long-distance routes, the ton-kilometer unit transport cost is US$0.09 below the level in

Table 3.6   Road Freight Costs, by Origin-Destination
US$ per ton

Origin-Destination	Bogotá	Medellín	Cali	Other regions
Barranquilla	88	71	111	91
Cartagena	94	68	116	96
Santa Marta	83	79	106	88
Búenaventura	54	56	16	75
Cúcuta (to Venezuela, RB)	79	81	108	97
Ipiales (to Ecuador)	91	94	47	103

Source: Roda and Perdomo 2011.

Table 3.7   Transport and Logistics Costs, by Trip Distance

Distance (km)	VOC (US$/ton)	Loading, unloading, and waiting time		VOC and logistics costs (US$/ton)	Per ton-km costs	Percentage of logistics costs
		Hours	US$/ton			
133	15.6	8.9	6.1	21.8	0.164	28
230	20.1	9.2	6.3	26.4	0.115	24
325	32.9	8.9	6.1	39.1	0.120	16
499	53.6	8.9	6.1	59.8	0.120	10
679	67.5	10.8	7.4	75.0	0.110	10
850	95.3	10.8	7.4	102.8	0.121	7
1,028	87.6	9.2	6.3	94.0	0.091	7

Source: 2007 Survey by EGIS BCEOM International.
Note: km = kilometer; VOC = vehicle operating costs.

Vietnam but higher than in India. For short routes, this cost almost doubles. This comparison illustrates how much savings can be achieved through increased efficiency and competitiveness by improving logistics platforms and operating transport schemes to ship cargos in less time (table 3.8).

The gravity model, a central piece in any economic geography study, suggests that the transport costs between two regions is a key determinant of the volume of trade between them. Further, it suggests that the flow of trade between two regions is directly proportional to the size of their economies and inversely proportional to the transport costs between them. This theory has been tested using various model specifications and fits quite accurately with the observed data.

Preliminary estimations using the gravity model (see table 3.9) suggest that reducing transport costs between two nodes by 10 percent would lead trade flows in the same route to increase by 10 percent. From this point of view, the benefits of improving transport infrastructure are not limited to direct savings in vehicle operating costs. Indirectly, lower transport costs catalyze new business opportunities and trade. Activities that today are unfeasible because of high transport costs might become feasible as transport costs decline, opening up new opportunities for cities. In the long run, lower transport costs can facilitate local industrial specialization and improve the efficiency and competitiveness of the national urban system.

Connectivity to international markets appears to be of great importance. The analysis presented in panel b of table 3.9 confirms the importance of international connectivity (measured by freight transport costs to the nearest seaport) in local economic growth (GDP growth). However, local GDP growth is not statistically associated with domestic connectivity, which is measured by freight transport costs to the nearest

Table 3.8 Origin–Destination Matrix of Freight Transport Costs

US$ per ton

	1	2	3	4	5	6	7	8	9	10	11	12	13	14	15	16	17	18	19	20	21	22	23	24	25	26	27	28	29	30
1 Arauca		98	135	69	85	122	115	141	84	132	86	160	140	107	118	143	146	101	151	101	129	133	139	99	131	137	59	127	68	43
2 Armenia	98		93	30	56	25	19	99	90	66	12	63	98	12	37	76	83	34	54	6	32	38	97	76	89	88	41	84	45	67
3 Barranquilla	135	93		88	51	117	111	13	73	134	82	155	30	89	71	144	29	102	146	96	124	111	23	134	10	20	85	27	103	105
4 Bogotá	69	30	88		45	81	74	79	64	18	91	93	38	47	74	29	33	66	83	33	60	65	91	47	83	89	13	79	16	39
5 Bucaramanga	85	56	51	45		81	74	57	35	97	77	45	118	56	53	47	107	62	66	110	33	59	87	91	47	53	35	42	60	55
6 Buenaventura	122	25	117	81	81		16	123	108	79	140	88	161	42	95	50	150	26	108	152	100	144	30	100	113	108	66	108	69	91
7 Cali	115	19	111	74	74	16		116	108	77	62	116	160	71	62	108	96	52	38	21	96	50	60	93	106	101	59	102	62	85
8 Cartagena	141	99	13	79	57	123	116		79	140	88	159	47	95	64	26	84	150	152	100	144	30	35	140	21	16	91	33	109	111
9 Cúcuta	84	90	73	64	35	108	108	79		79	30	47	32	26	60	84	43	152	66	51	87	41	96	125	69	74	69	64	94	89
10 Florencia	132	66	134	18	97	79	77	140	79		54	74	160	94	89	54	142	65	54	69	69	74	139	110	129	135	76	125	79	102
11 Ibagué	86	12	82	91	77	140	62	88	30	54		74	87	22	44	38	142	32	66	16	43	48	85	64	78	83	30	73	33	56
12 Ipiales	160	63	155	93	45	88	116	159	47	74	74		160	71	37	141	78	10	65	65	38	93	159	138	151	145	103	146	107	110
13 Maicao	140	98	30	38	118	161	160	47	32	160	87	160		94	32	106	152	111	69	56	62	128	8	139	21	42	90	17	108	110
14 Manizales	107	12	89	47	56	42	71	95	26	94	22	71	94		32	84	78	43	85	40	40	17	84	84	85	83	50	81	54	76
15 Medellín	118	37	71	74	53	95	62	64	60	89	44	37	32	32		106	152	43	85	33	85	41	41	96	79	52	62	75	65	87
16 Mocoa	143	76	144	29	47	50	108	26	84	54	38	141	106	84	106		152	69	56	34	62	62	50	120	140	10	96	38	87	115
17 Montería	146	83	29	33	107	150	96	84	43	142	142	78	152	78	152	152		111	69	79	109	87	50	79	38	104	45	93	48	70
18 Neiva	101	34	102	66	62	26	52	150	152	65	32	10	111	43	43	69	111		69	47	47	70	106	129	98	137	95	104	98	120
19 Pasto	151	54	146	83	66	108	38	152	66	54	66	65	69	85	85	56	69	69		38	29	84	50	79	142	84	45	137	98	120
20 Pereira	101	6	96	33	110	152	21	100	51	69	16	65	56	40	33	34	79	47	38		34	62	100	127	92	114	34	87	48	71
21 Popayán	129	32	124	60	33	100	96	144	87	69	43	38	62	40	85	62	109	47	29	34		62	150	111	120	92	62	115	76	98
22 Quibdó	133	38	111	65	87	144	50	30	41	74	48	93	128	40	41	62	87	70	84	62	62		127	137	119	41	77	114	80	103
23 Riohacha	139	97	23	91	87	30	60	35	96	139	85	159	8	84	41	50	50	106	50	100	150	127		137	14	29	89	15	107	108
24 San Jóse del Guaviare	99	76	134	47	91	100	93	140	125	110	64	138	139	84	96	120	79	129	79	127	111	137	137		129	135	59	125	32	57
25 Santa Marta	131	89	10	83	47	113	106	21	69	129	78	151	21	85	79	140	38	98	142	92	120	119	14	129		29	81	23	99	100
26 Sincelejo	137	88	20	89	53	108	101	16	74	135	83	145	42	83	52	10	104	137	84	114	92	41	29	135	29		87	29	104	106
27 Tunja	59	41	85	13	35	66	59	91	69	76	30	103	90	50	62	96	45	95	45	34	62	77	89	59	81	87		76	28	28
28 Valledupar	127	84	27	79	42	108	102	33	64	125	73	146	17	81	75	38	93	104	137	87	115	114	15	125	23	29	76		94	96
29 Villavicencio	68	45	103	16	60	69	62	109	94	79	33	107	108	54	65	87	48	98	98	48	76	80	107	32	99	104	28	94		27
30 Yopal	43	67	105	39	55	91	85	111	89	102	56	110	110	76	87	115	70	120	120	71	98	103	108	57	100	106	28	96	27	

Source: Roda and Perdomo 2011.

Note: Blank cells equal zero.

Table 3.9   Econometric Analysis

a. The gravity model			b. The local economic growth model		
Dependent variable: ln(trade flow, i↔j)	Model 1	Model 2	Dependent variable: GDP growth, 2000–08	Model 1	Model 2
ln(transport costs, i↔j)	−1.264***	−0.994***	GDP 2000	1.192***	0.487***
	(−7.21)	(−6.18)		(5.87)	(4.27)
ln(GDPi + GDPj)	1.804***	—	Mining	0.314	0.249
	(14.33)	—		(1.84)	(1.74)
ln(GDPi × GDPj)	—	1.167***	Transport costs to the nearest port	−0.567***	
	—	(19.07)		(−4.86)	
Port dummy	1436***	1.143**	Transport costs to the nearest big three city	0.0799	
	(6.8)	(6.7)		(0.56)	
Constant	7.15**	1.311	Average transport costs to ports	—	−1.025**
	(2.8)	(0.55)		—	(−2.85)
N	367	367	Average transport costs to big three cities	—	−0.205
R²	0.21	0.649		—	(−0.88)
F-stat	137	198	Constant	−8.596*	6.662
				(−2.33)	(1.03)
			N	19	26
			R²	0.837	0.668
			F-stat	18.67	6.162

Source: Roda and Perdomo 2011.
t-stats in parentheses
* $p < 0.05$, ** $p < 0.01$, *** $p < 0.001$
Robust standard errors

Source: Roda and Perdomo 2011.
All variables are in log.
t-stats in parentheses
* $p < 0.05$, ** $p < 0.01$, *** $p < 0.001$
Robust standard errors

Note: The parameters of the gravity model for internal trade relations were estimated at the department level. The dependent variable is the logarithm of trade flows in tons between region i and region j. Three independent variables were considered: the logarithm of the costs of transport, a Port dummy (1 if a source or destination corresponds to a port, 0 otherwise) and the logarithm of the sum of GDP of region i to region j (model 1) or the product (model 2). Transport costs are obtained directly from the transport model and are parameterized in this study, for each pair of origin–destination. The local economic growth model compares the relative importance of international versus domestic connectivity in determining local economic growth. International connectivity is measured by freight transport costs to the nearest seaport, while domestic connectivity by freight transport costs to the nearest large city among Bogotá, Cali, and Medellín. — = Not applicable.

large city among Bogotá, Medellín, and Cali. It is important to stress here that this lack of correlation may also be a result of the current weakness of trade flows between areas in Colombia. The results also suggest the beneficial effects of agglomeration economies (measured by the size of the local GDP) in promoting local economic growth.[20] The results in this analysis are only indicative of the correlation among trade flows, GDP, and connectivity and should be interpreted with caution.

Improving connectivity between cities in Colombia will improve both domestic and foreign competitiveness of cities. Investments to improve connections among cities across the urban network will also have a strong impact on competitiveness. A recent study by the IDB confirms these results, suggesting that a reduction of 12 percent in transport costs in Colombia would lead to an average increase of 9 percent in exports.

Colombia also experiences higher-than-necessary transport costs because of delays at ports. These delays have declined over time but continue to be a significant source of additional costs, with some of the busiest ports experiencing the longest delays. Time spent waiting at port is not cost free. It is estimated that for every hour that cargo remains idle, the cost is Col$826 per ton (US$0.69 per ton).[21] A recent study on logistics platforms characterized and quantified the logistics costs faced by different trucks at port terminals.[22] On average, truck drivers reported a lag time of nine hours between queuing for entry into the port facilities for freight unloading and reloading and departing on a return or new journey (table 3.10).

These cargo-processing times are relatively low in Santa Marta, presumably because of the high share of coal in the freight flow at that port and the presence of dedicated facilities for handling coal. Cartagena demonstrates greater delays in terminal processing times. However, a recently revised rule for access to the Cartagena terminal imposed fixed hours for the entry of each vehicle. The new system is expected to significantly reduce waiting times.

With 2007 survey data, it is possible to characterize the distribution of processing times. For a number of vehicles, delays far exceed national averages. The data also suggest high uncertainty in terminal transit times, limiting opportunities to optimize truck cycles and paths. Figure 3.4 shows that while the average loading times in Buenaventura were lower than those in Cartagena, the dispersion of time, as a measure of uncertainty, at Buenaventura is higher in almost all processes. Therefore, while shippers may face longer waiting times in Cartagena, the advantage of shorter delays at Buenaventura is undermined by high uncertainty.

Table 3.10   Vehicle Service Time at Marine Terminals

	Barranquilla	Buenaventura	Cartagena	Santa Marta
Average loading	3.40	3.29	3.83	2.58
Average unloading	2.91	2.76	3.28	2.20
Average waiting	2.88	2.85	3.71	2.50
Total hours	9.18	8.91	10.82	7.28

Source: BCOM 2007 Survey.

Figure 3.4   Histogram of Total Port Hours

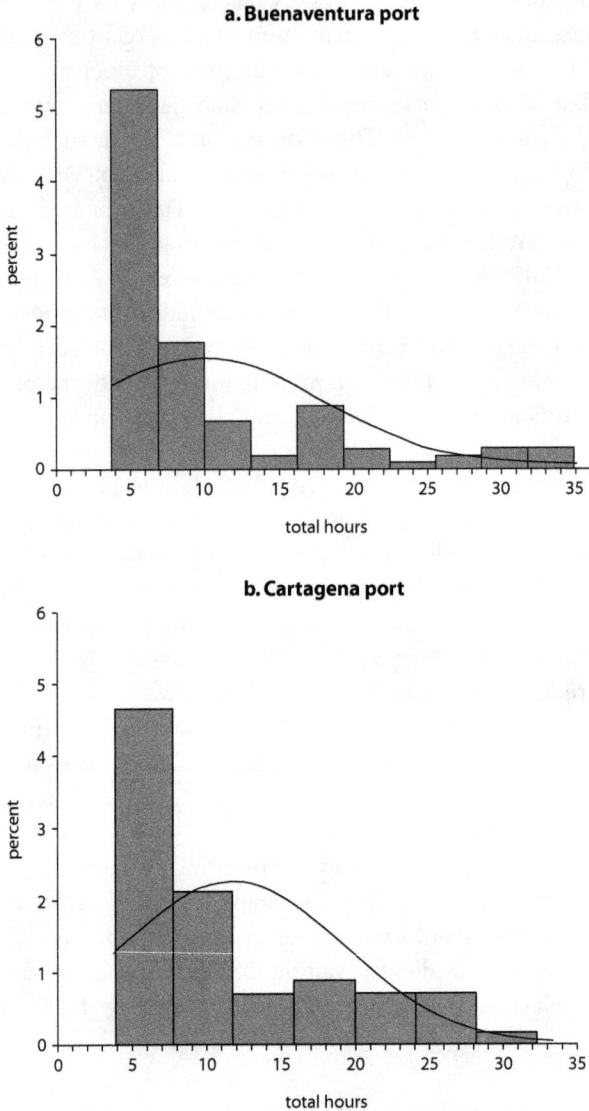

a. Buenaventura port

b. Cartagena port

Source: BCOM 2007 Survey.

Indeed, transport operators interviewed experienced high levels of congestion in the terminal and port area of Buenaventura while also reporting large variations in processing times.

Rail and fluvial transport are cost-effective for trips longer than 300 kilometers. These modes are significantly less expensive than road freight

transport, particularly for large volumes of heavy commodities. It is estimated that rail transport would cost only 25–30 percent of estimated
truck costs for long-haul trips. The transport model indicates that the rate
over long distances (800 kilometers) may be around US$0.023 (per ton-
kilometer) for flat terrain and US$0.035 for mountainous terrain. That is,
shipping by train would cost between one-third and one-fourth of the
cost of shipping by truck.[23] Colombia's current rail infrastructure, however, is very limited. Fluvial transport is even less expensive than rail, but
the high maintenance costs of frequent dredging appear to outweigh the
benefits. The costs of freight transport along the inland waterway between
Barrancabermeja and Barranquilla, according to the model, are estimated
at US$0.011 per ton-kilometer—almost a tenth of the unit cost by road.
If cargo cannot be assembled in the appropriate scale, the unit cost can
double, but this remains well below the cost of road transport.[24]

If intermodal logistics platforms were in place, rail would be economically viable for most routes longer than 300 kilometers. The
results of a preliminary simulation analyzing the competitiveness of
these three modes finds that, under the assumption of direct access to
marine terminals, as shown in figure 3.5, panel a, rail is more competitive than river transport, and these two modes are more competitive than road transport.[25] The difference in transport costs widens as
distance increases.

In a second scenario, the assumption is that neither the river nor the
rail transport system has direct access to marine terminals (as is the case
for Barranquilla and Cartagena by rail and Santa Marta by river). In this
scenario, an additional cost associated with the transfer of load to trucks

Figure 3.5   Simulation of Freight Transport Costs in Different Modes

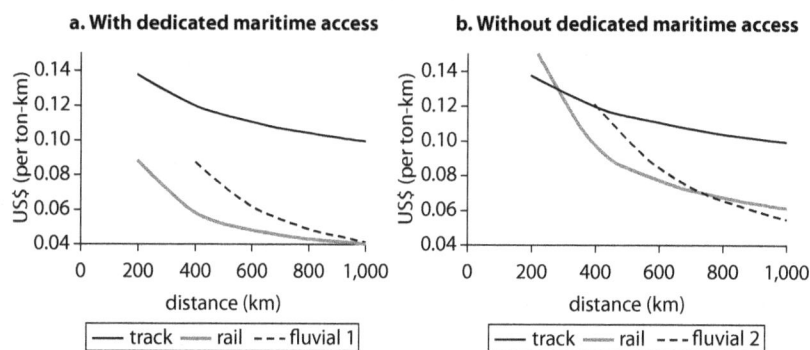

a. With dedicated maritime access   b. Without dedicated maritime access

Source: Roda and Perdomo 2011.
Note: km = kilometer.

is incurred for transporting goods to the seaport. As shown in figure 3.5, panel b, under this configuration, trucks are more cost effective for shorter distances under 300 kilometers, rail for medium distances between 300 kilometers and 700 kilometers, and river transport for distances more than 700 kilometers.

Trucks are faster and more flexible than either rail or water transport. Speed reduces logistical costs and maintains timely flow of goods. Because of these reasons, fluvial transport is also limited to low value per ton, but the financial costs associated with storage and warehousing requirements are lower.

The use of rail and river infrastructure for freight movement is limited and ineffective. In the case of railroads, the only reliable commercial operation is limited to routes between Chiriguaná–Ciénaga and Cerrejón–Puerto Bolívar, which only carry coal. In the case of the river, some freight service is available to the public, but a large percentage of transport consists of the movement of oil and its derivatives between Barrancabermeja and Cartagena (Ecopetrol operation). Many municipalities have rivers as their only means of transport, which means these municipalities can ship only low volumes of cargo. In general, no river in the country has the seaworthiness necessary to transfer and mount large-scale operations; nor is the equipment and infrastructure for doing so available.

The lack of alternative transport modes on major trade corridors reduces competition and efficiency. Each route has very little competition from other modes of transport. The lack of competition reduces efficiency within each mode. Truck transport completely dominates major trade corridors, such as that between Bogotá and Cartagena. A rail line along the same route, for example, would significantly increase efficiency because shippers could choose the best transport mode after considering specific cargo characteristics. Modal sharing will also reduce road traffic congestion.

The absence of intermodal infrastructure is a major driver of high transport costs and reduces Colombia's competitiveness. Transporting 1 ton-kilometer costs an average of US$0.091 by truck, US$0.055 by rail, and US$0.041 by river. Although truck transport has many advantages, such as reduced requirements for transfer (allowing direct shipment from the factory gate) and flexibility in lower frequencies and transit times, it is clear that for long-haul and low-value goods that are easily stored, rail and river transport are more efficient.

The study, based on the transport model, shows that savings in transport costs depend on the distance and modal shifts. This exercise allows us to conclude that trade would benefit if Colombia could build an inter-modal/multimodal corridor along the Magdalena route. The profitability of a massive system like this depends on significant freight demand to pay for initial investment costs, such as mining cargo from inland reservoirs. Once it has this critical mass, logistics platforms should be made at the transport nodes to extend logistics services to other products.

Thinking About Investment Priorities: An Analysis of Alternative Corridors

Establishing priorities for transport infrastructure investments requires targeted investment planning to maximize the impact on economic growth at the national level. The previous section suggested that infrastructure investments need to focus on main trade corridors with high freight traffic—and particularly on the routes connecting large Andean cities to international markets. The econometric analysis also suggests that reducing transport costs could have commensurate effects on increasing inter-regional trade and local economic growth.

To guide infrastructure investment planning, the study developed model simulations of various hypothetical investment scenarios, building on the newly developed transport model. These simulations rely on route-specific freight trade flows and their associated transport costs. The simulations identified six major corridors and the Atlantic ports for potential investment. This analysis focuses on the demand side of infrastructure investment by looking at trade flows. However, to choose among these six alternatives on the basis of costs and feasibility, an additional set of studies is required.

The analysis suggests that the corridor along the eastern mountain chain, connecting Bogotá to the Atlantic Coast ports, is under the greatest pressure and has the most investment potential (map 3.5). Second in importance is the route connecting the highlands to the Pacific ports (from Bogotá to Buenaventura). Finally, the western mountain chain route, stretching from the Pacific ports through Cali and Medellín to the ports of the Atlantic, is significant for imports and exports from the Pacific. This section discusses current conditions and investment planning of each trade corridor, as well as the Atlantic ports (map 3.6).[26]

Corridor 1: Eastern Corridor

The eastern corridor encompasses 55 percent of the country's economic activity. After Bogotá, which alone accounts for almost half of the national

Map 3.5   Allocation of Total Load Flows

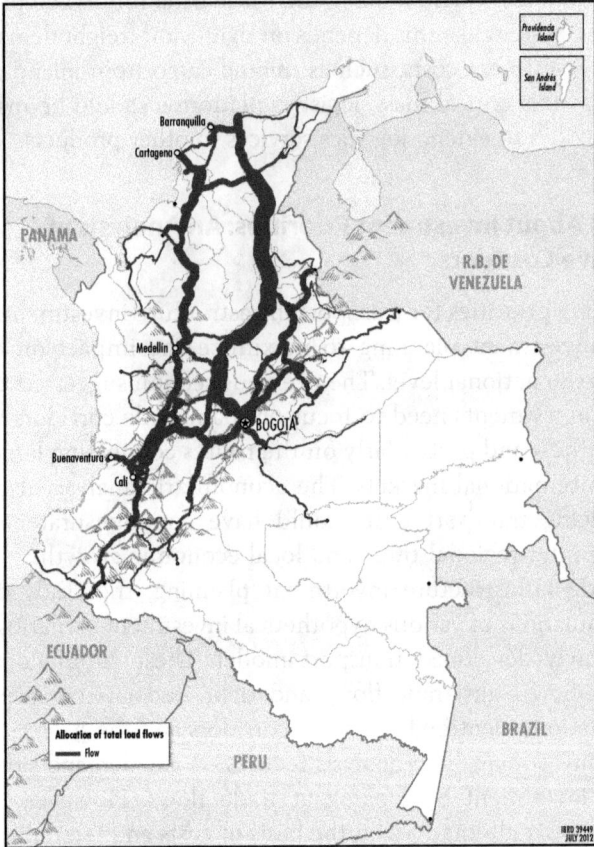

Source: Roda and Perdomo 2011.

economic activity, the corridor passes through the eastern plains region of Cundiboyacá, Santander, and cities along the upper Magdalena, and reaches the northeast coast. International trade flows are concentrated between Bogotá and the Atlantic Coast.

The Atlantic Coast ports account for most origins and destinations of Bogotá freight flows, but the corridor also plays an important role in mobilizing flows to subregions. Existing infrastructure is insufficient for the current volume and limits growth. In addition, transport costs are high, especially from the large urban centers of production in the Andes to the Atlantic ports (table 3.11).

Map 3.6   Main Trade Corridors

Main trade corridors
1. Eastern Corridor (Bogotá) to Atlantic Coast
2. Western Corridor Pacific Coast (Cali/Medellin) to Atlantic Coast
3. R.B. de Venezuela to Pacific
4. R.B. de Venezuela to Medellin
5. Bogotá to Medellin
6. Atlantic ports

IBRD 39450
JULY 2012

Source: Roda and Perdomo 2011.

The Carare coal railway represents a unique opportunity and a logical first step in consolidating intermodal transport and logistics hubs. It could also be used to bring inputs to cities more efficiently. This project is an alternative to transporting coal from internal to external markets through the Caribbean ports. The coal would provide the critical mass of freight necessary to make the project viable. Loads without coal and

Table 3.11   Transport Costs of the Eastern Corridor

Route to the Atlantic Coast	Distance (km)	VOC (US$/ton)	VOC and logistics costs (US$)
Amazonia	1,525	144.6	152.1
Sur	1,160	97.9	105.4
Llanos	1,224	108.7	116.2
Bogotá	1,104	93.5	101.0
Cundiboyacá	958	90.8	98.3
Santanderes	714	62.7	70.1
Norte	390	33.7	41.2

Source: Roda and Perdomo 2011.
Note: km = kilometer; VOC = vehicle operating costs. The table reports the estimates of transport costs between different origin-destination pairs of the corridor, as calculated by HDM-IV for a semi-trailer accounting for terrain, congestion, and the logistics costs associated with the ports of destination and the main cities.

other minerals are not sufficient to support the investment and operating costs of this infrastructure. From this point of view, if the Carare coal railway can be extended to carry other freight, the project could focus on a new multimodal corridor to reduce transport costs for both inputs entering the cities and export of the products.

The Carare railroad already has a preliminary structure[27] that ensures access to the Fenoco line and, consequently, guarantees some degree of financial viability. Currently, the railroad carries only 46 percent of the coal freight sent to the ports on the coast. Estimated investments are nearly US$1 billion for rail infrastructure and US$560 million for equipment. The annual operating cost is estimated at US$15 million, including the payment of tolls for the use of the core Fenoco network. Eventually, the railway can be extended to serve Medellín.

Expansion of the Carare railroad could save 47–51 percent of transport costs. The impact of the project on transport costs is immense, as shown in table 3.12. According to model simulations, the current road freight costs would be reduced by 47 percent in scenarios 1 and 2 and by 51 percent in scenario 3.[28]

Fluvial transport options are possible, but only if the private sector takes the lead. The Magdalena River could be an alternative for exporting large flows of coal and other minerals, as discussed in the government's expansion plan for mining and energy. However, when building a multimodal system, the cooperation of the private sector is necessary to develop dry ports for transfers to other modes, particularly in large cities, and to develop seaports in Barranquilla or Cartagena.

Table 3.12   Simulation of Transport Costs between Bogotá and the Atlantic Ports under Different Scenarios for the Carare Railroad

Route	Destination	Transport costs (US$/ton)	Distance (km)	Unit transport cost (US$/ton)	Relative to the current costs (%)
Highway	Ciénaga	151,825	964	0.087	100
Rail Carare–Fenoco	Ciénaga	71,501	924	0.043	47
Rail Carare–Fluvial transfer	Barranquilla	71,803	1,047	0.038	47
Rail Carare–Dibulla train	Dibulla	76,953	1,056	0.040	51

Source: Roda and Perdomo 2011.
Note: km = kilometer.

In addition, investments can be prioritized to strengthen the double-lane 1,000-kilometer Ruta del Sol highway and consolidate the corridor from Bogotá to the Caribbean ports. This route can be supplemented with the following investments: a lane between Girardot and Honda and a bridge between La Bodega and Yati.

Corridor 2: Western Corridor

The western corridor connects Medellín and Cali to the Atlantic and Pacific ports, linking areas that produce 35 percent of the national GDP. Medellín would be the primary beneficiary of the corridor, from increased import-export activity to the Caribbean and, to a lesser extent, Pacific ports. Imports to Medellín are split relatively evenly between the Pacific and the Atlantic coasts.

Total freight flows along this corridor are high but are dominated by intraregional movement. About 70 million tons of freight flowed along the western corridor in 2010, equivalent to 41 percent[29] of the total load of the country. However, while the western corridor can be considered a major artery, it primarily links economic activity in the western half of the country, with only 20 percent of the load generated in the corridor destined for other regions.

Freight transport costs are higher for segments linking highlands to the Atlantic Coast (table 3.13). In the case of Medellín, the transport costs to the two coasts are almost same. Route selection depends mainly on the origin-destination of foreign trade and other parameters not related to route-specific transport costs.

Simulations indicate that investing in an alternate route from Medellín to the Caribbean ports could generate cost savings of US$232 million

Table 3.13   Transport Costs of the Western Corridor

Route	Distance (km)	VOC (US$/ton)	VOC and logistics costs (US$/ton)
To the Atlantic Coast			
Ecuador	1,531	160.8	168.2
Intermedia Sur	1,333	140.8	148.3
Cali	1,087	116.3	123.7
Intermedias Eje Cafetero	873	97.9	105.4
Medellín	679	67.5	75.0
Intermedias Norte	218	21.1	28.5
To the Pacific Coast			
Costa Atlántica	1,123	122.9	129.0
Intermedias Norte	907	105.1	111.2
Ecuador	582	61.4	67.5
Medellín	511	56.5	62.6
Intermedia Sur	385	41.4	47.5
Intermedias Eje Cafetero	275	28.5	34.7
Cali	133	15.6	21.8

Source: Roda and Perdomo 2011.
Note: km = Kilometer; VOC = vehicle operating costs.

annually in general transport, which implies a present value savings of US$2 billion for over a 20-year period, using a 10 percent real discount rate. The immediate recommendation is to study the project in detail; if the project costs are lower than the quoted amount of savings, investment is warranted.

The investment plan for the western route would contain the following elements: (1) integrate Medellín with the southwestern divided highway system (mountain highway), connecting Manuela–La Pintada and La Pintada–Bolombolo–Medellín; (2) ensure efficient flows from Medellín to the Atlantic, through a more-thorough evaluation of the following alternatives: Medellín–Puerto Berrio (Ruta del Sol), Medellín–Puerto Valdivia (current route), Santa Fe de Antioquia–Puerto Valdivia (geographic corridor through the valley of Cauca), Bolombolo–Santa Fe de Antioquia, or Medellín–Santa Fe de Antioquia; (3) develop divided highways, where necessary, between Popayán and Jamundí, in the coffee highlands, and between Puerto Valdivia and Sincelejo; and (4) consolidate access to Urabá from Medellín and Montería.

Corridor 3: República Bolivariana de Venezuela–Pacific Corridor

This corridor connects the border with República Bolivariana de Venezuela with the Pacific ports and includes many key cities of the eastern Andes (Bogotá, Santanderes, Boyacá, and Llanos Orientales). Export goods flow predominantly from the central Andean cities to the coasts. Domestic freight flows on this route are fragmented and load specific.

Improving the connection between the foothills and the Venezuelan plains is perhaps the most important project for the Pacific–República Bolivariana de Venezuela corridor. According to the model, the cost savings in transport are nearly US$549 million in present value. It is necessary to enable improved border crossing in Arauca (Arauca and Saravena). Indeed, the path between Villavicencio and Caracas is mostly flat, unlike the Cúcuta route, which has extensive sections in mountainous terrain (table 3.14).

The recommended strategic investments would include projects for (1) expanding the missing sections of the routes Bogotá–Buenaventura, Ibagué–Cajamarca, Calarcá–La Paila, and Media Canoa–Buga with divided highways, and as a secondary priority, completing the second line tunnel and the Citronella–Buenaventura expansion; (2) promoting the development of an outer port in Buenaventura; (3) developing logistics platforms to promote access for trucks and freight handling in Bogotá; (4) consolidating the divided highway where the level of service is inadequate, such as Zipaquirá–Bucaramanga, Bucaramanga–Cúcuta,

Table 3.14   Transport Costs of the República Bolivariana de Venezuela–Pacific Corridor

Route	Distance (km)	VOC (US$/ton)	VOC and logistics costs (US$/ton)
To the Pacific Coast			
Bogotá	499	53.6	59.8
Cundiboyacá	649	65.5	71.7
Llanos	618	68.8	75.0
Santanderes	887	97.6	103.7
Sur	293	36.6	42.7
To Venezuela, RB			
Cali	918	107.9	116.7
Eje Cafetero	749	91.9	100.7
Sur	663	79.1	87.9
Llanos	697	94.1	102.9
Bogotá	587	78.9	87.7
Cundiboyacá	446	68.9	77.7

Source: Roda and Perdomo 2011.
Note: VOC = vehicle operating costs.

and Bogotá–Villavicencio; (5) consolidating the network of the foothills and the border crossing to República Bolivariana de Venezuela (divided highway where traffic is required, such as between Cumaral and Tame [New Track Hato Corozal–Tame]), branches to Saravena and Arauca, Granada–San José del Guaviare, and Puerto Lopez–Puerto Gaitán; and (6) consolidating modern logistics facilities on the border with República Bolivariana de Venezuela for unrestricted cross-border freight movement.

Corridor 4: República Bolivariana de Venezuela–Medellín Corridor

Freight flows to and from República Bolivariana de Venezuela have been historically volatile, due to frequent changes in tariff and subsidy policies (table 3.15). Cúcuta is an important receiver for exports from Medellín, Manizales, and Bucaramanga. Transport costs are high and are hindered by the lack of logistics facilities at the border.

The key investments would include, depending on the level of service, broadening the capacity of the divided highways between Hatillo–Puerto Berrio and La Lizama–Bucaramanga. In addition, a feasibility study should examine extending the operation of the railway to Medellín (Puerto Berrio–Bello) and developing a dry port to facilitate the handling of the containerized freight logistics of the city.

Corridor 5: Bogotá–Medellín Corridor

Freight flow between the Bogotá and Medellín is relatively low. The two cities have similar economic structures and, consequently, act as substitutes rather than complements. Transport costs between Bogotá and Medellín do not seem excessive and are probably not the explanation for the weak relationship between these cities (table 3.16).

The worst stretch on the Bogotá–Medellín route is Honda–Puerto Triunfo as this section was affected by the failed Comsa concession. The

Table 3.15 Transport Costs of the República Bolivariana de Venezuela–Medellín Corridor

Route to Venezuela, RB	Distance (km)	VOC (US$/ton)	VOC and logistics costs (US$/ton)
Medellín	559.3	81.0	87.1
Coffee region	661.9	86.8	92.9

Source: Roda and Perdomo 2011.
Note: km = kilometer; VOC = vehicle operating costs.

Table 3.16   Transport Costs of the Bogotá–Medellín Corridor

Destination	Distance (km)	VOC (US$/ton)	VOC and logistics costs (US$/ton)
Medellín	458	50.7	56.3
Bogotá	458	50.7	56.9

Source: Roda and Perdomo 2011.
Note: km = kilometer; VOC = vehicle operating costs.

stretch of Guaduas–Honda is interrupted as of the time of this publication. The area between Villeta and Honda is perhaps the busiest in the entire national road network and a real bottleneck to trade. These improvements are already included in the Ruta del Sol project.

As described in other corridors, the divided highway between Bogotá and Puerto Triunfo is part of the Bogotá Coast Ruta del Sol and will likely correct the current congestion problems. Because of weak economic relations between Bogotá and Medellín, the need for a divided highway between Puerto Triunfo and municipalities in eastern Antioquia is not anticipated.

Corridor 6: The Atlantic Ports

Ports along the Atlantic Coast are centers for import and export as well as centers of intraregional manufacturing and industrial activity. Trade flows among Barranquilla, Cartagena, and Santa Marta are relatively low. There is an imbalance of flows between Barranquilla and Cartagena—in favor of the former, which may be explained by the larger size of Barranquilla and the diversity of its production.

Investment priorities would include (1) constructing a divided highway between Ciénaga and Barranquilla; (2) improving access to ports such as Santa Marta (road and rail), Barranquilla (urban access and maritime channel access), and Cartagena (expanding access to the sea and consolidating a divided highway between Cartagena and Gambote); and (3) considering an outer harbor logistics service to support the three ports by rail or road mode.

Priority Policy Agenda

Spatial Planning for Infrastructure Investment

Reshaping Colombia's economic geography has significant bearing on the future of the Colombian economy and its global competitiveness.

Given the complex economic geography challenges in Colombia, the study indicates two key growth pole corridors that connect the largest economic engines in Colombia (Bogotá) to international markets and pass through emerging industrial clusters are vital to trade. These corridors are the eastern corridor, which travels from Bogotá to the northeast coast, and the western corridor, which connects Medellín and Cali to the Atlantic and Pacific ports. In addition, the expansion of the road between Bolombolo and Puerto Valdivia along the Cauca River and improvements to the border crossing in Arauca could significantly reduce transport costs and facilitate international trade.

In terms of the eastern corridor from Bogotá, the study indicates that infrastructure investments can best be directed toward facilitating intermodal linkages with ongoing railway projects spurred by the mining boom. The model simulation of the study estimates that railway transport between the Bogotá and Caribbean ports using the Carare–Fenoco railways can reduce current transport costs for road freight by one-half.

While increased intermodal transport could promote trade with U.S. and European markets in the Atlantic, the focus in the Pacific (western) corridor should continue to focus on road transport for trade with U.S. and Asian markets. The Pacific corridor from Bogotá currently transports international freight much cheaper than the eastern (Atlantic) counterpart. The current transport cost from Bogotá to Buenaventura is as low as US$54, compared to Caribbean ports (US$83 to US$94). Even though railway transport along the eastern corridor would reduce transport costs significantly, the Pacific corridor can compete with the eastern corridor thanks to its short-distance trip and competition in different transport modes.

Finally, an expansion of the road between Bolombolo and Puerto Valdivia along the Cauca River would be highly beneficial for Medellín, Colombia's second-largest industrial center. This road could provide an alternative route to access the Atlantic ports by using less mountainous terrain. The consolidation of the road system in the eastern plains, and development of the crossing in Arauca, would facilitate regional trade with República Bolivariana de Venezuela.

Overall, the analysis indicates that provision of alternative transport modes and competition among different routes and transport modes will optimize the use of transport infrastructure and increase the overall efficiency of the transportation sector. It would catalyze industrial specialization across the system of cities and, consequently, increase the competitiveness of Colombia.

Thinking Beyond Infrastructure: Institutional and Regulatory Reforms in the Transport Sector

While this study did not enter into a detailed assessment of the regulatory environment for freight transport in Colombia, the following conclusions and recommendations build on the studies and policy reports of various stakeholders, including the World Bank, multilaterals, and technical consultants. Key areas for institutional and regulatory reforms in the transport and logistics sector include (1) institutional and regulatory reforms to match responsibilities and financial resources; (2) new legal frameworks for concessions, public access to dedicated transport facilities, and subsidies and fees; and (3) the development of intermodal infrastructure with strong government leadership and intervention.

Transport lags far behind the regulatory and institutional frameworks of several other public services, including energy, communications, and water. Each of these sectors has an independent regulatory commission and a set of principles for tariffs, interconnection, access, and market structure. These interventions aim to increase efficiency and support service gains in these markets. Unfortunately, the transportation sector operates under a law originally developed for maritime transport; as a result, some of the key regulatory "pieces of the puzzle" are missing. The sector does not have a fully independent regulatory commission with the necessary fiscal, technical, and human resources to begin building a solid regulatory framework.

Jurisdictional authority and financing mechanism should be clarified. There is no solid framework to guide how the transport sector is financed and how it fits into the decentralization process. Regulations that directly address day-to-day planning, operations, and execution of contracts are noticeably absent. For example, it is essential to ensure that third parties have access to transport infrastructure of central corridors for external trade. It is also important to implement a framework of tariffs and subsidies to level the field and facilitate competition among the different modes of transport.

Initiatives such as creating a fund to provide a stable flow of resources to maintain the road network would facilitate clearer interjurisdictional coordination by establishing new legal vehicles. Specific responsibilities should be assigned to existing jurisdictional structures, along with clear legal authority and responsibility for oversight. For example, it is important to consolidate the decentralization process by assigning responsibility for the roads to whomever can best manage them. An efficient institution is needed to lead these processes and optimize economies of scale.

The national road network comes under the responsibility of two entities. The first is the National Roads Institute (INVIAS), which is in charge of construction, rehabilitation, and maintenance of the road network not operating under concessions. The INVIAS issues traditional public service contracts with third parties but has neither sufficient equipment for direct interventions nor adequate resources to maintain the additional 27,000 kilometers of tertiary roads. The second entity is the National Infrastructure Agency (ANI), recently created out of the National Concessions Institute (INCO), which is responsible for the road network that operates under concessions. ANI was created to tackle institutional weakness in INCO, which was responsible to structure, assign, and supervise more than 20 concession contracts covering almost 4,500 kilometers. As the process of institutional transition is ongoing, it is not yet clear how this reorganization will affect the operation of the road network under concession. The concessions scheme—which was implemented in the 1990s to accelerate the construction and expansion of roads—has become increasingly inefficient. Most contracts have been renegotiated, losing sight of market competitiveness and best practice, and many signed agreements lack efficiency in cost and investment.

The freight transport sector has a particularly low level of regulation. Countless small and informal associations of truckers dominate the sector. Trucking rates are, in theory, market driven; until early 2011, however, they were based on government-published tables. A sector cost analysis model replaced this system. Freight pricing is made more difficult by the uncertainty and long wait times when handling loads. Under-regulation in other public services, such as parking areas, creates higher operating costs. A vice ministry was recently created to tackle the economic and technical regulation of freight and passenger transport.

The regulation of railways and ports is also insufficient. Colombia has experimented with several models of managing a public-access railway. To date, all have failed, including public corporations, infrastructure and operational concessions, and integrated concessions. Developing intermodal transport requires rethinking the expansion of publicly accessible rail. Publicly owned port operators, in contrast, were dissolved in the early 1990s, and operations were concessioned. A more comprehensive development of coastal ports was envisioned, but a lack of "top-down" planning and legal authority resulted in a proliferation of diverse private initiatives and prevented the efficient consolidation of a few terminals that are correctly connected to transport networks.

Dedicated infrastructure is expanding, but public access is under-exploited because of a weak regulatory environment. Providing this access is a growing challenge. Colombia is experiencing a mining boom concentrated in large holdings by multinational companies. These companies have had the vision and the financial muscle to develop their own rail and port infrastructure specialized in handling coal. These lines are typically efficient, and indeed two of the main lines move more than 60 million tons of coal each year in the Caribbean region. However, owners are deterred from renting this infrastructure to third parties as a result of high costs and uncertainties related to insufficient regulation.

The transportation sector in general is marked by unstable and uneven financing. Subsidies and fees are often inconsistent between modes and are insufficient. In addition, unstable funding can disincentivize proactive investment. In the case of roads, this has resulted in a deteriorating condition of the network and higher operating costs.

Creating maintenance funds could help to counter the problems associated with unstable financing. A road maintenance fund, for example, could address the backlog in maintenance across the network. In addition, such a fund would also allow users to participate in setting priorities, determining fee levels, and structuring efficient monitoring mechanisms.

On concessioned roads, regulated transport tariffs include a component for covering the costs of administration, operation, and maintenance. On roads not under concession, in contrast, maintenance depends on an unstable flow of insufficient resources, with little leeway for proactive interventions. This equilibrium is not efficient for the government because it results in more spending in the long term and sacrifices the road assets. The equilibrium also negatively impacts users, as the poor condition of the network results in higher operating costs. A road maintenance fund established with revenue from user charges, in addition to solving the backlog in maintenance at all levels of the network, could introduce new elements. For example, users could participate in setting the priorities for the fund, determining fee levels, and structuring efficient monitoring mechanisms.

As is discussed in greater depth in chapter 4, Colombia underwent a process of extensive decentralization that was consolidated in the 1991 constitution. In the transportation sector, this process has led to the responsibility for roads being distributed among 33 departments and about 1,100 municipalities. However, this responsibility for roads was not matched with resources for road network maintenance, and it did not take into account that road maintenance has economies of scale. In addition, some municipalities lack institutional capacity (equipment and human resources) and even departments to meet the decentralized responsibility for roads with the desired efficiency.

In addition, national transport planning has been driven by uncoordinated regional interests and, in large part, by regional politics. Initiatives such as Plan 2500, the "competitiveness arteries," and allocation of concessions have been developed without reference to models or research into traffic flows. National planning requires stronger backing in assessing needs and gathering information. There are indications that this is shifting under the current administration. This is important because intermodal logistics platforms require governmental intervention. Private sector actors do not have the capacity or collaborative structures to develop intermodal/multimodal corridors and logistics platforms on their own. The government should give clear signs about long-term plans and invest strategically to direct private resources to consolidate multimodal solutions.

Freight transport operations must be modernized, and a critical mass of large companies that can guarantee norms and advocate for more efficient turnaround times with businesses is essential. Subsidies have been discussed as a means to provide companies with incentives to comply with standards. Public sector contracts, as well as those done through concessions, are beset by problems. Several large factors are to blame: the legal framework, the financial model, the weakness of the judiciary, opportunistic bidding behaviors, insufficient studies, and the ability to renegotiate concessions.

Railways can have competitive advantages over road for medium- to long-distance freight transport. However, the railways' viability depends on ensuring a minimum demand. The government should play a central role in promoting initiatives that could allow railways to operate in strategic corridors. Ideally, the operation of railways needs to be aligned (perhaps from the ownership structure) with that of ports and other intermodal transfer centers of dry ports and waterways.

Similarly, it would be useful to implement electronic systems that integrate information from various forms of transport and thereby permit the seamless movement of domestic cargo (cargo manifest) and foreign cargo (customs and freight list manifest). Such a system would streamline the transfer process at ports and borders, improve information for planning purposes, allow increased control over these flows, and reduce waiting times at ports and for customs procedures.

Notes

1. National Decree 2828.

2. Along with equality of opportunity and consolidation of peace.

3. See World Bank (2004, 2005), Fay and Morrison (2007), Cárdenas and Escobar (2005), Pérez (2005), and ALG (2008).

4. Across income levels in Latin America and the Caribbean, food is the primary purchase of households accounting for 20–30 percent of all expenditures, depending upon the country. In Colombia, the poorest decile of the population spends almost half of its disposable income on food (Schwartz et al. 2009). "Logistics, Transport and Food Prices in LAC: Policy Guidance for Improving Efficiency and Reducing Costs."

5. This is not the case of Medellín, which receives cement and other materials from other locations.

6. India is an example where manufacturing firms are increasingly locating in suburban areas around the largest seven cities (*India Urbanization Review* [World Bank forthcoming]).

7. Valle del Cauca, Antioquia, and Cundinamarca.

8. Bolívar, Atlántico, Magdalena, and Cauca.

9. The total road flows were taken from the National Survey of Cargo 2008, which was administered by the Ministry of Transportation. This is a survey of a sample of truckers conducted in more than 60 strategic points of the road network for a short period of time. The survey records the type of truck, age of the truck carrying the product, its origin and destination (municipality), and the tonnage transported. The firm conducting the survey extrapolated these results to estimate the annual flows at the national level, taking into account the seasonality of the products detected and traffic counting stations, among other variables. The Ministry made available to the study team the most recent Freight Survey 2008. To reconcile the internal load with the foreign trade flows, it took year 2008 as the base year and 2010 used as the economic performance of each sector and "driver" of the freight during these two years.

10. The bulk of the foreign trade data was obtained from the database updated annually by the National Bureau of Statistics (DANE) and the Directorate of Taxes (DIAN). This database feeds on the customs documents and, consequently, includes all foreign trade transactions. Among other variables, it includes some information of value (cost, insurance, and freight and FOB), weight (kilograms), origin and destination internal (department) and external (country) of entry or exit, and the value of freight and insurance. For this year, the government made available to the study team base year 2010; consequently, the analysis reflects the current conditions of Colombian foreign trade.

11. The implicit price per ton of flower exports was estimated at US$5,607.

12. For example, coffee is trucked from the mountains to ports and then shipped, while sugar is grown in the Cauca Valley and exported through the Pacific port of Buenaventura.

13. It is noteworthy to mention that the internal load calculation is an approximation and makes comparisons with the flows of production and consumption. The load is derived from the extrapolation of survey results from one sample to the total load. Foreign trade data are gathered from all the universe of transactions from the trade tax database. From this point of view, any error in the expansion factors of the survey result in estimation errors of the internal trade load. Also, one ton of product may be involved in more than one trip (transfers) and, as a result, the remainder of the tonnage of the foreign trade to the total load might yield uncertain values. Specific products are subject to multiple transfers with their weight in the moved cargo greater than the total production. This is the case for coffee, which is transported from the plantation to a thresher at a storage facility and from the storage to the port. For the statistics of cargo, 1 ton of coffee is counted under the transport optics up to three times.

14. To compare these figures in Mexico, for example, 466 million tons of load were moved by road (2.6 million in Colombia) with a distance of 218,000 million kilometers traveled (three times that recorded in Colombia), which means the routes are located at 469 kilometers per trip, slightly higher than the 399 kilometers of Colombia (Statistical Handbook 2009 of the Transport Sector, Ministry of Communications and Transport). Presumably, there are fewer secondary routes in the country where production facilities are close to the seaports.

15. Methodological limitations are as noted in previous note.

16. For example, in early 2011, the government stopped recommending minimum freight rates for each trip.

17. World Bank, World Development Indicators Database, http://siteresources .worldbank.org/DATASTATISTICS/Resources/GDP.pdf; Salin and Mello (2009).

18. It includes cargo handling fees at ports.

19. Only for maritime costs, excluding port fees.

20. The ordinary least squares estimation used in this econometric analysis implies statistical association between regressors and the dependant variable, and not necessarily the direction of causality.

21. *The Sistema de Información de Costos Eficientes del Transporte Automotor de Carga* (Information System of Cost Efficient Transportation by Motor Vehicle) transport model.

22. Study of the feasibility of logistics platforms at Bogotá and the region of the Savannah of Bogotá, by BCOM (EGIS BCEOM International) in 2007.

23. This simulation was performed for a flow of 3 million tons per year proportionate load. The optimal scenario requires 8 locomotives dragging 50 wagons with a capacity of 30 tons each. Like the river, if the load is unbalanced, the costs are multiplied by two.

24. This exercise assumes a distance of 550 kilometers and an annual flow of 1.5 million tons. According to the model, the pattern of operation requires 22 tugs dragging 44 barges of 400 tons, which takes 8 days for a round trip, which takes place with a convoy for 45 trips a year.

25. It was assumed that trucks carry the load directly from the factory gate to the seaport. In the first graph, a truck transports a load to a hypothetical railway station located in the metropolitan area. The railroad in this scenario directly downloads the product at the marine terminal. The load is assumed to be transported by truck for 200 kilometers for fluvial transport because none of the major Colombian cities are located on the banks of the rivers. Fluvial loads are assumed to transfer directly to the seaport, without a further modal shift.

26. Consult the background paper for a detailed description of each trade corridor.

27. In particular, the Brazilian company Odebrecht performed the conceptual layout of the line in a corridor that minimizes the slopes connecting the highlands with the Magdalena Valley up to the mouth of the Carare River (near Puerto Berrio). Subsequently, the consortium Sumatoria Incoplan prestructured the project, which estimates the investment and operating costs, the demand from surveys of miners, the financial model, and as a result, the rate per ton. This project has a sponsor, Corpoferrocarare, which brings miners to the area.

28. Three alternative rail routes were modeled, using the transport model. The first line modeled is to build the Carare railroad, and ensure access to the railway line that operates under a grant from Chiriguana Fenoco and Ciénaga. The second provides for a transfer to the Magdalena River at the river port of Capulco and for the development of a specialized coal shipping terminal in Barranquilla. The third includes the construction of a new railway line between Dibulla and Chiriguaná and bordering the Sierra Nevada on the eastern side.

29. The corridor originates and receives 83 million tons per year by road, which represents 47 percent of the total freight in the country in this way. Not all of this puts pressure on the freight corridor. Those flows originating and destined within the same area, in practice, do not use this inter-municipal corridor but use city streets or highways.

Bibliography

Advanced Logistics Group. 2008. *Diseño Conceptual de un Esquema de Sistemas de Plataformas Logísticas en Colombia y Análisis Financiero y Legal (Primera Fase)*. Bogotá: Departamento Nacional de Planeación.

Blyde, J., and C. Volpe Martincus. 2011. "Shaky Roads and Trembling Exports: Assessing the Trade Effects of Domestic Transport Costs Using a Natural Experiment." Paper presented at the Forum for Research in Empirical International Trade, Ljubljana, Slovak Republic, June 9–11. http://www.freit.org/LETC/2011/SubmittedPapers/Christian_Volpe_Martincus74.pdf.

Cárdenas, M., and A. Escobar. 2005. "Infraestructura y Crecimiento Departamental 1950–1994." *Planeación y Desarrollo* 26 (4).

Fay, M., and M. Morrison. 2007. *Infrastructure in Latin America and the Caribbean: Recent Developments and Key Challenges*. Washington, DC: World Bank.

Haussman, R., and B. Klinger. 2008. "Achieving Export-Led Growth in Colombia." CID Working Paper 182, Harvard University, Cambridge, MA.

IDB (Inter-American Development Bank). 2011. *Program to Support the National Logistics Policy (CO-L1090) Loan Proposal*. Washington, DC: Inter-American Development Bank. http://idbdocs.iadb.org/wsdocs/getdocument.aspx?docnum=36261654.

Pérez, G. 2005. "La Infraestructura del Transporte Vial y la Movilización de Carga en Colombia." Documentos de Trabajo sobre Economía Regional 64, Banco de la República, Cartagena de Indias, Colombia.

Renner, G. T. 1927. "Colombia's Internal Development." *Economic Geography* 3 (2): 259–64.

Roda, P., and F. Perdomo. 2011. "Costos de transporte y eficiencia económica en Colombia: Revisión del proceso de urbanización en Colombia. Fase II." Background Study for the *Colombia Urbanization Review*.

Salin, D., and E. Mello. 2009. *Snapshot of Colombian Transportation and Infrastructure*. Washington, DC: Office of Global Analysis, United States Department of Agriculture Foreign Agricultural Service.

Schwartz, J., J. L. Guasch, G. Wilmsmeir, and A. Stokenberga. 2009. "Logistics, Transport and Food Prices in LAC: Policy Guidance for Improving Efficiency and Reducing Costs." Sustainable Development Occasional Paper Series 2, Inter-American Development Bank and World Bank, Washington, DC.

Stokes, C. J. 1967. "The Freight Transport System of Colombia, 1959." *Economic Geography* 43 (1): 71–90.

World Bank. 2004. "Colombia: Recent Economic Developments in Infrastructure (REDI). Balancing Social and Productive Needs for Infrastructure." World Bank, Washington, DC.

————. 2005. *Colombia Public Expenditure Review.* Washington, DC: World Bank.

————. 2006. *Infraestructura Logística y de Calidad para la Competitividad de Colombia.* Washington, DC: World Bank.

————. Forthcoming. *India Urbanization Review.* Washington, DC: World Bank.

World Bank. 2011. World Development Indicators Database. http://siteresources .worldbank.org/DATASTATISTICS/Resources/GDP.pdf.

World Bank and IFC (International Finance Corporation). 2011. *Doing Business Report on Colombia.* Washington, DC: World Bank. http://www.doingbusiness .org.

World Economic Forum. 2011. *Global Competitiveness Report 2010–2011.* Geneva: World Economic Forum. http://www3.weforum.org/docs/WEF_ GlobalCompetitivenessReport_2010-11.pdf.

CHAPTER 4

Interjurisdictional Coordination

Nancy Lozano-Gracia, Alexandra Panman, and Alejandro Rodriguez

Introduction

Decentralization has left its mark on administrative reforms throughout the developed and developing world. In many cases, increased decentralization was promoted under the theory that creating a competitive environment between individual jurisdictions is a manifestation of good governance. As recent evidence shows, however, decentralization is not an all-purpose solution for a more-efficient local government. Decisions taken in a vacuum can cause a host of unintended consequences, which often spill over jurisdictional boundaries.

For example, recent work covering U.S. jurisdictions that introduced smoke-free bar laws suggests that these jurisdictions have suffered from an increase in drunk-driving-related accidents (Adams and Cotti 2008). This type of increase has not been observed in jurisdictions without bans. This work finds evidence consistent with two possible explanations for the increased accident rate: (1) smokers driving longer distances to

This chapter was written with input from Robert Yaro and Nicolas Ronderos (Regional Plan Association) and Francisco Rodriguez Vitta. The background paper, "International Metropolitan Governance: Typology, Case Studies and Recommendations" (Yaro and Ronderos 2011), is available on the World Bank's Urbanization Review website (http://www.urbanknowledge.org/ur.html).

bordering jurisdictions without bans and (2) smokers driving longer distances within the same jurisdiction to bars that allow smoking through noncompliance or outdoor seating. The first explanation indicates that lack of coordination between jurisdictions leads to a negative externality from the new regulatory regime, an "interjurisdictional" spillover. The second explanation suggests an "intrajurisdictional" spillover, with smokers driving longer distances within the same jurisdiction. In both cases, the spillover effects, that is, a negative externality, undermine higher social gains from the new regulatory regime. This is only one example of many cases in which the effectiveness and efficiency of governmental actions depend on conditions in neighboring jurisdictions.[1]

In a metropolitan context, multiple jurisdictions are often understood as a unified region, where economic, social, and environmental decisions are assumed to be in perfect alignment with the administrative landscape. In reality, local public policies are often designed and implemented within jurisdictional silos that do not reflect the reach of the driving forces of economic and social interaction. These administrative boundaries are often established to correspond with "natural" borders that become obsolete as the environmental and socioeconomic landscapes of cities shift. As a result of these artificial divisions, adjacent jurisdictions often take policy decisions without considering the spillover effects of their actions on their neighbors. In addition, jurisdictions often ignore the effect their neighbors' decisions will have on them. This spatial-administrative mismatch translates into redundancy and lost opportunities for the mutually beneficial development of common institutions (environmental, land, and business regulations and common utility networks), connective infrastructure (transit systems to integrate labor markets), and coordinated resource management (environment, heritage, and housing).

Large, interconnected metropolitan areas that span multiple administrative boundaries exist across the world. As urban expansion continues, government officials struggle to adjust to the needs and activities of large urban agglomerations shaped by forces such as natural increases in population, migration, land-use and density policies, and economic activity, among many others. The city of São Paulo, for example, is located near the center of a metropolitan area of 220 square kilometres that encompasses 20 million people and 39 municipal authorities. This city, like many others around the globe, has limited capacity to tackle cross-jurisdictional challenges; it has insufficient tools to provide efficient and effective public services, exploit economies of scale, and address the externalities of urban development. These externalities often extend beyond the urbanized "edge" and need to be addressed through a regional lens that emphasizes sustainability and competitiveness.

Coordination can foster economies of scale in service provision and help mitigate the negative externalities associated with rapid urbanization. Water, sewerage, solid waste management, electricity, and transport networks logically flow across administrative divisions in a metropolitan area. It is possible to harness efficiency gains by, for example, organizing transportation at a regional scale to capture the synergies and flows of people and capital across localized areas. Coordination can also prevent wasteful duplication of policies or unintentional contradictions between urban development policies of neighboring jurisdictions. With respect to mitigating externalities, benefits can range from preventing regional epidemics that might erupt out of limited access to treated water in one jurisdiction, to reducing congestion and pollution through the development of an integrated road transportation plan across jurisdictions. Despite these benefits, however, strong political economy incentives discourage the delivery of coordinated services and planning across administrative boundaries. In decentralized systems, such as Colombia, local administrators and politicians are strongly disincentivized to facilitate coordinated regional action on these challenges. There is often strong resistance to aggregation or any "clawing back" of power and responsibility from the local level.

Colombia's National Development Plan (NDP) reflects the importance of improving interjurisdictional coordination in the country. Interjurisdictional coordination is relevant to many of the key themes of the 2010–14 NDP. In particular, the chapters on Equality of Opportunity for Social Prosperity and Cross-Cutting Support and Democratic Participation emphasize how to address the urban-rural gap, close regional disparity in key service indicators, and amplify the gains from the pro-poor growth felt in Colombian cities to other areas. The National Planning Department (DNP) has defined strengthening the relationship between territorial entities and the nation as a strategic priority. The DNP's goals include identifying instances and mechanisms through which policies can be better articulated between entities, to stimulate capacity building and to cause convergence among territorial entities. To date, Colombian municipalities have applied a range of coordination mechanisms and instruments with varying degrees of success. All the cases reinforce the importance of interjurisdictional coordination. These cases highlight the potential of amplifying the gains from urbanization by building on their successes and applying the lessons learned from their weaknesses.

Efforts to address interjurisdictional coordination are particularly timely in light of new legal reforms. The Colombian legal and institutional framework is one of the important elements defining incentives for cooperation among territorial entities. This framework establishes the "rules of the game," plays a large role in determining the costs and benefits of cooperation for actors and stakeholders, and defines what instruments are available to facilitate cooperation in practice. The new law regulating spatial planning—*Ley Orgánica de Ordenamiento Territorial* (LOOT)—responds to the need to develop a clear institutional framework to support the aggregation of municipal functions and coordination between territorial entities. The law opens up new space for voluntary collaboration in institutional interjurisdictional arrangements and creates organizational entities (or commissions) to collaborate on territorial planning issues. The law, consequently, resolves much of the legal uncertainty that had hindered the implementation of many previous coordination instruments. It does not, however, go as far as to establish clearly defined coordination responsibilities. It is critical for the analysis of the dynamics of interjurisdictional coordination in Colombia to identify what coordination structures might function most effectively in this new context.

International experience shows that urban areas that have adapted interjurisdictional arrangements to changing conditions have more successfully responded to evolving challenges. A number of cities have adopted new institutional arrangements as they have expanded. Cities such as Toronto have responded over time to the changing pressures of urbanization by adapting their interjurisdictional arrangements. Toronto moved from a one- to two-tiered government in the 1950s, created a metropolitan-wide coordination office in the 1970s, and amalgamated municipal arrangements under one "City of Toronto" in the 1980s. In addition, province-wide and sector-specific entities, such as the Greater Toronto Transportation Authority, have been introduced and reformed over time. This case study and the experiences of other cities demonstrate that reforming metropolitan governance systems requires political recognition of the regional geographic scope of these metropolitan areas, as well as institutional leadership and incentives for cooperation through established and recognized authority.

In Colombia, improved interjurisdictional coordination could catalyze enhanced service delivery and the efficiency of land use. Growth over the past few decades has been accompanied by improved living conditions across the country, but disparities in access to basic services and other social services persist. In terms of access to basic services, challenges are particularly acute in intermediate and small urban areas as well as in rural areas, where small utility companies face strong financial constraints and cannot exploit economies of scale. Quality of service is also a major challenge in these areas. Effective mechanisms for coordination across municipalities could exploit economies of scale in the provision of basic services and extend improvements in livability beyond large cities. Improved interjurisdictional coordination can also help reduce the housing deficit and improve economic density as it is associated with improved spatial and sectoral planning, as well as greater land-use efficiency.

It has been observed in Colombia and other countries around the world that social services have improved around cities with good interjurisdictional coordination. Medellín, which is part of the Metropolitan. Area del Valle de Aburrá, has been more successful than other cities in Colombia in spreading its benefits, as measured by reductions in the number of deprived households (NBI) between 1993 and 2005. While reductions in the number of deprived households in municipalities neighboring Medellín were, on average, 14 percentage points, Barranquilla's neighbors only experienced reductions of 4 percentage points in the NBI index during the same period. While the cities of Medellín and Bucaramanga have been able to work with their neighboring municipalities to design coordinated frameworks for transport, investment, financing, and in the case of Medellín, environmental issues, other cities, such as Bogotá and Cali, have been less successful.

Coordination is particularly vital because Colombia is one of the most-highly decentralized countries in Latin America. Almost 45 percent of annual central government revenue is transferred to subnational governments through the *Sistema General de Participaciones* (SGP). In this system, local governments are responsible for the execution of basic service provision expenditures, without any incentive to coordinate—not even the services that benefit from significant economies of scale, such as transportation, water, and sewage. Efforts to improve coordinated delivery of services across different levels of government and between jurisdictions could have an important impact on the quality of service in intermediate and small urban areas.

In this context, international experience suggests that voluntary cooperation structures and national government incentives can play an important role in fostering greater coordination. Voluntary coordination structures are appropriate because they are flexible in response to changing circumstances and are less likely to meet resistance from stakeholders who fear "claw back of powers." National government incentives such as fiscal and regulatory incentives are critical to align the costs and benefits of coordination for individual actors. Coordination of infrastructure provision can be fostered through incentive-based mechanisms for access to the resources available through the new *Bolsa de Regalías* (royalties funds). It should be noted, however, that small municipalities may have limited ability to design and present quality projects to the national government. Public-private partnerships (PPPs) and Bolsa de Regalias–funded knowledge transfer activities could be used to improve the quality of projects presented.

This chapter is divided into four sections. First, it provides an overview of interjurisdictional coordination in Colombia with reference to the LOOT. It also discusses the characteristics of associated schemes that preceded the law, identifying their strengths, weaknesses, and challenges. These cases are brought into the new framework LOOT provides. In this context, some opportunities for reform are identified, including an international perspective on interjurisdictional coordination. By providing an overview of the international coordination models, this section proposes structures that may prove useful in the Colombian context. Later, drawing on international experience, the role of the central government is discussed in promoting coordination, and concluding remarks are presented.

Interjurisdictional Coordination in Colombia

Territorial coordination was first discussed in Colombia in the 1950s. The first laws emerged in the 1960s and 1970s in response to rapid urbanization and as a way to introduce models of regional integration between municipalities (Massiris Cabeza 2010). Under the 1991 Constitution, which consolidated the Colombian decentralization process, certain instruments for regional coordination were strengthened. However, while legal institutions to support decentralization were clear, those for regional cooperation and coordination were lacking (see box 4.1).

A key component of decentralization of land-use planning was the use of territorial entities. These entities took on responsibilities from the national government in a specific region. The territorial entities are legally and administratively independent and are the sole entities that can access the intergovernmental transfer system. The territorial entities

Box 4.1

Governance and the Political Economy of Decentralization in Colombia

Colombia is a highly decentralized country. Thirty-two regions, called departments (*departamentos*), are each headed by a popularly elected governor, considered to be the representative of the president of the republic for the region. There are also regional councils composed of elected councilors. The responsibilities of the regional councils include approving the regional budget. In addition, there are about 1,100 municipalities with elected mayors and municipal councils. Ten of these municipalities have the status of districts, which manage the expenditures of regions. These subnational administrations are heavily dependent on the national government for funding their operating budgets; they collectively execute expenditures worth roughly 8 percent of gross domestic product (GDP)—about a third of total public expenditures—and raise roughly 3 percent of GDP in tax revenue (about a fifth of total tax revenue).

Regional interests have traditionally been strongly asserted in Colombia (Chamorro 1997 and Moncayo 2002). The process of political decentralization that took place between 1986 and 1991 has contributed to a widening division between national and subnational governments. The decentralization process lowered barriers to entry for new actors in the political arena, fostering greater competition and political pluralism at the subnational level and eroding the political duopoly of the Conservative and Liberal parties (Escobar-Lemmon 2003, 2006). Political parties are an important vehicle in how regional interests are articulated (Gutiérrez 2007), as a result, internal party discipline is weak. Nongovernmental armed groups, such as narcotraffickers and right-wing paramilitary groups, remain a part of the political system (Monsalve and Gaviria 2004), and decentralization has arguably facilitated the capture of aspects of some subnational governments by these groups.

The exercise of power is dominated by short-term incentives and has become increasingly unpredictable. Elections for mayors and governors are held at different times and usually in different years from national elections, a pattern that typically leads to more autonomy from national politics. Mayors and governors are elected for four-year terms and cannot be reelected in successive terms, which—compared to the political systems in, for example, Argentina or Brazil—limits their influence. This system creates incentives for short-term benefits or other policies with little long-term payoff. The powerful rationale followed by

(continued next page)

Box 4.1 *(continued)*

other parties in Latin America—they negotiate the inter-temporal tradeoff implied in decentralization: "parties give today in order to receive tomorrow" (O'Neill 1998)—does not hold very true for Colombia. The exercise of power has become less predictable and incentives for short-term measures have become more dominant. Rules governing the election of congressional representatives in Colombia also tend to undermine party discipline and reduce the likelihood that they will support national, as opposed to regional, interests. Presidents are often pitted against these strong and assertive regional interests, which creates incentives to enhance legitimacy through direct interventions at local or departmental levels.

Source: Adapted from the "Colombia Decentralization: Options and Incentives for Efficiency," World Bank, August 2009.

can also create new subentities to provide services and regulate land-use planning within their jurisdiction.

Regional planning capabilities in Colombia are determined by poorly aligned political, administrative, and regulatory norms. The two key dimensions of territorial management in Colombia are (1) the political and administrative institutions required to support regional activities (any social, economic, political, or cultural entity that spans over administrative boundaries); and (2) the regulations and norms that define land use and changes in land use. While the first dimension is determined by the recently approved Law of Territorial Ordering, land use planning is ruled by more "standard" laws, such as Law 9 of 1989 for Urban Reform and Law 388 of 1997 for Territorial Development.

Lack of clarity over the instruments and institutions of coordination has led to several governance problems, including, for example, the lack of consistency between Territorial Ordering Plans (POTs) and Development Plans (DPs) that include sectoral projects.

The Law of Territorial Ordering

The Colombian Congress has adopted a new law to provide the legal, administrative, and financial framework for coordinating spatial units across the country. The new law of territorial ordering—LOOT, or Law 1454 of 2011—was approved in Congress and signed into law by President Santos on June 28, 2011, after 20 years of debate and 20 unsuccessful proposals. This highly anticipated law will reinforce municipal authority over local projects and create organizational enti-ties (commissions) to collaborate on territorial planning issues. It will also open up an institutional space for voluntary, collaborative inter-jurisdictional arrangements. The law has five main objectives: (1) define norms for territorial planning; (2) provide consistency between norms and legislation; (3) define principles for territorial planning; (4) define the institutional framework for territorial development; and (5) allo-cate competencies between the national government and territorial entities.

The LOOT identifies and seeks to clarify the competencies of four main administrative units for territorial planning. These administrative units are territorial entities, coordination committees, associative schemes and units that provide services that span over one or more territorial enti-ties, and Regions for Planning and Management or Regions for Planning and Administration (figures 4.1 and 4.2). To elaborate:

Figure 4.1   Administrative Units under Law 1454 of 2011 (LOOT)

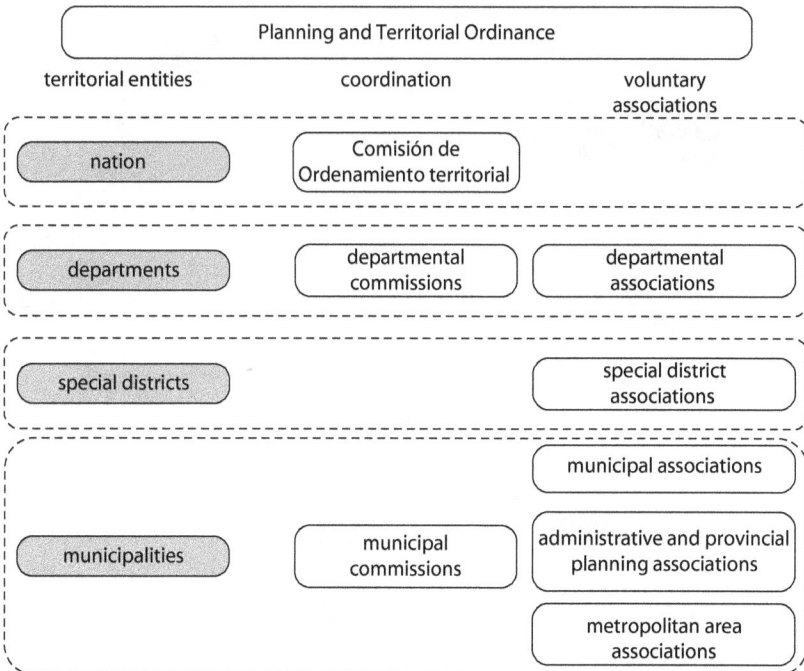

Source: Rodriguez Vitta 2011.
Note: LOOT = Territorial Ordering Act.

Figure 4.2 Coordination before and after LOOT

		Pre LOOT				Post LOOT		
		Planning	Territorial ordinance	Financing		Planning	Territorial ordinance	Financing
Coordination mechanisms	**Territorial coordination committees**	In charge of studies and recommendations on territorial division in light of constitutional regulations	Organize territorial conformation		**Territorial coordination committees**	Technical assistance role to evaluate, revise, and recommend policy and regulation	Technical assistance role to evaluate, revise, and recommend policy and regulation	Financed by the state without SGP participation
	National planning council	Consultative forum for the national development plan			**Regional territorial coordination committees (departmental and municipal)**	Not clearly determined by the LOOT	Not clearly determined by the LOOT	Not clearly determined by the LOOT
	Territorial integration committees	Implementation of POT and input for future territorial strategic vision		Although created under Law 614 of 2000, no established financing mechanisms available				
Voluntary associations	**Municipal associations**	Concieved as a management and planning instrument for public services, operates as intermediary between municipal and departmental levels		Independent of municipalities; no SGP or *Regalias* expenditures	**Departmental associations, municipal associations, special district associations, metropolitan area associations, joint commissions of autonomous regional corporations**	Joint public service delivery functions for planning competency to execute common interest functions	No binding competency	Financing determined through contracts and plan agreements between territorial entities, which will also determine specific projects and functions
	Other examples: RAPE in Bogotá-Cundinamarca and the Eje Cafetero Eco-Region							

Source: Rodríguez Vitta 2011.

Note: LOOT = Territorial Ordering Act; POT = Territorial Ordering Plans; RAPE = Región Administrativa y de Planeación Especial (Administrative Region for Special Planning); SGP = System of National Transfers.

- *Territorial entities.* The new law explicitly identifies the national government, departments, municipalities, and special districts as territorial entities, with the capacity to autonomously define social and economic development planning and environmental management policy.[2] Territorial entities are responsible for both development plans and POTs. They also have access to the System of National Transfers (SGP). The LOOT aims to support the capacity of territorial entities to plan, manage, and administer their territory.

- *Coordination committees.* The LOOT created the Comisión de Ordenamiento Territorial, which is a high-level committee to provide technical assistance and oversee all projects as well as cases where national competencies are transferred to local agencies. Two similar coordination committee structures were created at the departmental and municipal levels.

- *Associative schemes.* The law is a milestone because it provides a legal framework for administrative and planning regions as well as voluntary municipal planning associations. Through the definition of associative schemes, the law aims to allow municipalities to work together toward joint projects and to create regions that act as a space for collaboration between existing jurisdictions. These voluntary associations or associative schemes are defined under the law and can be associations of territorial entities, special districts, departments, municipalities, districts, or metropolitan areas for administrative and planning purposes. The central government aims to promote these associations through incentives. The law also opens the door for regional project financing, for example, from funds directed to regional development or from royalties (*Regalias*).

- *Regions for Planning and Managements, and Regions for Planning and Administrations.* The law creates the Regions for Planning and Managements and Regions for Planning and Administrations, following Article 85 of the Constitution. These regions can be created by any of the associations described above to handle investment projects of regional impact. These Regions for Planning and Managements will plan and execute the funds assigned through the Regional Development Fund.

The LOOT also aims to reduce the creation of parallel norms through the introduction of contracts and plan agreements. Contracts and plan agreements are agreements made between the national government and territorial entities, associations of territorial entities, or metropolitan areas for the execution of projects that are of strategic importance for regional development. These contracts or agreements will define the financial contribution of each party to specific projects. In addition, the national government will be able to transfer some of its responsibilities defined under the NDP to regional entities, whenever the project is consistent with the purpose of the entity and approval is given from the appropriate administrative level. These new arrangements are expected to provide scope for flexible negotiation between the national and territorial government institutions.

The LOOT provides an explicit definition of territorial entities and clarifies the departments' role in project coordination across municipalities. By recognizing the departments as territorial entities, their land-use plans become binding. As such, the LOOT strengthens departmental authority and, accordingly, may serve as an important instrument to enforce coordination among municipalities.

The new law establishes a framework that stresses the administrative role of several new regional entities (see figure 4.3). Elements of these entities could be drawn from within the current structure, as is the case with metropolitan areas, Regions for Planning and Managements and Regions for Planning and Administrations. Under the new law, these administrative units do not have power in terms of regional

Figure 4.3   Framework of Responsibility under LOOT

	Planning	Territorial ordinance	Financing
Territorial entities	Territorial entities have autonomy in planning and economic development as well as in social and environmental management. They should develop *Planes de Desarrollo* and *Planes de Ordenamiento*.	Territorial entities are the only entities that can develop binding norms in this area.	Territorial entities are the only entities that can participate in SGP transfers, giving them access to both this source of revenue and their own resources.
Metropolitan areas			
Institutions for regional planning	Planning for service delivery must be subject to the *Planes de Ordenamiento* established by territorial entities.	Entities or private firms do not have competency in the area of changes in service delivery.	Particular or from entities through agreements.
Regions for Planning and Administration			
Regions for Planning and Management			

Source: Rodriguez Vitta 2011.
Note: LOOT = Territorial Ordering Act.

planning and territorial ordering. While these units are expected to play a role in regional planning and fostering coordination, their decisions and plans will not be binding. For example, the law states that metropolitan areas must design DPs for territorial planning at the metropolitan level. However, because they are not considered territorial entities, metropolitan areas will have neither access to funding nor the ability to design binding land-use planning norms for municipalities inside the metropolitan area.

Lessons from existing associative schemes. As the country assesses the implications of the new LOOT law, there are useful lessons to learn from Colombian experiences with coordination and associative arrangements to date. Because of the lack of institutional clarity that preceded the introduction of the LOOT, Colombia has witnessed the emergence of a range of associative schemes and coordination mechanisms established by local governments and politicians to address interjurisdictional problems. Analysis of the different models that grew out of this process yields important insights into the strengths and weaknesses of different coordination efforts. Examples of associative schemes include metropolitan areas, associations of municipalities, and the committees for regional integration.

Metropolitan areas. Metropolitan areas are voluntary association of municipalities that are established to regulate issues spanning across jurisdictional boundaries. The objectives of a metropolitan area are defined by law and include: (1) to program and coordinate the development of the territory under its jurisdiction; (2) to coordinate public service provisions among jurisdictions and, if necessary, to provide services; and (3) to carry out works in the interest of the metropolitan area. The areas are organized around their central municipality, which forms the nucleus. The mayor of this municipality leads the metropolitan area and must approve the Metropolitan Area Development Plan, investment plan, and budget.[3] Metropolitan areas have access to different financing sources, including transfers from national, departmental, and municipal budgets; betterment levies (valorización) collected from metropolitan development projects; fees related to public services and other services provided; credit; and the gasoline tax collected within the jurisdiction of the area.

Colombia has six legally recognized metropolitan areas (map 4.1), all created since 1968: Valle de Aburrá, Bucaramanga, Barranquilla, Cúcuta,

Map 4.1   Metropolitan Areas of Colombia

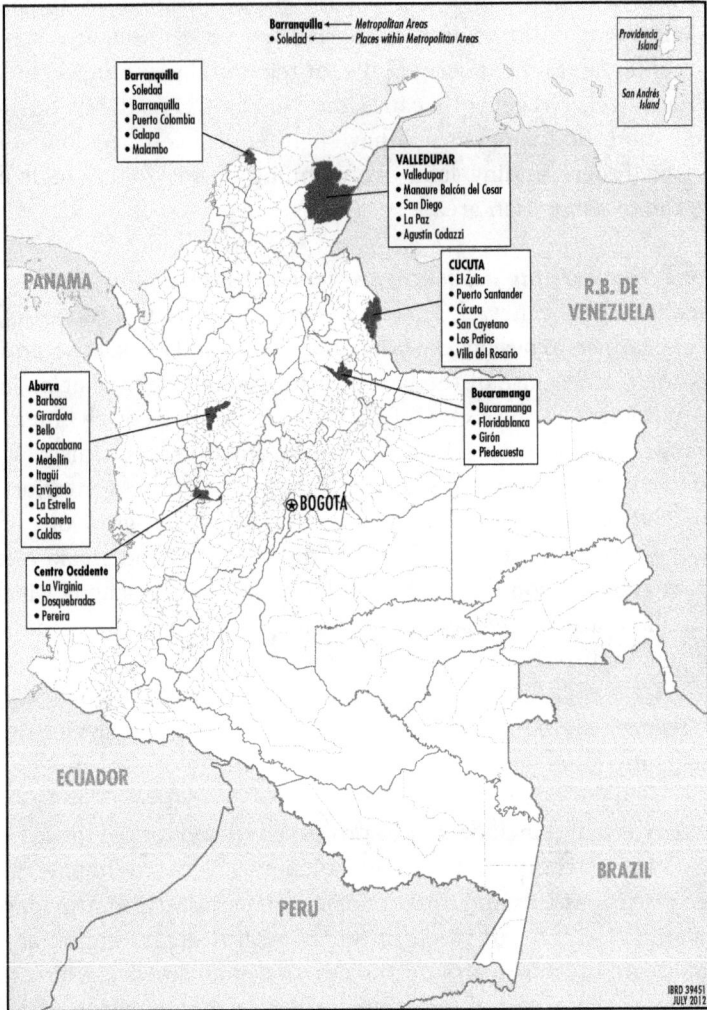

Source: Rodriguez Vitta 2011.

Centro Occidente, and Valledupar. They were officially recognized in the 1991 Constitution as administrative units formed by one or more municipalities to promote coordination across municipal boundaries.

The metropolitan area of Valle de Aburrá is widely regarded within Colombia as an example of successful coordination. This metropolitan area includes 10 municipalities, with Medellín as the anchor.[4] It was formed with the primary objective of stimulating economic development.

For this purpose, the metropolitan area defines an Integrated Metropolitan Development Plan that establishes a strategic framework for the area and allows for the coordination and definition of common objectives for all municipalities.

The structure of the Valle de Aburrá metropolitan area promotes dialogue and relies on strong political will. Projects require unanimous municipal approval and strong mutual understanding for implementation because decisions are not legally binding. To date, the metropolitan area has defined plans for territorial planning, transport networks, statistics and data collection, and housing and environment; these plans provide guidelines for the region as a whole. The metropolitan area undertakes a number of initiatives to promote coordination on these plans by, for example, sponsoring workshops to revise and adjust Territorial Ordering Plans (POTs) so that they align with the objectives of the region. Between 2004 and 2007, the metropolitan area invested more than Col$2,480 million in efforts to align municipal POTs. The metropolitan area also has promoted coordination beyond the metropolitan area through a voluntary agreement to align development objectives across levels of governance. The agreement was signed by the governor's office of Antioquia, the Metropolitan Area of Valle de Aburrá, and the municipality of Medellín—a group called Comision TriPartita.

Financial management of the Valle de Aburrá metropolitan area is remarkably solid for a voluntary association. The metropolitan area uses almost every possible source of financing in the framework of existing laws to generate revenue (figure 4.4). For example, Decree 3100 of 2003 imposed a pollution fee on constituent entities, charging for the discharge of pollutants into water bodies. The metropolitan area estimated the pollution generated by Empresas Públicas de Medellín (EPM), which was responsible for the wastewater generated by industries, households, and commerce, and collected the associated fees. It also estimated the pollution discharges and collected fees from industries not connected to the public sewer.

The metropolitan area of Valle de Aburrá also acts as the Environmental and Transport Authority in the Medellín area. Environmental and transport issues are laid out as part of the development strategy of the area. By creating a Metropolitan Environmental Council, the metropolitan area has been able to provide a regional perspective on environmental management. No other city in Colombia manages its environmental policy and planning under a regional framework. However, some institutional fixes are still needed. Two environmental authorities coexist within the

Figure 4.4   Income Source of the Metropolitan Area of Valle de Aburrá

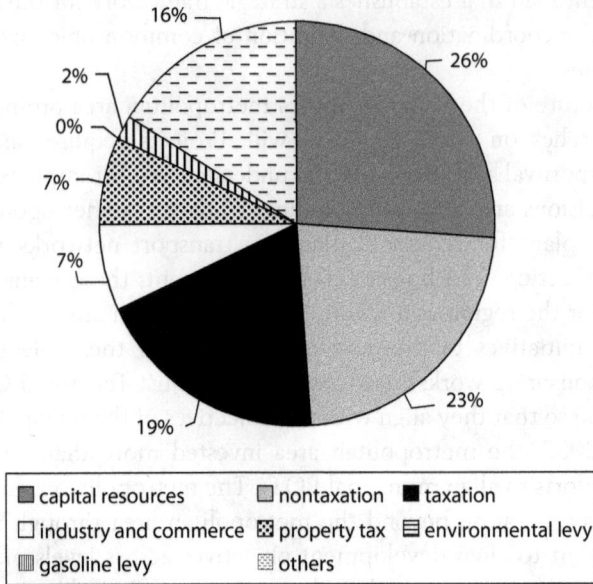

Pie chart with the following segments:
- 26%
- 23%
- 19%
- 7%
- 7%
- 0%
- 2%
- 16%

Legend:
- capital resources
- nontaxation
- taxation
- industry and commerce
- property tax
- environmental levy
- gasoline levy
- others

Source: Rodriguez Vitta 2011.

same region—the metropolitan area and Corantioquia for rural areas. The administrative boundaries of these two authorities do not correspond to the natural boundaries of the ecosystem in the area. The resulting difficulties for environmental planning and policy implementation are likely to be further exacerbated by recent modification to the Corporaciones Autónomas Regionales (CARs) to exclude local environmental authorities from ruling over water resources within urban boundaries.

The metropolitan area of Valle de Aburrá has the responsibility to plan, organize, monitor, and control metropolitan transit. It also has the mandate to develop policies that encourage an efficient, safe, and economically viable and integrated mass transit system. However, there is not enough revenue to fully exercise this authority. The metropolitan are lacks resources and institutional capacity to effectively plan, regulate, monitor, and manage that system. For example, the Metro system was not developed in coordination with a restructuring of the existing public transport system. This situation generated two parallel systems within the metropolitan area, creating inefficiencies across the network. Several protests and strikes from bus and taxi companies from the neighboring municipalities of Medellín, especially Bello and Envigado, have taken place in recent years.

The metropolitan area of Bucaramanga is a widely cited example of effective metropolitan coordination on social and economic development issues. This area is composed of four municipalities (Bucaramanga, Giron, Floridablanca, and Piedecuesta), with a population of approximately 1.1 million, or 53 percent of the Department of Santander and most of its formal employment. Since the creation of the metropolitan area in 1981, quality of life and social indicators have shown marked improvement across member municipalities. Between 2007 and 2010, the area of Bucaramanga increased its labor force participation from 59.2 percent to 71.2 percent (see figure 4.5). Similarly, poverty decreased by over 20 percentile points between 2002 and 2009; in striking contrast to other metropolitan areas (table 4.1). Economic policies have been coordinated across municipalities, and key economic clusters have been identified regionally, as in the case of the leather and shoe industries. Municipalities do not compete. There is a high degree of economic integration within the metropolitan area, led by a clear effort to consolidate a common market.

However, this integration is not reflected in environmental and planning issues. The metropolitan area of Bucaramanga is located in an envi-

Figure 4.5   Bucaramanga's Labor Force Participation

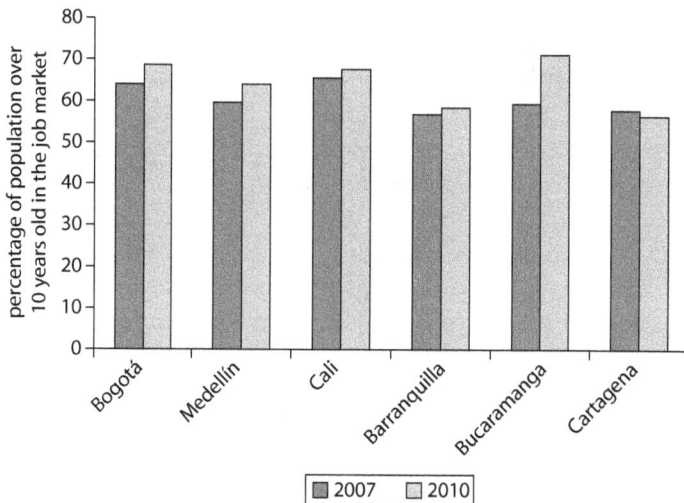

Source: Bucaramanga Metropolitana Como Vamos.

Table 4.1   Share of the Population below the Poverty Line
percent

City	2002	2009	Change
Bucaramanga	39.9	18.5	−21.4
Bogotá	35.7	22.0	−13.7
Medellín	49.7	38.4	−11.4
Cartagena	43.2	36.0	−7.2
Barranquilla	41.6	40.7	−0.9
Cali	33.3	32.6	−0.7

Source: MESEP (Misión para el Empalme de las Series de Empleo) database.

ronmentally sensitive system of canyons and rivers. Management of this system requires integrated planning across the metropolitan area. At present, however, there is no coordination of fundamental issues such as solid waste disposal, which has negative repercussions for the entire area in terms of water source pollution.

To the north of Colombia, the metropolitan area of Barranquilla is characterized by striking disparities in administrative capacity between its nucleus and surrounding municipalities. There is marked income inequality between the municipality of Barranquilla and the municipalities of Galapa, Soledad, and Malambo, which account for only 23.3 percent of the metropolitan area's income combined. As figure 4.6 shows, this difference in income between the nucleus and peripheral municipalities is considerably more pronounced than in other metropolitan areas in Colombia. There is also a gap in administrative capacity between Barranquilla and the other municipalities, which may be accentuated by the proximity of the municipalities to the nucleus. Given the average distance from periphery municipalities to the municipality of Barranquilla of 9 kilometers, it is likely that municipal governments feel less pressure to improve services as periphery population have access services in the central municipality.

In this context, the commitment to strengthen the metropolitan area is weak. Indeed, periphery municipalities contributed only 55 percent of the funds they committed to the metropolitan budget in 2012. Coordination within the metropolitan area has been limited to environmental issues, and the shared concerns that arise from all of the municipalities (with the exception of Galapa) bordering significant bodies of water: the Magdalena River (the longest river in Colombia) or the Atlantic Ocean. The natural area of the metropolitan area is an alluvial plain that extends for several miles across municipalities. Not

Figure 4.6   Economic Distances and Physical Distances

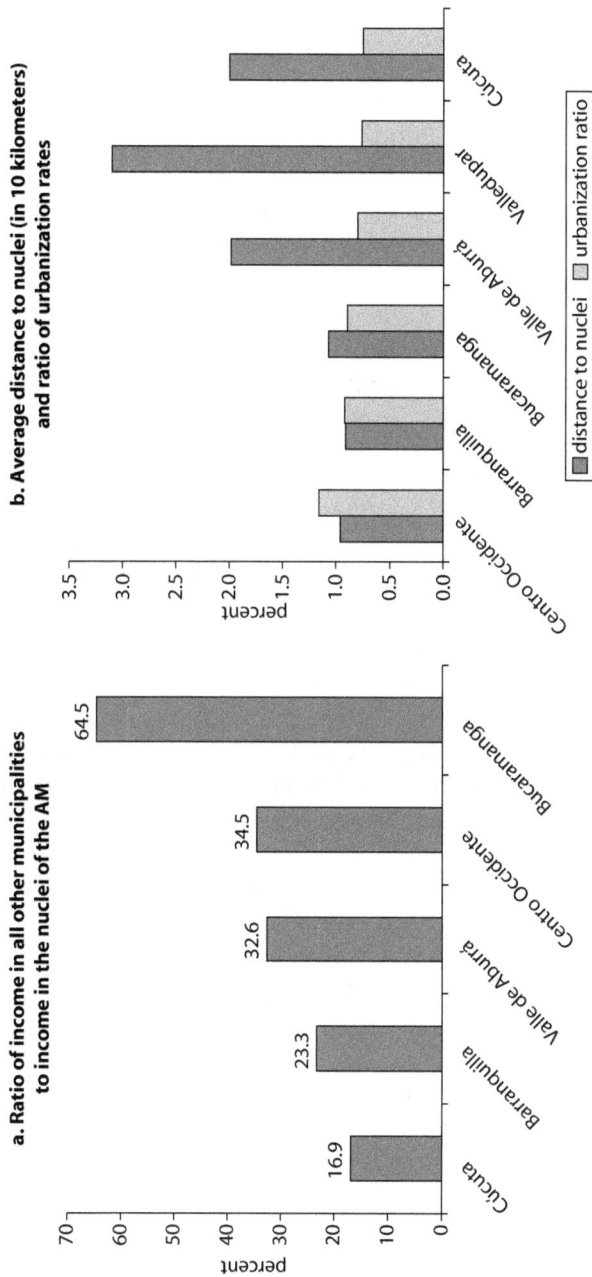

a. Ratio of income in all other municipalities to income in the nuclei of the AM

b. Average distance to nuclei (in 10 kilometers) and ratio of urbanization rates

Sources: DNP 2009; AMVA.
Note: The ratio of urbanization rates is defined as the ratio between the average urbanization rate in the periphery and the urbanization rate in the nuclei.

surprisingly, most of the projects financed through the metropolitan area are either related to environmental protection, such as Ecopark Mayorquín, or to infrastructure risk prevention, such as the Canals El Salao—El Platanal.

In general, urbanization rates tend to be higher in peripheral municipalities that are close to the central city than in more distant municipalities. Examples are in the metropolitan areas of Barranquilla and Centro Occidente. However, the quality of this urbanization tends to be lower in metropolitan areas with economically weak peripheries. For example, social services have much better quality in the periphery of Pereira (the nucleus of Centro Occidente metropolitan area) than in Barranquilla, given the similar budget of municipalities in the metropolitan area of Centro Occidente.

Municipal associations. These are supra-municipal entities created under the Constitutional reform of 1968 as instruments for spatial planning and the joint management of public services. The association allows municipalities to enter into agreements for the provision of public services, investment projects, or other administrative activities with the main objective of reducing costs and bringing about efficiency gains in the provision of services. At present, there are 42 municipal associations in Colombia.

In the absence of a strong regulatory framework, municipal associations have increasingly been used as an instrument to channel resources. They are entitled to manage resources gained through efficiency improvements and those transferred by participating municipalities. Municipal associations also can create administrative agreements and work on infrastructure projects that are not part of development or territorial plans. As a result, the associations have become involved primarily with resource management functions, despite being originally established for a broader range of purposes including from technical assistance to planning and management.

The newly sanctioned LOOT will strengthen the regulatory framework of municipal associations to carry out their intended functions. The new law promotes the creation of municipal associations as well as other forms of associations among territorial entities, including the Regions for Planning and Managements and Regions for Planning and Administration. Under this law, investment plans and resource allocation decisions for associative schemes are legally binding.

Committees for territorial integration. Comites de Integración Territorial (Committees for Territorial Integration), instituted in 2000, under Law 614, are designed to coordinate Territorial Ordering Plans and oversee regional land-use strategy. This law did not specify financing mechanisms— most Committees are financed through contributions from member municipalities—but it did create the space for Committees for Territorial Integration to work as executors for the national government in regional projects that were defined as part of the National Development Plan. An example is the Committee for Territorial Integration for *Centro Occidente*. This committee was created in 2008 by 10 municipalities, spanning two departments.

Committees for Territorial Integration have not been introduced widely, as was envisaged when they were instituted. Law 614 made them obligatory for all municipalities within metropolitan areas; districts with populations of more than 500,000 within their influence area; and for one department. However, this did not translate into practice. The LOOT opens the possibility to redesign Committees for Territorial Integration and clarify their role as planning instruments in the new framework. Committees for Territorial Integration can serve as intermediate-level institutions to promote strategic regional plans and work closely with the committees for territorial ordering, as defined in the new law.

Lessons from International Experience

Urban growth patterns and low-density commuter watersheds give rise to issues such as sprawl and traffic congestion. Transportation and service delivery networks, park systems, housing supply and demand, and employment markets are issues that are not contained within artificially imposed administrative boundaries. Rather, they extend to a regional or metropolitan scale, and only by looking at them on this larger scale will governments be able to provide appropriate solutions to the issues brought about by urbanization. Regional- or metropolitan-scale planning promotes the development of more efficient cities by addressing issues such as sprawl and traffic congestion.

There has been an international trend toward metropolitan manage-ment and away from policy decisions taken within isolated administrative boundaries. This evolution has occurred over the twentieth century as governance theories and practices responded to changing forces, such as urbanization, decentralization, and globalization. This trend reflects the understanding that (1) the governance challenge for metropolitan areas is based on the need to provide public services across a multitude of local jurisdictions with differing geographic scopes and (2) metropolitan arrangements and institutions must be flexible to accommodate rapid changes in the urban environment. International experience also indicates that metropolitan management requires concerted efforts to incentivize or mandate cooperation through established and recognized authority structures, as well as political clout and leadership within institutions.

In the context of Colombia's new LOOT, voluntary agreements appear to be the road toward increased cooperation. International experience suggests that voluntary cooperation structures and competencies are powerful mechanisms to foster planning and interlocal collaboration. The structure for promoting collaboration can be formalized in the long term. As many examples around the world indicate, successful structures for coordination are flexible and adjust as the needs of the cities change. In the long term, these voluntary agreements may be formalized and incentives can be provided for regional/metropolitan agencies to assume financial and service provision independent from the central government. However, financial and regulatory incentives from the national government may be required to promote coordination at the metropolitan and regional scale.

Flexible and inclusive metropolitan institutional arrangements are more versatile and adaptive. Generally, municipal governance models can be categorized according to their degree of participation and formalism. Participation refers to the types of actors included in decision making while formalism is the level of bureaucracy or institutionalism of the arrangement. The governance[5] model that a city chooses has an effect on service delivery, public finances, accountability, and level of citizen participation (Slack 2007). In this context, arrangements that are inclusive of more-diverse actors and, at the same time, have a lower degree of institutionalization are more versatile and provide the needed flexibility to cope with changing economic, social, and political conditions.

In the remainder of this section, we provide international examples to illustrate important features of interjurisdictional coordination that should be considered as agreements of this type are designed and promoted in Colombia. Rio de Janeiro provides an example of a large metropolitan area that brings together autonomous localities with sector-based national government oversight and coordination. Because localities remain autonomous in service provision and planning, coordination is relatively weak and the coordination mechanisms are not considered to have been effective. The experience of Barcelona suggests that over time, a metropolitan area can build on the success of initial voluntary agreements around specific projects and sectors to promote a more-formalized structure of metropolitan governance. The relevance of multiple organizations, including both special-purpose district authorities and civil organizations, is highlighted in the history of metropolitan New York. Sydney provides an example of how metropolitan functions can be undertaken by states without needing to create additional governmental structures. Toronto and London provide examples of governance structures that are probably less applicable to Colombia at present, but the experiences of these two cities still provide an important lesson: as needs of cities change, a flexible set of norms is crucial to allow governance structures to best adjust to these changes.

Fostering Coordination: International Examples and Typology

A typology of five interjurisdictional coordination models emerged from the analysis of metropolitan management case studies. The first type of government pattern observed is characterized by a unitary institution with complete regional authority; for the purposes of this report, this will be termed *metropolitan government*. The second type of institution is a *metropolitan council*, where an umbrella organization of local units promotes the shared objectives. The third type is *territorial polycentrism*, where territorial fragmentation and local semi-autonomous governments prevail. The fourth includes institutions that seek service consolidation through interjurisdictional coverage; we refer to that model as *single purpose districts*. Finally, there are voluntary agreements, or what will be termed the *interlocal cooperation* model, where regional pragmatism prevails and multiactor inclusion is the main objective.

Interjurisdictional practices vary by the geography, population size, and number of local government organizations of a given metropolitan area. Figure 4.7 summarizes a set of 15 international best-practice examples, according to the five types of metropolitan governance defined above. The vertical and horizontal axes of the graph plot the average area and number of governments (jurisdictions) involved, while the average population size is represented by the size of the bubbles. The figure shows that metropolitan governments or unitary governance models tend to emerge in regions with a relatively low number of local governments, a small area, and a small population compared to the other models. This suggests that more-formal and institutionalized ways of governance might work better in small areas with small populations. Metropolitan councils, on the other

Figure 4.7   Average Area and Population of Cities by Metropolitan Governance Model

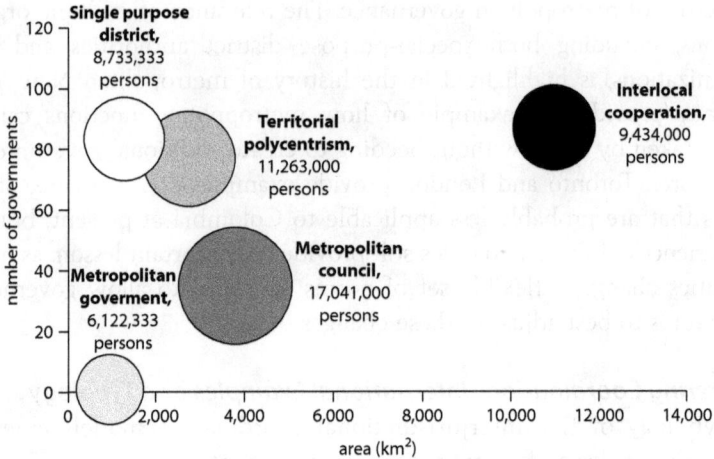

Source: Yaro and Ronderos 2011.
Note: km^2 = square kilometer.

hand, have a medium number of governments, large land areas, and large populations. Single purpose districts are characterized, on average, by a large number of governments, a small area, and a small population. Single purpose districts are, for example, a good alternative for the provision of services when a large number of governments are involved.

There are exceptions to general trends in city characteristics within the typology. Shanghai, for example, has a very large population and a consolidated metropolitan government. New York uses single purpose districts to manage its regional transportation and water systems, despite its large population and land area. A more-detailed characterization of 15 cities is presented in table 4.2. The first column of the table identifies the type of government structure, while the third column indicates the extent of the region. The remainder of this section provides a more-detailed characterization of the five types of government coordination structures identified in the context of metropolitan areas.

Metropolitan Government

The metropolitan government model is of a single body that exercises general and multifunctional authority over an entire metropolitan territory. This distinguishes the model from most other governance models

Table 4.2   International Examples within the Typology of Interjurisdictional Coordination

Model	Examples	Management	Participation
Metropolitan government	Shanghai Singapore Toronto	Vertical organization and implementation	Metropolitan decision-making and engagement
Metropolitan council	London Paris Tokyo	Vertical/horizontal organization and implementation	Metropolitan/local decision-making and engagement
Territorial polycentrism	Buenos Aires Los Angeles Rio de Janeiro	Fragmented organization and implementation	Localized decision-making and engagement
Single purpose district	Barcelona Madrid, Mexico City	Horizontal organization and implementation	District decision-making and local engagement
Inter-local cooperation	New York Sydney, Lima	Horizontal organization and implementation	Multiple-actor decision-making and engagement

Source: Yaro and Ronderos 2011.

and impacts its structure. A typical structure is centered on the metropolitan town that provides the most services, including planning and sector-based delivery. Municipal governments are typically financially autonomous and only supervised by internal checks and balances and the national government. In this model, decision making and engagement is determined by metropolitan institutions that regulate participation in the political process. Compared to the other models discussed, metropolitan governments tend to have smaller population sizes, and provide a wide functional and administrative range of duties over a relatively small geographic area. International examples of metropolitan governance include Shanghai, Singapore, and Toronto.

The City of Toronto: Metropolitan government model through progressive reforms. The City of Toronto developed a metropolitan government model through progressive reforms that responded to evolving metropolitan challenges. The City of Toronto has adopted a wide spectrum of metropolitan arrangements, including: (1) unitary government, (2) two-tier government, (3) sectoral coordination institutions, and (4) a single city encompassing six municipalities. This gradual transformation reflects progressive reforms to meet evolving urban conditions.

In the 1950s, the City of Toronto adopted a two-tier government structure in response to rapid growth in bordering municipalities. At the beginning of the 1950s, the City of Toronto was surrounded by 12 municipalities. Land scarcity stimulated the development of new housing in neighboring municipalities, which faced an increasing demand for services such as education, roads, lighting, and water and sanitation systems. Furthermore, while the City of Toronto had a solid financial base, both from its commercial and residential tax base, its neighboring municipalities had weaker financial systems, lower local capacity, and a smaller tax base. To address these issues, the Metropolitan Toronto Act of 1954 established a two-tier government structure for the metropolitan area, which brought together the City of Toronto and 12 surrounding municipalities.[6]

This two-tier system shared many costs between local governments. Local responsibility for service delivery was retained in a context of unified metropolitan coordination and planning functions. Initial responsibilities of the metropolitan government included matters concerning planning, borrowing assessment, transportation, and justice administration. Local governments maintained responsibility for fire protection, garbage collection and disposal, licensing and inspection, local distribution of hydro-electric power, policing, public health, general welfare assistance, recreation and community services, and tax collection. Most interestingly, costs were shared by local governments based on the property tax base, which led to the City of Toronto being responsible for covering 62 percent of the costs of the metropolitan government in that year. Responsibility for parks, planning, roads, traffic control, sewerage disposal, and water supply was shared across lower- and upper-tier governments.

Ten years later, the metropolitan area became a single legally defined "city," with the amalgamation of the six municipalities with the City of Toronto. In the 1970s, the challenges of the city and the metropolitan area changed; the nucleus of rapid growth shifted to outside the metropolitan area, placing new pressure on broader service provision. In response, in 1988, the province of Ontario created the Office of the Greater Toronto Area to encourage the coordination of the metropolitan area and all its surrounding regions in terms of waste disposal, regional transportation, land use, and infrastructure planning. Following this, the province created the Greater Toronto Services Board (GTSB) to oversee regional transit, but with no legal or taxing authority. Given its limited powers, the GTSB was disbanded in 2001, only to give way to the Greater Toronto Transportation Authority in 2006.[7]

Metropolitan Councils

Metropolitan councils allow local governments to coexist with metropolitan structures but have relatively weak integration instruments. This formula combines proximity between local authorities and their citizens, while transferring the responsibility of metro issues to a supra-community entity. There is no subordinate relationship between the two territorial levels—they act in tandem to coordinate functions. The metropolitan umbrella organization is usually responsible for planning, monitoring, and coordinating tasks, but its budgetary resources remain limited. Metropolitan councils are not considered to be well suited for regulating the policies of their component parts because of the weakness of their integration instruments and relatively autonomous financial arrangement. Most service delivery is local, although some infrastructure services can be provided at the metropolitan level or are supported through regulatory incentives for cooperation by the central government.

The City of London: Metropolitan council model. Greater London Authority and the city's 32 boroughs share responsibility under a metropolitan council model. Between 1964 and 1998, London had a two-tier governance structure, where the upper tier of government was in the hands of the Greater London Council, and 32 boroughs formed the lower-tier component. In 1986, the metropolitan area was disassembled, and London's governance became the responsibility of the central government. The disappearance of a metropolitan government led to the appearance of ad hoc arrangements for regional planning, such as the Government Office of London. These arrangements brought together regional offices of ministries, the representatives of the 32 neighboring boroughs, and the other agencies involved in London's planning. After its disintegration in 1986, a metropolitan government reappeared in 1999 with the creation of the Greater London Authority (GLA), which included the Corporation of London and 32 boroughs.

Under this structure, coordination between the mayor and the metropolitan authority is essential. When political interests are not aligned, the transaction costs are often high. The main objective of the GLA is to promote economic and social development, together with environmental sustainability. Housing, education, social, and health services remain the responsibility of the boroughs. The metropolitan area has four institutions for transport, development, policing, and fire and emergency planning, which are not part of the GLA, but are accountable to it through the unique elected mayor for the MA. Planning remains a responsibility of the boroughs and the mayor does not have the authority to promote the approval of developments by any borough. However, the mayor may direct boroughs to reject large-scale development applications if he or she considers them to be in conflict with metropolitan strategy.

Territorial Polycentricism

The territorial polycentrism model combines autonomous localities with the sector-based oversight and coordination of the national government. This model is often applied in large physical areas in which localities retain autonomous planning and service delivery competencies. Because coordination is relatively weak, losses in technical efficiency often occur, and public servicing decisions can be fragmented. These issues are particularly acute in localities where home rule is emphasized.

Rio de Janeiro: A highly fragmented example of territorial polycentrism. The metropolitan region of Rio de Janeiro was originally created by Law 20 of July 1, 1974, but its structure has evolved over time. In part, this reflects changes in the national context, including the introduction of a new national constitution in 1988, which transferred key urban policy responsibility to municipalities,[8] and a new city statute in 2001, which further increased local autonomy in land-use and development planning. Metropolitan governance in Brazil is one of the most-complex issues in the Brazilian federative regime, which recognizes three levels of autonomous government (federal, state, and municipal). Municipalities are responsible for matters of local interest, including urban planning, while states have the authority to define metropolitan regions through a complementary law. Municipalities can enter into voluntary agreements with states, but membership of metropolitan regions is not optional: once a municipality is part of a metropolitan region, membership is mandatory.

The evolution of the metropolitan structure also reflects changes in the metropolitan context of Rio de Janeiro, which is the one of the largest metropolitan areas in Brazil, with 19 municipalities.[9] The metropolitan region has experienced decades of intensive population growth, despite changing economic fortunes in the 1960s and 1970s due to the transfer of the capital city to Brasilia and deindustrialization. This unbalanced growth has placed a strain on governance and service delivery across all municipalities in the metropolitan region, which suffers from severe spatial divisions in social conditions and wide disparities between the institutional and financial strengths of different municipalities.

Although there are clearly defined priorities for cooperation between municipalities, few of the established mechanisms have been effective. The Foundation for the Development of the Metropolitan Region (Fundação para o Desenvolvimento da Região Metropolitana), for example, was created in 1975 and disbanded in 1989 because its functions were increasingly curtailed by the absence of political support. Law 87 of 1997 also highlighted the benefits of coordination, established a deliberative council for metropolitan management, and specified key sectors for services of common interest in the metropolitan region,[10] without, however, designating any funding source for this metropolitan management. The law is not considered to have successfully instituted any of the envisaged plans and is currently being challenged in the Supreme Court[11] over issues that include the definition of "common interest" services. The established institutional frameworks have generally been undermined by fragmentation, inefficiency, and "sectorized" policy actions (Britto and Formiga Johnsson 2009).

Single Purpose District

Single purpose districts are service-based on a functional metropolitan scale and can have hybrid administrative boundaries. Intergovernmental relations of single purpose districts tend to be horizontal across institutions; all localities participate as equals. Decisions are made at the district level while engagement tends to be localized. Single purpose districts can be created by means of an agreement between municipalities and other actors. Legislation can prescribe or simplify such arrangements in designated sectors or services. An intermunicipal agreement, which is the most-popular arrangement, can operate even in the absence of a specific metropolitan institution.

Under these types of agreements, territorial fragmentation persists, but specific sector-based integration overcomes the challenges of administrative divisions. These agreements are common in sectors such as water and sanitation, electricity, transportation, and waste management. These are usually financed by intralocal transfers, user fees, or other charges. Single purpose district agreements are usually overseen by the regulatory wings of the national government.

Barcelona: Voluntary and sector-based cooperation in a single purpose district model. Barcelona provides an example of how a metropolitan area can first promote collaboration across jurisdictions based on voluntary agreements and then build on this successful collaboration to promote a more formalized structure of metropolitan governance. In 1997, after the dissolution of the Barcelona metropolitan corporation, three sectoral institutions were created in the metropolitan sphere. This led to three organizations with different territorial coverage, because city councils had the option to join the sectoral institutions on a voluntary basis. In 2011, the new Barcelona Metropolitan Area organization was formed. It encompasses and absorbs the three existing institutions in a two-tier council structure to foster increased coordination.[12]

The institutional arrangement for the Barcelona metropolis until 2011 was the result of cooperation between different local governments within the region on specific sector-based issues, including planning, transportation, and the environment. The Barcelona Metropolitan Area was composed of the amalgamation of three institutions covering different territorial areas: the Mancomunitat de Municipis (31 municipalities), the Entitat Metropolitana del Transport (metropolitan transport organization, 18 municipalities) and the Entitat Metropolitana del Medio Ambient (environmental organization, 33 municipalities). These institutions were coordinated through the Macomunitat until 2011, when they came under the control of the newly established Barcelona Metropolitan Area that includes 35 local areas.

The Mancomunitat de Municipis was a voluntary association of municipalities in the metropolitan area, with the objective of bringing a common metropolitan perspective to planning and sector specific issues. It acted in the area of planning for and improving metropolitan infrastructure, public space, housing, and land, the last through the public company Institut Metropolità de Promoció del Sòl i Gestió Patrimonial. The metropolitan transport organization (EMT) and the organization for the environment were also associations of voluntary participation. EMT coordinated the organization, management, and planning of the public transport system; the provision of the subway service in seven municipalities; and the organization and control of the taxi system and traffic and road-network programming. The organization for the environment was responsible for the construction and maintenance of hydraulic infrastructures, water supply, drainage, and wastewater and the treatment of urban and industrial waste. All of this sectoral activity was carried out in coordination with the respective municipal services.

The metropolitan organizations are financed through a diverse set of resources, including taxes, charges, and other fees and transfers from the municipalities. The Barcelona Metropolitan Area assigns these resources to the planning, transport, or environmental functions within its jurisdiction. Each local government has a representative within the metropolitan council, which elects the administrators of the metropolitan area organization.

The concept of "territorial management" frames competencies within the emerging Barcelona Metropolitan Area. The metropolitan area includes planning, territorial policy, housing, infrastructure, and political coordination among the 35 local governments. It has undertaken competency in areas that were within the purview of the previous organizations that were merged. This includes transport, environmental issues, and planning. Economic development and strategic planning are new competencies being added to the new model.

Mexico City: Coordinating single purpose districts over an ever-expanding megalopolis. Recently formed entities in greater Mexico City illustrate a concerted effort to coordinate special purpose districts on a large urban scale. Around Mexico City, coordination initiatives continue to evolve and expand their spatial scope and authority in response to shifts in urban scale and development needs. Greater Mexico City dwarfs Barcelona in population and geography; over 20.1 million residents now live in the 7,733 square kilometers included in the Metropolitan Area for the Valley of Mexico (ZMVM). Mexico City has historically been home to nearly 20 percent of the national population, and there have long been efforts to coordinate planning and services for the area. In the 1980s, a Central Conurbation Commission was formed, including the federal district and counties from the states of Mexico, Hidalgo, Tlaxcala, Puebla, Morelos, and Queretaro. The Metropolitan Coordination Executive Committee (CECM) was created in 1998 to coordinate efforts by the federal district and the state of Mexico.

Although it began slowly, the CECM has grown to a trilateral effort with a policy agenda, a modest fund, and six special-purpose subcommissions. The executive commission is based out of the federal district's Office for Metropolitan Program Coordination, the Department of Metropolitan Development in the state of Mexico, and the Department of Planning and Regional Development in Hidalgo. One of the CECM's first tasks was to facilitate the 2005 establishment of the ZMVM for greater Mexico City. The ZMVM currently encompasses a total of 101 jurisdictions—16 *delegaciones* of the Mexico City federal district, as well as 56 and 29 municipalities from the adjacent states of Mexico and Hidalgo, respectively. ZMVM expansion is regulated by the CECM. As a sign of the changing demand for planning at scale, the ZMVM fits into a larger multimetropolitan area zone to encourage coordinated growth and development across the regional urban conglomeration.

Today, the CECM oversees six single purpose subcommissions operating in the Valle de Mexico Metropolitan Area. These subcommissions advocate and follow up on sectoral issues for the entire metropolitan area on the environment, water and drainage, public safety, civil protection, informal settlements, and transport. Special-purpose commissions work directly with the states and municipalities, and occasionally put forward special projects to be funded by the Metropolitan Area Fund, which is financed by contributions by the federal and state governments. In this way, the network of sector-specific commissions has gradually given rise to more formal interjurisdictional entities.

The central nucleus of the metropolitan area is formed by the federal district of Mexico City, which has long enjoyed a privileged status with the federal allocation of funds and a prominent role as the national capital. The relationship between the formally defined metropolitan area and the ZMVM is reflected in the practice of some businesses paying taxes in the federal district where their headquarters are located, while some of their other establishments and operations are outside Mexico City. By law, the federal district is the repository of national and state powers. While this position as a capital city and metropolitan area leads to Mexico City having a strong national and state role in terms of governance, the state of Mexico has also taken the lead on many of the ZMVM initiatives.

The CECM is the authorized entity to facilitate bilateral coordination in metropolitan matters between the governments of the state of Mexico and the federal district. The first is represented by the Metropolitan Development Secretariat and the second by the General Coordination Body of the metropolitan programs of the government. The executive committee debates and approves plans, programs, and projects of a metropolitan nature and proposes and advocates for legislative changes to further its agenda.

The CECM is financed separately by the federal, state, and municipal governments to address their respective jurisdictional responsibilities on an as-needed basis. The CECM is staffed by officials from the federal, state, and municipal federal district, who are appointed to serve in the executive and sectoral committees.

Interlocal Cooperation

Interlocal cooperation arrangements have a regional functional and administrative spatial boundary. In these arrangements, localities participate horizontally in intergovernmental relations while multiple actors participate in decision making through robust civil society engagement. A variant of this model are state-run metropolitan areas; in Sydney, for example, governance is the jurisdiction of the state.

While interlocal cooperation arrangements take a variety of organizational and implementation structures, they tend to emphasize pragmatic solutions in which stakeholders, different governments, or civil society come together to solve specific problems. Flexible structures to coordinate local participation around targeted initiatives are common and have become more so over time. This interlocal cooperation model is usually focused only on planning and coordination functions rather than service delivery. Activities are financed by local or other actor efforts that coordinate regional actions. National governments usually provide incentives to deepen the extent of this collaboration.

New York: A sectoral and civic governance system. New York City is an example of interlocal cooperation through sectoral agreements and a civic governance system. Greater New York has one of the largest metropolitan boundaries of all the cities analyzed in this chapter, encompassing 30,671 square kilometers. The administrative definition of the metro area boundary for Census purposes includes portions of 3 U.S. states, 31 counties, and more than 900 incorporated municipalities. It also has a very large population, with 17.8 million people, representing 6 percent of the national population.

New York has a tradition of establishing sector-based interjurisdictional entities for coordination. An interesting example is that of transportation, where long-range metropolitan plans have been developed through engagement with a tri-state civic group—the Regional Plan Association—which was an ad hoc group formed in 1922 to develop the regional plan for New York and its environs.

The plans are developed in coordination with: (1) the New York City the Port Authority of New York and New Jersey (PANYNJ),[13] which is a public authority responsible for the maintenance and operation of bridges, tunnels, airports, and ports in the area between the two states, as well as major urban development projects such as the World Trade Center in lower Manhattan; and (2) the Metropolitan Transportation Authority (MTA), which was established in 1968 to operate one of the world's largest regional transit systems and a network of eight bridges and tunnels, including the subway system and commuter rail facilities. The MTA has undertaken an ambitious capital investment program since 1982, investing more than US$80 billion to restore its vast transit system to a state of good repair.[14]

This first regional plan was completed in 1929, and the Regional Plan Association was incorporated as a permanent nonprofit organization later that year, to oversee the plan's implementation.[15] In response to new economic, mobility, environmental, and social challenges, the second and third regional plans were completed by RPA in 1968 and 1996 to address these concerns. Over the years, the vast majority of the actions proposed by the RPA in its three regional plans have been implemented.

The PANYNJ, MTA, and RPA each have their own financing sources. The direct service provision of the Port Authority is financed by tolls, fees, and other charges for using the transportation infrastructure under its jurisdiction. Leadership, including the chairperson, executive director, and members of the board of directors of the organization, at the Port Authority is appointed by the governors of New York and New Jersey. The RPA is financed through its business, grants, and donations from members and supporters. Although it is reliant on federal and state grants for capital improvements, the MTA has assembled a relatively stable source of operating funds from user fees, taxes, and service contracts.

Sydney: A State and intralocal cooperation metropolis. Sydney is a case in intralocal cooperation, in which the state coordinates local area planning and management. The Sydney Metropolitan Area spans over 43 jurisdictions and housing 16 percent (3.5 million) of the country's population. Given the highly fragmented system of local governments in the region, the Sydney Metropolitan Area is governed by the state of New South Wales, which controls the local government areas within its borders.

There is no specific metropolitan institution with overall jurisdiction for the 43 city councils of the metropolitan area of Sydney. A majority of metropolitan responsibilities are exercised by the government of the state of New South Wales. These include public transport, main roads, traffic control, police, primary school education, and the planning of major infrastructure projects. The commonwealth or federal government takes part in the planning of urban policies in the areas of immigration, trade, housing, and health. The federal government also makes transfers to states and local governments.

The state of New South Wales has its authority based on Australia's federal system of government, whose first constitution dates back to 1856. The government of New South Wales is responsible for the following areas: education (primary and secondary schools), health (hospitals, ambulances, refuges, and community health services), transport (public transport, major highways, and vehicle registration), state development (investment attraction, employment, work compensation, information technology, sports, recreation, gaming, and tourism), natural resources and the environment (development of agriculture, electricity and gas supply, sewerage and water supply, forests, land management, and environmental protection), law and order (courts and tribunals, legal aid, police, and prisons), community services, housing, the fire brigade, and emergency services.

Public institutions in the State of New South Wales include the Rail Corporation of New South Wales (RailCorp) and the Sydney Catchment Authority. RailCorp was created on January 1, 2004, from the merger of two state agencies: the State Rail Authority of New South Wales and the Railway Infrastructure Corporation. RailCorp is a public company that plans and manages the railways in the state. The company provides train services to passengers through two bodies: CityRail and CountryLink. In Sydney, RailCorp is also in charge of the city rail network. The Sydney Catchment Authority is a New South Wales government agency that manages Sydney's water. Its responsibilities include water distribution, sewerage, and the management of flood prevention systems. It was created in 1999 by the Sydney Water Catchment Management Act 1998.

Metropolitan functions for the Sydney Metropolitan Area are financed through allocations of the New South Wales government, which focuses its expenditures on metropolitan issues through the different governmental units and departments within its organization. These units also appoint representatives for the management and operation of the metropolitan function in this region.

Governance in Sydney is dominated by the state, with local governments essentially playing a supporting role. Given the centrality of the Sydney metropolis within the state as an economic and population center, management of metropolitan areas is clearly one of the most-important functions of the state. It exercises tight control over metropolitan planning, including dealing directly with major development proposals and special-purpose agencies for urban transport, main roads, water, sewerage and drainage, pollution control, major cultural facilities, and other functions that might otherwise be the responsibility of the local government. A key factor limiting local government and favoring state metropolitan governance that coordinates among these different local governments is its division into 43 local governments, half with populations of 75,000 or fewer and several with fewer than 40,000 people.

This fragmentation undermines the potential of local governments to handle metropolitan planning and management issues. Local governments have resisted amalgamation and have made only limited moves toward regional cooperation and resource sharing. The resulting governance structure is not a separate metropolitan government but a coordination of the local areas. This model creates political venues through the state parliament and election of the premier by which interlocal cooperation is achieved through a representative democracy.

The Role of the National Government in Promoting Coordination

The competencies, roles, and relationships between metropolitan regions and higher levels of government are closely intertwined. International experience indicates that central government best practices are generally supervision and standard setting to support and review decisions, monitor performance, and provide targeted intervention to solve market and government failures. National governments should provide the financial and regulatory framework for metropolitan areas to develop and promote growth and other societal goals through vision setting, service provision, and internal cooperation at metropolitan level. To achieve these ends and encourage regional independence in planning and service delivery, central governments can assign relative fiscal and regulatory autonomy to metropolitan areas to promote their capacity building.

The financial structure of a metropolitan region is an important factor in the distribution of capacity and the central government's role in promoting coordination. Direct competencies, such as planning or service delivery, cannot be separated from their financial structure because the arrangements for financing public services in metropolitan areas are largely driven by the service delivery responsibilities assigned to the various governments and enterprises. From the perspective of the leaders in metropolitan regions, effective governance often depends upon bringing wider regional and national organizations and resources to bear on their mission. In this context, intervention by higher-level governments can also supplant metropolitan cooperation and initiative. Based on the subsidiarity principle, the larger the scale of governance, the more difficult it is to provide effectively for the participation of local units, neighborhoods, civil society, or individual citizens making the case for metropolitan subsidiarity.

Building metropolitan governance capacity depends greatly on the type of incentives set by higher levels of governments. Incentives set by these levels are important factors in building metropolitan governance because local and regional areas are almost always dependent on fiscal frameworks established by the national government. Positive incentives, such as grants, financial subsidies, and increased competencies, can promote area-wide governance through planning coordination or service delivery. Negative incentives, including an imposed metropolitan government solution, can also be effective. The success of incentives depends greatly on the abilities and willingness of the metropolitan entities to perceive incentives as such and then make use of them. Large events, such as the Olympics, are also components of an incentive structure to promote capacity. Coordinated and specific projects between the national and regional governments can also promote metropolitan capacity. Table 4.3 summarizes some incentives offered by national governments in Germany, Switzerland, France, and the United States.

Positive financial incentives could be a forceful instrument to promote coordination in Colombia. As the case studies below indicate, there are many examples from around the world in which central governments have successfully encouraged better interjurisdictional coordination by altering the incentives structure that these entities face. In particular, there is scope to use the positive incentive of making funds available for coordinated projects, as has occurred in Germany. There is also scope to encourage greater coordination by withholding transfers, as in the case of federal transportation funds in the United States. The relatively important

Table 4.3   Examples of National Financial Incentives for Metropolitan Coordination

Nation	Incentive
France	New framework for the creation of governance structures
Germany	State incentives granted for cooperation in metropolitan areas
Switzerland	Federal incentives for regional cooperation and specific projects
United States	Federal fiscal transfers dependent on regional plans and investment priorities

Source: Yaro and Ronderos 2011.

role that national transfers play in Colombian municipal finances and indeed, the anticipated increases in revenues from natural resources in the near future, suggest that these lessons are particularly applicable to Colombia. (See chapter 5 for further information on the structure of municipal finances.)

The experience of Germany confirms that positive fiscal incentives can be an effective strategy in highly fragmented local contexts. There, the federal government offered fiscal incentives for regions and states to cooperate on regional issues. In Germany, as in Colombia, there was a strong statist and local tradition that relied heavily on institutions to solve societal problems. In this system, regional cooperation faced high transaction costs. In the 1990s, however, the need for greater regional and economic self-governance arose with trends such as the increasingly competitive nature of the global economy and the fiscal crisis of the public sector. This represented a paradigm shift in which local governments united to solve metropolitan problems. The federal state played an important role in promoting this cooperation by "regionalizing" restructuring policy and enticing collaboration through fiscal incentives that reward cooperation on regional issues through transfers for metropolitan-coordinated efforts. This paradigm shift boosted regional cooperation and raised the attractiveness of the regional level as a political arena. The paradigm shift has been reinforced by European Union Structural Funds, which have coordinated with the German incentives to further entice metropolitan planning and coordination.

In Switzerland, where there is a strong tradition of the predominance of local mandates, the Confederation has introduced policies to incentivize cooperation on metropolitan issues. In 1999, a new article was introduced to the federal constitution to create a "tri-partite agglomeration conference" with the objective of developing coherent policies and strategies for metropolitan management across the three levels of government. In 2000, this was supplemented with an "agglomeration policy," which offers financial support to urban projects in specific metropolitan areas that are developed with the cooperation of the city, locality, and state. Although the financial commitment of the federal government has been modest to date, substantial sums have been reserved to finance the improvement of public transportation infrastructure at the regional scale.

In France, the central government has provided incentives for coordination by giving financial support to supra-communal cooperative bodies that integrate several jurisdictions. The 1999 "Chevenement Law" laid the groundwork for policies to reinforce and simplify metropolitan governance structures and vehicles. The law allowed prefects to force a commune to integrate with a supra-communal cooperative body, the Communaute d'Aglomeration (CUA). This reform marked a significant change in a country that has a strong tradition of local political fragmentation. The powers of the CUA can include economic development, urban planning, social housing, urban regeneration, and policing of petty-crime. The CUA are funded through national contributions—which is proportional to the number of competencies they adopt—as well as local corporate taxes.

In the United States, financial incentives for federal transportation are applied to encourage metropolitan planning and coordination. A federal requirement for urban transportation planning was first introduced in the United States in the 1960s. The Federal-Aid Highway Act of 1962 attached conditions to the federal financial assistance associated with the Interstate Highway System, which required transportation projects in urbanized areas of 50,000 or more people, based on a continuing, comprehensive, urban transportation planning process undertaken in cooperation between the state and local governments. This condition is known as the 3Cs—"continuing, comprehensive and cooperative"—planning process. Other instruments include the Regional Transportation Plans and federal funding through the Transportation Improvement Program (TIP).

RTPs are developed with a 25-year horizon, but updated every 4 years to support long-term planning. The TIP provides funding for projects identified in the RTP that have also been evaluated under the Project Development Work Program (PDWP).

Concluding Remarks

Flexible and voluntary coordination structures are the most relevant tools to improve planning and collaboration in the Colombian context. Financial and regulatory incentives are needed to create regional plans in metropolitan areas in the country by the national government. Incentives can be provided for these entities to assume financial and service provision independence from the central government in specific projects agreed upon by the metropolitan and national governments (box 4.2). In the long term, and as these plans are implemented, the potential to increase their institutional formalization should be explored.

Box 4.2

Road Map for Implementing Interjurisdictional Coordination

Promoting improved metropolitan governance and planning systems is not an overnight process. It will require efforts starting from the use of diagnostics to understand the past evolution and future development of each metropolitan area in the country, moving then toward identifying constraints in regional/metropolitan coordination and, finally, identifying mechanisms to promote a regional perspective in these areas. A roadmap of important steps in moving toward better metropolitan governance and planning systems is provided below. This roadmap provides a list of the important steps to follow, both in the short and long term.

1. Develop 10-, 20-, and 30-year population and employment forecasts for each major metropolitan area, and calculate the number of additional housing units and industrial, retail, and commercial spaces needed to accommodate this growth. These forecasts can be used to project the land areas needed to accommodate the projected growth and to shape the urban growth patterns that need to be managed.
2. Identify the major systems that must be managed at the regional scale to produce more-productive, efficient, and sustainable metropolitan regions. These should include:

   • The "eco-structure" of natural systems, for example, the public water supply, watersheds, and other large natural systems needed to sustain each region for decades to come
   • The major infrastructure systems, including the roads, transport, and goods movement systems, water supply and wastewater management systems, and parks needed to sustain the region's functionality and quality of life
   • The "urban structure" of the built environment, including central business districts, residential communities, and future designated growth areas
   • The "infostructure" of major fiber optic hubs and other information management systems, which will become a focal point for each region's economic development

3. Assess the effectiveness of existing metro governance institutions and regional planning systems in each metropolitan area.

(continued next page)

Box 4.2 *(continued)*

4. Identify the gaps in regional governance and planning systems in each metropolitan area.
5. Assess the options for filling these gaps with new institutions or by improving existing institutions or processes.
6. Identify the incentives or mandates from the central government that could result in improvements to existing regional institutions or the creation of new ones.
7. Create an on-going process to finance and implement plans and institutions and benchmark their progress toward agreed-upon goals.

Source: Robert Yaro and Nicolas Ronderos, Regional Plan Association, New York.

In Colombia, infrastructure is perhaps the most accessible area to move forward with improved coordination structures. However, it is likely that larger municipalities will attract all incentive-based funds because of their better capacity to structure and design projects to be presented to the national government. The capacity to structure realistic projects in smaller municipalities needs to be improved with the participation of the private sector, where PPPs may play an important role. These projects can be financed with the *Bolsa de Regalías* through a component of knowledge transfer to smaller municipalities. Within a large regional urban system, all infrastructure within the nuclei, in fact, supports the metropolitan infrastructure. Many of these projects need to have the active involvement and participation of municipalities outside the nuclei to guarantee their success. For example, Bogotá should move beyond coordinating infrastructure for Soacha and invite this municipality to take an active role in the managing and structuring of projects inside the capital.

A national framework is needed to support improved coordination. One important component is ensuring new laws for metropolitan and regional coordination are aligned with a broader framework of territorial development. Law 388 needs to be updated to incorporate all recent developments on national and subnational regulation for interjurisdictional coordination. In addition, it should be noted that current reforms to the metropolitan tax framework do little to support fiscal coordination, which is vital to align political incentives for collaboration. Indeed, the proposed text to modify Law 128 of 1994 for metropolitan areas makes only one reference to taxation. Steps should also be taken to support better territorial and fiscal planning for urban conglomerations. At present, for example, there is little incentive to consolidate land cadasters into central offices in metropolitan areas, as this cannot be undertaken without consolidating all the municipalities into a single territorial unit at the expense of municipal autonomy. Currently, the only way possible for municipalities to have a centralized office to manage taxes is the unification into a district. However, this also implies that they will transform into one single territorial unit and lose all autonomy. It is clear that a "race to the bottom" in tax policies will leave all municipalities worse off.

One size does not fit all. The experience of metropolitan coordination in Colombia to date shows that the existence of a metropolitan institution does not guarantee successful coordination. Bucaramanga, for example, has been more successful in promoting social convergence than Barranquilla or Cali. While it is clear that the creation of metropolitan areas can give cities an additional tool to become more competitive and manage their needs as they grow, it is also clear that these institutions need to be relevant to their context. A pragmatic approach based on voluntary agreements that build on existing governance institutions and traditions could help consolidate successes and build toward more formal coordination structures.

Financial incentives for planning and coordination from the national government will help promote the process. Steps to implement this would include (1) identifying the region and its jurisdictions and the business and civic actors to be included in the coalition and (2) defining the role of the coalition and identifying the planning and coordination tasks to be accomplished by the coalition. The central government can support this process by providing financial incentives to create regional strategic plans that include issues on urban growth management, transport, economic development, and environmental and water management, among others. In the framework of the new LOOT, the central government can promote the coordination of POTs and PDs through the Commission of Territorial Ordering and working in parallel with the departmental commissions.

These institutions can be formalized based on the success of these voluntary coalitions. In the long term, the voluntary cooperative structures could be formalized into nonprofit organizations or sector-based structures to undertake specific projects, following the civic and single purpose district models documented in this chapter. It is possible that different regions across the country could utilize either the civic-based or sector-based structure or a combination of both. Initial steps for the implementation of this agreement and the creation of the associated institutions would first require identifying the needs of each successful metropolitan coalition and single purpose districts. Finally, it is important to recognize that new institutions would have financial needs and act accordingly to ensure their financial sustainability.

Notes

1. The ideas presented in this paragraph refer to World Bank (2010) Cross-jurisdictional Service Provision in Indian Metropolitan Areas.

2. Regions, provinces, and indigenous territorial entities are not included.

3. This was initially established in Law 128 of 1994 and has now been confirmed under the new LOOT.

4. This metropolitan area includes the municipalities of Caldas, Estrella, Sabaneta, Envigado, Itagüí, Bello, Copacabana, Girardota, and Barbosa.

5. Governance may be defined in different ways. The definition used in this study is that used by United Nations Development Programme (UNDP), and reads as follows: "the exercise of political, economic and administrative authority in the management of a country's affairs at all levels. It comprises the mechanisms, processes and institutions through which citizens and groups articulate their interests, exercise their legal rights, meet their obligations and mediate their differences." The most important aspect of this definition for developing a typology of metropolitan governance is that it is focused on management. This includes the mechanisms, processes, and institutional arrangements for decision-making.

6. In 1967, the number of municipalities forming the metropolitan area was reduced to six.

7. Urbanization Review—Colombia.

8. Including the power to enact laws pertaining to urban development, scope for increased popular participation in urban decision making, and the obligation for cities of populations above 20,000 to develop master plans for urban expansion. See World Bank (2006).

9. The municipalities include Rio de Janeiro, Belford Roxo, Duque de Caxias, Guapimirim, Itaboraí, Japeri, Magé, Maricá, Mesquita, Nilópolis, Niterói, Nova Iguaçu, Paracambi, Queimados, São Gonçalo, São João de Meriti, Seropédica, Tanguá, and Itaguaí.

10. These sectors include (1) integrated regional economic and social development; (2) water and sanitation; (3) gas distribution; (4) integrated and rational

use of water resources; (5) mapping and basic information for metropolitan planning; and (6) housing and land use.

11. See "Arranjos Institucionais para a Gestão Metropolitana," Projeto Observatório Das Metrópoles (October 2009).

12. With a total area of 803 square kilometers, Barcelona can be considered a small metropolitan area from a spatial perspective. It is also small in terms of population because it houses about 10 percent of Spain's population (3.9 million people). The metropolitan area is formed by 36 governments, which makes it a middle-range metropolis in terms of number of jurisdictions.

13. The Port Authority of New York and New Jersey is a bi-state port district that runs most of the regional transportation infrastructure within the Port of New York and New Jersey. Its management board provides equal representation to members elected by the states of New York and New Jersey. The district was established in 1921 (as the Port of New York Authority) through an interstate compact to run infrastructure that includes bridges, tunnels, airports, and seaports. The Port Authority operates the Port Newark-Elizabeth Marine Terminal, which handles the third-largest amount of shipping of all ports in the United States and the largest on the Eastern Seaboard, as well as the Hudson River crossings. The Port Authority also runs the bus terminal, Trans-Hudson rail system, LaGuardia Airport, John F. Kennedy Airport, Newark Liberty International Airport, Teterboro Airport, and Stewart International Airport. The agency has its own 1,600-member-strong Port Authority Police Department, which is responsible for providing safety and deterring criminal activity at Port Authority–owned-and-operated facilities.

14. The authority is now engaged in a program to expand the transit system through the creation of two "mega projects"—the East Side Access commuter rail link and the Second Avenue subway transit line. The authority uses surplus toll revenues from its bridges and tunnels to cross-subsidize its transit operations.

15. RPA is a civic group with a board of directors with representatives from the major business and institutional entities in the metropolitan area. RPA provides a coordination role among the municipalities, counties, and special governments in the region. After the completion of each of its three regional plans, the RPA has advocated for public and private actions needed to implement major policies and investments proposed in the plan.

Bibliography

Adams, S., and C. Cotti. 2008. "Drunk Driving after the Passage of Smoking Bans in Bars." *Journal of Public Economics* 92: 1288–305.

Britto, A. L., and R. M. Formiga Johnsson. 2009. "Water Governance and Climate Change in the Rio De Janeiro Metropolitan Region: Discussing Reduction in Urban Water Supply Vulnerability." http://www.cityfutures2009.com/PDF/44_Ana_Lucia_Britto_Rosa_Maria_Formiga_Johnsson.pdf.

Chamorro, L. H. 1997. "Balance del Proceso de Conformación de Regiones en Colombia." *Planeación y Desarrollo* 28 (4): 115–15.

Escobar-Lemmon, M. C. 2003. "Political Support for Decentralization: An Analysis of the Colombian and Venezuelan Legislatures." *American Journal of Political Science* 47 (4): 683–97.

———. 2006. "Executives, Legislatures, and Decentralization." *The Policy Studies* 34 (2): 245–63.

Gutiérrez. 2007. "Lo que el Viento se Llevó? Los Partidos Políticos y la Democracia en Colombia 1958–2002." Editorial Norma.

Massiris Cabeza, A. 2010. "Ordenamiento Territorial: experiencias internacionales y desarrollos conceptuales y legales realizados en Colombia." Angel Massiris Cabeza. http://www.banrepcultural.org/blaavirtual/geografia/orden/7.htm.

Moncayo, Edgard. 2002. "Las Políticas Regionales en Colombia." Archivos de Economía (7 Separatas), Departamento Nacional de Planeación, Bogotá.

Monsalve, A., and I. Gaviria, eds. 2004. *Colombia, Democracia y Paz.* Vol. VIII. Medellín: Universidad de Antioquia.

O'Neill. 1998. "Understanding the Great Power-Giveaway: Decentralization in the Andes." Paper presented to the 1998 Meeting of the Latin American Studies Association, Chicago.

Rodriguez Vitta, J. F. 2011. "Inter-Jurisdictional Coordination, Metropolitan Management, and Regional Integration." Background Report for the *Colombia Urbanization Review.*

Slack, E. 2007. "Managing the Coordination of Service Delivery in Metropolitan Cities: The Role of Metropolitan Governance." Policy Research Working Paper WPS4317, World Bank, Washington, DC, September 24–26.

World Bank. 2006. "Inputs to a Strategy for Brazilian Cities: A Contribution with a Focus on Cities and Municipalities (Two Volumes) Volume I: Main." Report 35749-BR, World Bank, Washington, DC.

———. 2009. *Colombia Decentralization Options and Incentives for Efficiency.* Washington, DC: World Bank.

———. 2010. "Cross-Jurisdictional Service Provision in Indian Metropolitan Areas." Report, World Bank, Washington, DC.

Yaro, R., and N. Ronderos. 2011. "International Metropolitan Governance: Typology, Case Studies and Recommendations." Background Report for the *Colombia Urbanization Review.*

CHAPTER 5

Infrastructure Finance

Yoonhee Kim, Alexandra Panman, and Alejandro Rodriguez

Introduction

Infrastructure investment is closely linked to urban economic growth and productivity. There is broad consensus among researchers that improved intra-urban and interurban infrastructure connectivity contributes to increased output and lowered production costs. Several empirical studies have concluded that infrastructure makes a positive and significant contribution to output in the Latin American region (Calderón and Servén 2003). Furthermore, improving the level and quality of infrastructure can have considerable payoffs in terms of higher growth and reduced inequality. For example, a 2004 World Bank study estimated that if Colombia reached the same level of infrastructure as Costa Rica, the region's leader in terms of quantity and quality of infrastructure, per capita gross domestic product (GDP) growth rates could be higher by as much as 3 percent.

The infrastructure financing gap in Colombia is considerable. Colombia needs to mobilize significant amounts of capital to bridge this gap. In 2007, the World Bank estimated that Colombia would need to invest about

This chapter was written with input from Juan Benavides, Mauricio Olivera, Oscar Arboleda, and Claudia Patricia Quintero. The background study, "Financiación de infraestructura y el desarrollo urbano" (Benavides et al. 2011), is available on the World Bank's Urbanization Review website (http://www.urbanknowledge.org/ur.html).

4 percent of GDP a year for 20 years—far more than it is investing now—
if the country aims to reach the same infrastructure levels as the Republic
of Korea. In Bogotá, for example, there is a considerable gap in road maintenance investments alone. In 2007, the city of Bogotá classified 40 percent
of the road network in bad condition, and estimated a backlog of US$3.5
billion in road maintenance investments. The University of Los Andes
increased this estimate to US$5.0 billion in 2009. The allocated investment
for 2007–11, however, was only US$300 million. Similarly, it is also esti-
mated that Bogotá requires an investment of approximately US$1.6 billion
to upgrade basic infrastructure in informal settlements against an actual
investment of US$143 million during the 2007–11 period.

Other principal Colombian cities face significant challenges in terms of
financing infrastructure. Medellín is perhaps one of the most fiscally sol-
vent cities in Colombia because of sound management and the role of the
city's profit-making publically owned utility, Empresas Públicas de
Medellín (EPM). EPM contributes 30 percent of all profits to the city
administrative budget, a total of US$345 million in 2011. Nonetheless,
Medellín faces important challenges. The city recently estimated that city-
wide flood-risk-mitigation infrastructure would cost approximately US$4.0
billion, against an annual budget of US$12.6 million for the MetroRio
program, the principle source for capital investment in the sector.

Infrastructure bottlenecks contribute to Colombia's stagnant productivity levels. Colombia has been lagging in terms of its productivity
performance over the past three decades (World Bank 2008). Since
1995, productivity growth has been especially disappointing. Between
1995–2000 and 2001–05, total factor productivity (TFP) declined by
one percentage point every year. Economic growth resumed after 2000,
accompained by an average TFP annual growth rate of 1 percent
between 2005 and 2008 (Caballero et al. 2011). Colombia's productivity performance was below the entire average of Latin America and the
Caribbean for the period 1996–2000. From 2001–05, productivity
improved only marginally to match the regional average. The infrastructure gap is an important factor behind slow productivity gains.
Numerous empirical studies point to the fact that poor infrastructure
affects integration with the global market.[1] As discussed in chapter 3 of
this review, high transport costs create disincentives for regional specialization and limit the production of competitive goods for export. In
addition, lack of infrastructure provision hinders the capacity of firms
to export and the ability of countries to attract foreign investment. This
can reduce opportunities for increased international integration,
enhanced competitiveness, technological advances, and innovation.

As Colombian decentralization has advanced, cities have assumed responsibility to provide social services and basic infrastructure in urban areas. Cities finance social services, such as education and health, and basic infrastructure, such as water, urban drainage, solid waste, and public transportation. These services are primarily financed through fiscal transfers from the central government, and are supplemented by capital resources from their own budgets, and use of other financing instruments. Municipalities of different sizes rely on different sources of financing; in general terms, less urban municipalities, which either have small cities or are mainly rural, depend on the national transfer system as their main source of financing, where as own source revenues gain importance for mid and large sized cities. Cities such as Bogotá, Cali, Barranquilla, and Medellín have moved beyond more traditional funding sources and have experimented with more-innovative financing instruments.

The objective of this chapter is to contribute to policy dialog on infrastructure financing in Colombian cities. In analyzing the current structure of municipal financing for urban infrastructure, it aims to shed light on both the strengths and weaknesses of the current system. The recommendations and policy options explored to improve financing mechanisms are differentiated by municipality and city size. This reflects variation in the challenges and sources of financing between municipal categories.

For smaller cities and rural areas, the central government has an important role in increasing the efficiency of infrastructure investments through the national transfer system (Sistema General de Participaciones, SGP) and the design of performance-based incentives. There is scope for the central government to promote a careful evaluation of the efficiency of fiscal transfers and local expenditures on water, sanitation, and transport. Introducing output- and performance-based incentive systems focused on sector outcomes might lead to higher efficiency and effectiveness in both SGP transfers and overall municipal investment. More systematic data recording of expenditures could facilitate the measurement of investment and provide more concrete evidence on what institutional strengthening efforts could be beneficial to improve the quality of investments. Monitoring and evaluation would also clarify what the impacts of specific conditions, such as earmarking, are on the efficiency of investment. Finally, providing technical assistance to these small cities and rural areas to implement infrastructure projects and improve expenditure efficiency also seems to be a key role of the central government.

As municipalities urbanize and cities become larger, more-sophisticated financing instruments can be used to finance an increasingly complex urban infrastructure and redevelopment investment portfolio. Instruments may include user charges and local government debt, as well as land-based financing instruments such as property taxes, exaction and development impact fees, and land sales or leases. Land-based instruments can provide cities with an opportunity to enhance urban efficiency by intensifying land use and managing densities, while sharing the cost of infrastructure provision with private landowners and developers.

The chapter is divided into four sections. The first section reviews public infrastructure finance in Colombian cities. The second section analyzes national government–supported investment programs in urban transport and the water and sanitation sector. The third section explores differentiated policy options, drawing on key lessons and challenges from the application of urban infrastructure finance instruments. In particular, Colombia's experience with land-based finance instruments, such as betterment levies and *valorización*, is assessed, as well as international experience with instruments that have not yet been used in Colombia. A specific focus is given to tax increment financing (TIF) and transferable development rights (TDRs). This section highlights the advantages of these instruments as well as the challenges they may raise in Colombia. The chapter concludes with a section outlining key policy recommendations organized around the system-of-cities approach, under which guidance is tailored to cities and municipalities at different stages of the urbanization process.

Diagnostics: Review of Public Infrastructure Finance in Colombian Cities

The political decentralization process in Colombia increased municipal responsibility for infrastructure investment and service delivery, with important implications for public finances. Colombia has undergone extensive decentralization over the past several decades. Direct elections of mayors were introduced in 1986. This process was consolidated by constitutional reform in 1991 and a series of legal reforms. Political decentralization involved the devolution of responsibility for service provision and infrastructure finance to the municipal level. This increased municipal responsibility required greater expenditure; indeed, municipal investment doubled in per capita terms between 1996 and 2009. As figure 5.1 shows, the upward trend in investment has been fairly constant throughout the period 1995–2009, and is manifested in both absolute and per capita terms. Municipal investment peaked at

Figure 5.1   Municipal Investment, 1996–2009
thousands of constant 2000 pesos

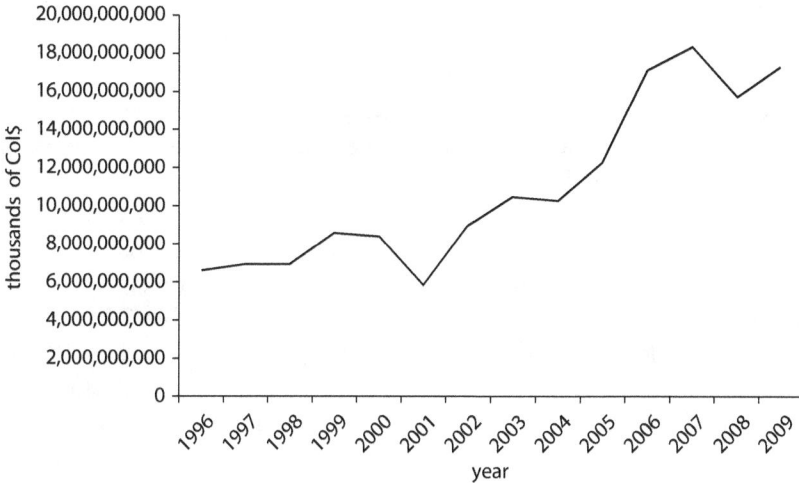

Source: SICEP.
Note: The analysis is predominantly based on data from the Sistema de Información para la Captura de la Ejecución Presupuestal (SICEP) between 1996 and 2009, where possible; data limitations, for example, restrict analysis of the transportation sector to 2002–09.

Col$18 billion in 2007, when it was equivalent to 6.5 percent of the national GDP.

The legal framework for decentralization specifies detailed roles and responsibilities for municipalities. The constitutional reform of 1991 and Law 60 of 1993 guaranteed that: (1) departmental and municipal governments assume responsibility for health, education, and water and sanitation services; and (2) funds were dedicated to build and maintain necessary infrastructure for these services. Under these institutional arrangements, 23 percent of government revenue was earmarked for transfer to departments, with designated portions for health (60 percent) and education (20 percent) expenses. Law 60 further specified that a growing portion of national revenues would be transferred to municipalities (15 percent in 1994, rising steadily to 22 percent by 2001) for investment in education (30 percent), health (25 percent), water and sanitation (20 percent), sports, leisure and culture (5 percent), and other municipal priorities (20 percent).

Through the process of decentralization, new municipal revenue flows were established to fund the increased municipal costs associated with decentralized responsibility for service delivery. The key sources of municipal revenue in Colombia are (1) SGP; (2) taxation, categorized as "own revenue;" (3) royalties from natural resource extraction (*Regalías*), which are distributed directly in municipalities and departments that produce the resource (direct *Regalías*) or in nonproducing areas (indirect *Regalías*); (4) national[2] and departmental cofinancing for specific projects, which is allocated according to the central government's analysis of regional need[3]; and (5) credit.

As the infrastructure investment challenges in Colombia vary significantly across the urban portfolio, it is important to differentiate analyses by categories of cities. Law 617 of 2000 categorized municipalities into seven groups, according to their size and revenue. As table 5.1 outlines, these categories range from isolated municipalities of less than 10,000 inhabitants to large cities that have experienced rapid urbanization and population growth. "Special Category" municipalities account for nearly 30 percent of the population of Colombia and incorporate Colombia's most-important cities, including Bogotá Medellín, Bucaramanga, and Cali, as well as some of the municipalities around Medellín.[4] Municipalities in categories 1 and 2 are dominated by midsized cities, while municipalities in categories 3 and 4 are considered small cities and towns for the purposes of this book. Finally, category 5 and 6 municipalities are primarily rural areas and towns.

The challenges associated with the urbanization process vary across this range of municipalities. Smaller municipalities and rural areas continue to experience the challenges associated with extending networks and developing institutional capacity for service provision. Midsized cities and more-urban municipalities face challenges in terms of improving service quality and developing increasingly mature planning and management instruments in the face of complex urban challenges. Larger cities have pressure from increasing densities and rapid urban expansion beyond municipal boundaries and are, as a result, confronted with the complex challenges associated with upgrading and extending structural infrastructure on a metropolitan scale, while developing and leveraging a sophisticated urban management capacity.

However, as noted above, the infrastructure finance gap is considerable across the system of cities. In order to close this gap, it is important to understand the weaknesses in current financing mechanisms. The following section looks at infrastructure expenditure and identifies patterns in the sources of finance for different municipalities.

Table 5.1   Municipal Categorization

	Municipal	Number of municipalities	Percent	Minimum wage (Col$)	Population	Additional characteristics
Large cities	Special	6	28.8	More than 400,000	More than 500,001	Municipalities categorized
	1	16	14.2	100,000 to 400,000	100,001 to 500,000	as "special" count on tax-
	2	16	9	50,000 to 100,000	50,001 to 100,000	ation as their major source
Midsized cities	3	18	4.6	30,000 to 50,000	30,001 to 50,000	of revenue. Category 6
	4	25	4.5	25,000 to 30,000	20,001 to 30,000	municipali- ties are
Smaller cities and mostly rural munici- palities	5	24	2.7	15,000 to 25,000	10,001 to 20,000	dependent on central government
	6	997	36.1	Less than 15,000	Less than 10,000	transfers.

Source: Law 617 of 2000.
Note: Total population in 2010 was 45,508,205 (Departamento Administrativo Nacional de Estadística, DANE).

Infrastructure Investment: Different Sources for Different Municipalities

The most important sources of municipal revenue for municipalities are national transfers and taxation revenue, as indicated above. These sources accounted for, on average, 40 percent and 26 percent, respectively, of municipal finances between 1995 and 2009 (figure 5.2). National transfers and tax revenue have increased steadily in absolute terms since 1995. Over this period, the importance of *Regalías* has grown steadily and now exceeds the relative share of credit in municipal funding. Still, by 2009, the national government was transferring more than Col$10 billion to municipalities; this is equivalent to Col$200,000 per person or 3.5 percent of the national GDP.

Under the theoretical framework established for decentralization, it was anticipated that transfers would be allocated for capital investments, while municipalities would use local revenues to meet operational costs of programs. This division is upheld in general terms by the law. However, in the specific classification of expenditures, some significant operational costs, such as teachers' salaries, remain funded by transfers.

The most important fiscal transfer program is the SGP, which was developed in response to the economic crisis of 1999. The SGP was established by Legislative Act 01 and Law 715 of 2001, which as

Figure 5.2   Municipal Revenue by Source

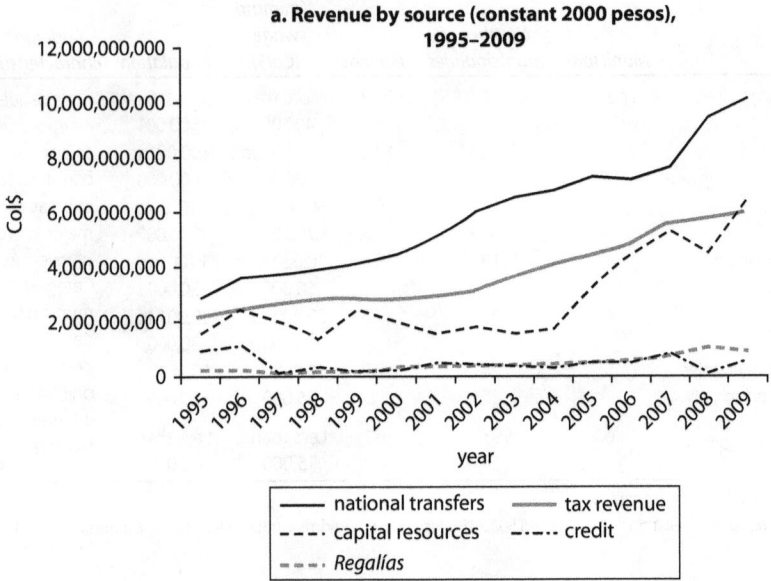

a. Revenue by source (constant 2000 pesos), 1995–2009

Legend:
— national transfers   — tax revenue
--- capital resources   –·–·· credit
–·–·· *Regalías*

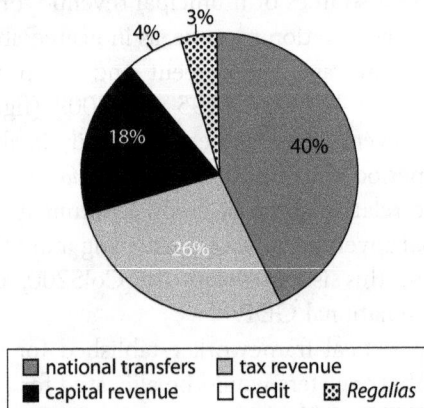

b. Revenue by source (% of total investment), average, 1995–2009

40%
26%
18%
4%
3%

Legend:
■ national transfers   ▨ tax revenue
■ capital revenue   □ credit   ▨ *Regalías*

Source: SICEP.

figure 5.3 indicates, specified the distribution between key sectors and expenditure categories. This allocation was further refined through Legislative Act 04 of 2001 and Law 1176, which placed additional emphasis on water and sanitation investment. SGPs are also tied to

Figure 5.3   The Composition of SGP by 2008 According to Law 1176

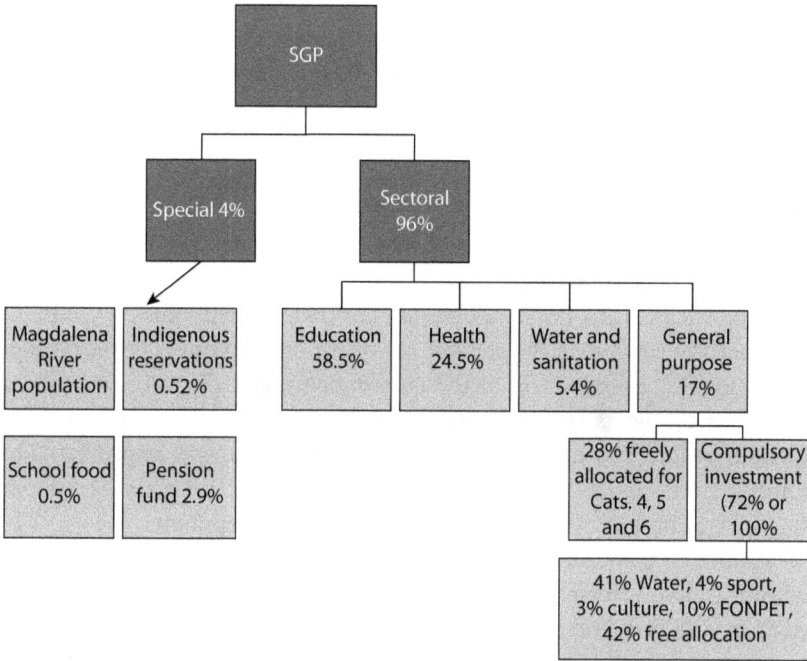

Source: Rodriguez Vitta 2011.
Note: FONPET = National Fund for Pensions of Territorial Entities. 53.4 percent of education, 28.7 percent of health, and 15.0 percent of water and sanitation SGP are directed to departments.

minimum criteria measures to improve efficiency in the use of public resources and administration, for example, efforts to expand service coverage and measures of poverty (Unsatisfied Basic Needs, NBI).

The fiscal transfer system of *Regalías* is growing in importance as a source of municipal funding for basic service provision and infrastructure finance. *Regalías* are royalties from natural resources and extractive industry production. *Regalías* can be "direct" or "indirect." Direct *Regalías* are royalties assigned to territorial entities where the nonrenewable resources are produced, including extraction areas and transportation corridors. Indirect *Regalías* are resources assigned to finance priority investment projects in nonproducer areas. The proportion of *Regalías* that are redistributed directly into producer areas is determined by a formula that accounts for the level of production in any given year. Broadly, however, regions can receive 47.5 percent to 52.0 percent of petrol royalties and between 42.0 percent and 45.0 percent of carbon royalties; municipalities receive between 12.5 percent and 32.0 percent of direct petrol royalties and between 32.0 percent and 45.0 percent of carbon royalties.

Two key laws govern the allocation of *Regalías*. The first is Decree 1747 of 1995, which specifies that *Regalías* producing departments or municipalities must spend 60 percent or 70 percent (respectively) on attaining minimum standards for infant mortality, basic health and education, and water and sanitation. Once met, 90 percent of the remaining revenue from direct *Regalías* remains earmarked for investment projects. The second law is Law 863 of 2003, which specifies that 50 percent of indirect *Regalías* are designated for the National Fund for Pensions of Territorial Entities (Fondo Nacional de Pensiones de las Entidades Territoriales, FONPET) and that the remaining 50 percent are distributed among: (1) promotion of mining; (2) preservation of the environment; and (3) priority regional investment projects, specified in the 2006–10 National Development Plan (NDP).[5] More recently, in June 2011, a new law was approved that improves the spatial distribution of royalties through the use of Territorial Compensation Funds and Funds for Regional Development.

Municipal tax collection has also increased with decentralization and administrative reforms. The most important sources of municipal taxation in 2009 were: (1) industrial and commercial activity, which accounted for 38 percent of tax revenue; (2) real property tax (*predial unificado*), which made up 29 percent of the total; and (3) gasoline tax, which provided an additional 11 percent of the "shared tax base"[6] for departments and municipalities. Under Law 715 of 2001, municipalities have the autonomy to determine tax revenue expenditure, but they are required to invest between 15 percent and 25.9 percent of the real property tax in the *Corporaciones Autónomas Regionales*, which then directs these resources to priority environmental and renewable resource projects in keeping with municipal development plans. Municipalities also often direct revenue from gasoline taxes to the maintenance of the road network and investments in mass transportation systems.

Municipal capacity to raise real property taxes is closely connected to the efficiency of the cadastral system. There is also a positive correlation between real tax revenue and the accuracy of the cadastral system. Large cities have more comprehensive land cadastres than rural areas: Bogotá, for example, has attained 100 percent registration of land, while only 43 percent of rural areas are included within the system. Further, only three cities in Colombia have independent cadastre offices (Bogotá, Medellín, and Cali)—all others are handled at the national level. Evidence also suggests that in some rural cases, local property tax rates are so low that the collection costs are greater than the collected revenue (see Kalmanovitz and Enrique 2006). Taxation revenue steadily increased for all categories of municipalities over the past 15 years (figure 5.4). As figure 5.5 indicates, this growth has been most significant in larger cities.

The contrasts between funding structures for municipal investment are clear when municipalities are disaggregated by size. The largest cities have greater resources for investment than cities in other municipal categories, both in per capita and absolute terms, but these funds are

Figure 5.4   Per Capita Municipal Taxation and Per Capita Transfers, 1995–2005

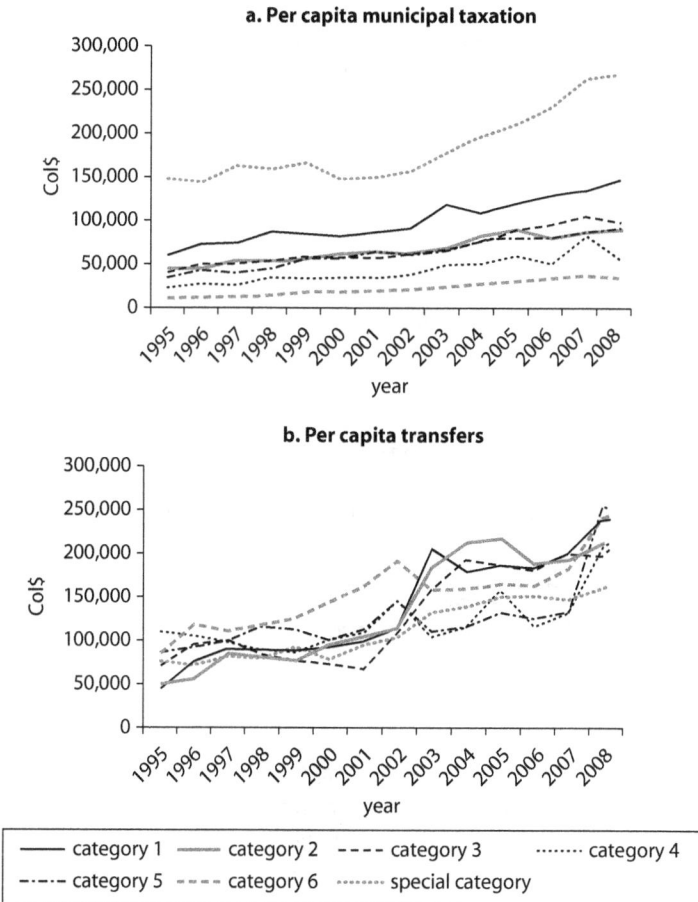

a. Per capita municipal taxation

b. Per capita transfers

Source: SICEP.

Figure 5.5   Special Category and Category 6 Sources of Revenue as a Percentage of the Total

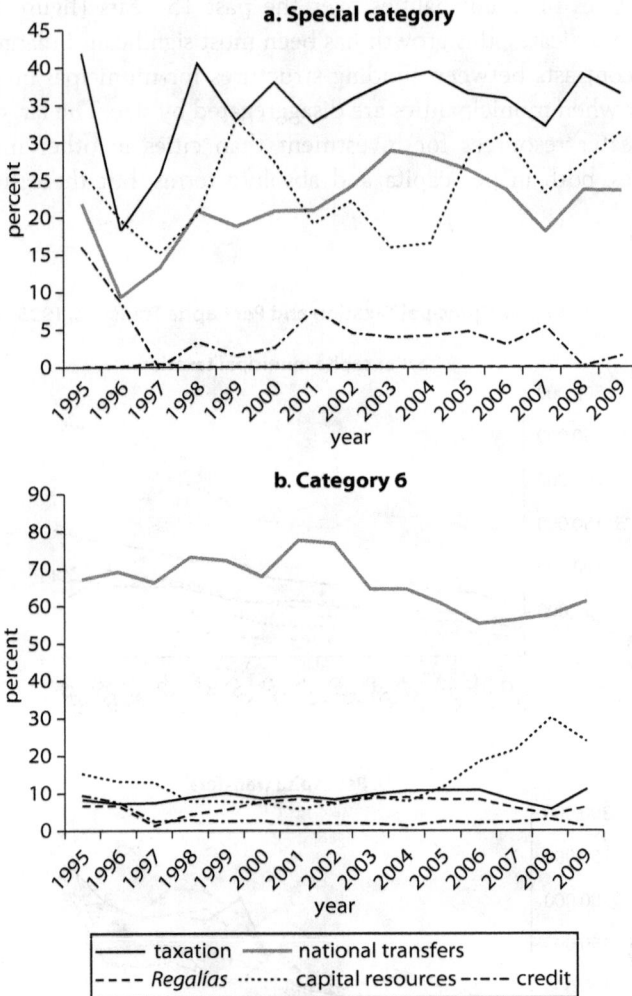

a. Special category

b. Category 6

taxation	national transfers
Regalías	capital resources	credit

Source: SICEP.

predominantly self-generated. On average, taxes accounted for 40 percent of the funds managed by the six largest municipalities between 1995 and 2009. This trend has been driven by large cities, such as Bogotá and Medellín, whose per capita taxation rates have increased more rapidly than their transfer rates (figure 5.6, panel a). The smallest municipalities, on the other hand, receive the second-largest volume of resource royalties in absolute terms. Although these municipalities receive less per capita in transfers than medium and large municipalities (in categories 1, 2, and 3), transfers nonetheless account for nearly 70 percent of their revenues, compared to about 30 percent for the largest municipalities.

Heavy reliance on transfers in smaller municipalities may weaken accountability and lead to spending inefficiency. Although transfer funds are spent at the local level, the political costs of raising the money are born at the national level. As a result of this distance, there may be reduced taxpayer scrutiny over the efficiency with which they are spent. This is important because quality of service remains a major challenge in

Figure 5.6   Large Cities' Per Capita Taxation and Transfer Revenue

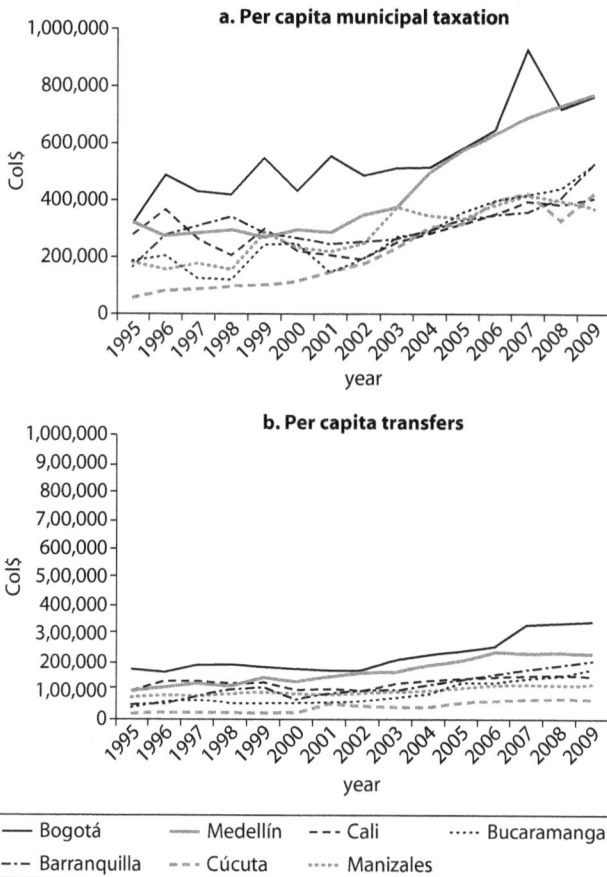

Source: SICEP.

Colombia. Earmarking transfers for spending on particular sectors might not be sufficient to ensure quality improvements without mechanisms to measure the effectiveness of the investments. Over-reliance on earmarking could also have the negative effect of discouraging municipalities from raising revenue and directing it to specific local needs. Indeed, recent work by the National Planning Department (Departamento Nacional de Planeación; DNP)[7] found evidence that funds from *Regalías* and transfers from departments to municipalities (but not SGP) were correlated with less-efficient education and health expenditure.

There is also the risk that transfers could cause "fiscal laziness."[8] Fiscal laziness may prevent transfers from having any net increase on municipal finances because they will simply "displace" the revenue that would otherwise have been raised through other avenues, such as taxation. Although findings in the literature on fiscal laziness are not definitive,[9] some evidence of this effect has been found in Colombia (Perry and Olivera 2009). Perry and Olivera (2009) find that "unearned" resources from redistributed petrol and mining royalties can have a "crowding-out" effect on other revenue sources, particularly when institutional quality is low.

There is a clear need for increased monitoring and evaluation of the efficiency of municipal investment. Improving the efficiency of investment is vital for addressing the significant challenge posed by the low access to and the low quality of services experienced in Colombia, outside of the largest cities. The Government of Colombia (GoC) has taken steps to link spending to output targets for service delivery, for example, through SGP transfers. However, there is very little systematic data recording to facilitate the evaluation of the efficiency of the invested resources. For example, only in the transportation and education sectors can infrastructure investment be disaggregated from operational expenditures. More systematic data recording of expenditures could facilitate the measurement of investment and provide more-concrete evidence on which institutional strengthening efforts could be beneficial in improving the quality of investments. Monitoring and evaluation would also clarify what the impacts of specific conditions, such as earmarking, are on the efficiency of investment.

The government might also consider analyzing and developing greater performance-based incentives within the SGP framework. Output- and performance-based incentive systems that focus on sector outcomes can potentially improve the efficiency and effectiveness of SGP transfers and overall municipal investment. Performance-based systems have been implemented in a wide range of developed and developing countries and—when appropriately designed—can create real incentives for subnational governments to improve performance in targeted sectors or in response to strategic priorities within sectors. The government might also consider developing fiscal management performance incentives for the SGP transfer system. Linking a portion of the transfer system to improved municipal fiscal management and performance (for example, updating cadastral systems, increasing property tax revenues, and improving effective tax effort) could mitigate negative externalities caused by incentives within the transfer system.

Sector Analysis

Municipal spending has increased in the sectors for which expenditures are earmarked, but spending in other sectors has remained stagnant. Investments in education, health, and water and sanitation have increased as these are sectors for which national transfers are earmarked. Investment in transportation and housing, in contrast, relies primarily on local resources and, consequently, make up a smaller portion of municipal investment, particularly for smaller municipalities.

Water and sanitation. Municipal per capita spending in the water and sanitation sector has increased over the past 15 years, particularly in smaller municipalities. The growth trend in this sector has predominantly been led by investment in categories 4, 5, and 6 municipalities. This can be seen in figure 5.8, which shows increasing per capita investment in these municipal categories, compared to declining investment in the largest cities. In absolute terms, Category 6 municipal investment increased from Col$200 million in 1995 to close to Col$760 million in 2009, and peaked at over Col$900 million in 2007.

These trends in municipal investment may reflect the combined influence of two factors: (1) increasing investment from the emphasis placed on extending coverage at the national level and the increased availability of specifically designated funds for this purpose, and (2) efficiency gains in the provision of these services through extensive regulatory reform. Regulatory reforms in this sector can be broadly divided into three stages: efforts to financially strengthen providers (1995–2003), efforts to improve efficiency in administration and transparency in investment (2004–08), and efforts to improve the efficiency of investment (2009 onward) (Andres, Sislen, and Marin 2011). This water sector modernization program is widely thought to have dramatically increased water and sanitation coverage and quality indicators and catalyzed a transformation in utility commercial and management performance in large and midsized

Figure 5.7   Investment in the Water and Sanitation Sector

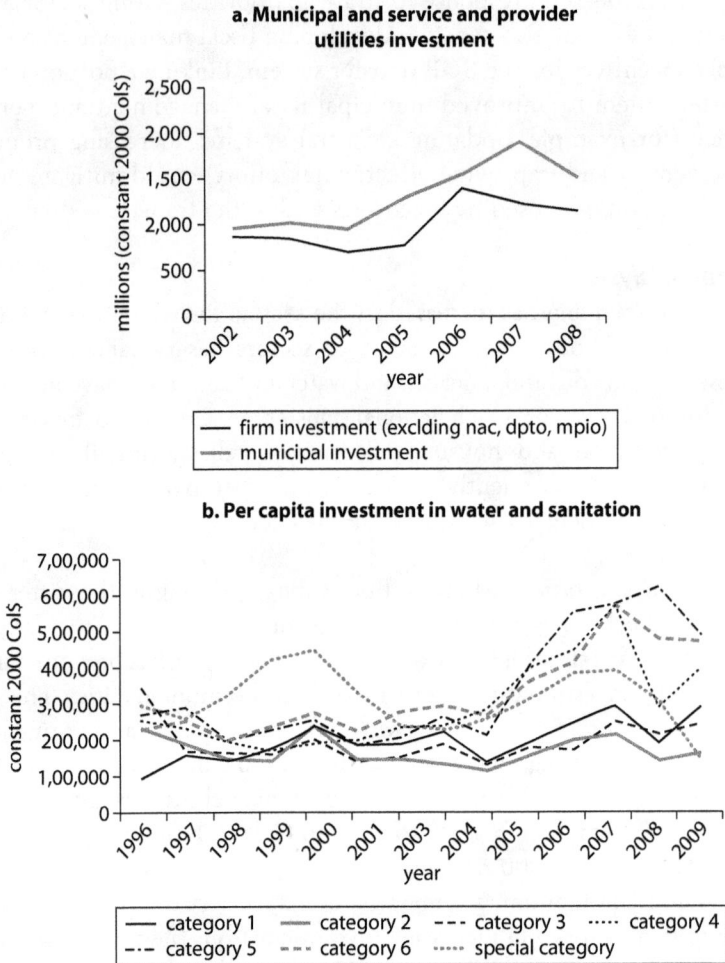

a. Municipal and service and provider utilities investment

y-axis: millions (constant 2000 Col$)
values: 2,500 / 2,000 / 1,500 / 2,000 / 500 / 0
x-axis (year): 2002, 2003, 2004, 2005, 2006, 2007, 2008

— firm investment (exclding nac, dpto, mpio)
— municipal investment

b. Per capita investment in water and sanitation

y-axis: constant 2000 Col$
values: 7,00,000 / 600,000 / 5,00,000 / 400,000 / 3,00,000 / 200,000 / 1,00,000 / 0
x-axis (year): 1996, 1997, 1998, 1999, 2000, 2001, 2003, 2004, 2005, 2006, 2007, 2008, 2009

— category 1   — category 2   – – category 3   ····· category 4
–·– category 5   – – category 6   ····· special category

Source: SICEP.

cities, such as Cartagena, Barranquilla, Montería, and Santa Marta. Revenue from user tariffs has increased since the 1996 introduction of tariff methodologies. This growth may be associated with increasing investment from utilities (both private and public) in this sector, as figure 5.7 highlights.

The most important sources of municipal investment funds in this sector over this period were SGP transfers, own resources, and *Regalías*. However, there has been a degree of volatility in the proportion of funding

Figure 5.8   Per Capita Investment in Water and Sanitation and Sources of Funds

a. Per capita spending by municipal type

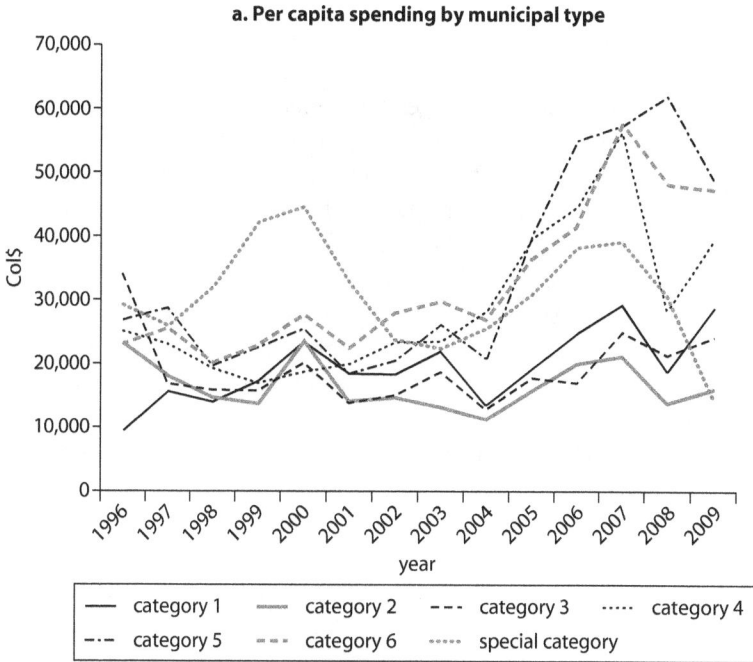

b. Source of funds

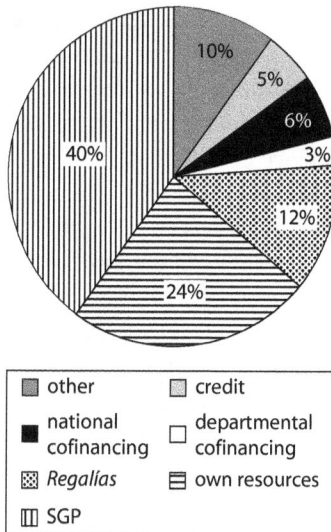

by source. While SGP transfers maintained a portion of investment close to 40 percent over the period, the relative importance of *Regalías* and own resources fluctuated significantly. Own resources declined as a source of investment from 37 percent in 2001 to less than half (12 percent) in 2009. This might reflect investment patterns in special category municipalities: declining spending and reliance on own resources, which fell from 80 percent in 1995 to less than 55 percent in 2009. This contrasts with an increase in the relative importance of *Regalías*, which accounted for 3.7 percent in 1995, 7.0 percent in 2001, and 28.0 percent in 2009.

The trend of increased reliance on *Regalías* is particularly marked in Category 6 municipalities, where the proportion of funding from this source increased from less than 5 percent in 1995 to almost 30 percent in 2009. Reliance on transfers has been associated with inefficient investment. Funds are assigned to individual municipalities in an atomized and segmented manner, with little incentive for municipalities to invest the funds in regionally coordinated and comprehensive investment plans. This causes inefficiency because the provision of water and sanitation services often benefits from economies of scale, which cannot always be achieved within a single municipal administrative boundary (Andres, Sislen, and Marin 2011).

Special Category municipal investment in water has declined, reflecting improvements in coverage levels and utility performance. Until 2000, Special Category municipalities invested more than any other municipal type, in absolute terms. It is probable that this decline in spending reflects higher levels of private investment as Colombia's largest cities have better performing utilities that are able to mobilize revenue from tariff collection and leverage private investment. It is also likely that the close-to-universal levels of service coverage attained by large cities in recent years have led to funds being channeled away from investment toward maintenance. Investment in Bogotá has recently gone against the trends of other cities, and declined noticeably, as seen in figure 5.9.

The fragmented nature of funding in this sector has led to a regional distribution of resources that is not necessarily in line with national investment priorities, and indeed, may generate incentives for some municipalities to avoid making adequate tariff efforts. There is also limited use of the national financial system, which is important in this sector as long-term credit and capital can introduce rigor to prevent scattered and incomplete investments. Although larger companies have access to long-term financing, including bond issuances, this situation demands the design of an explicit strategy for access to credit for the sector as a whole.

Figure 5.9   Per Capita Investment in Water and Sanitation—Large Cities

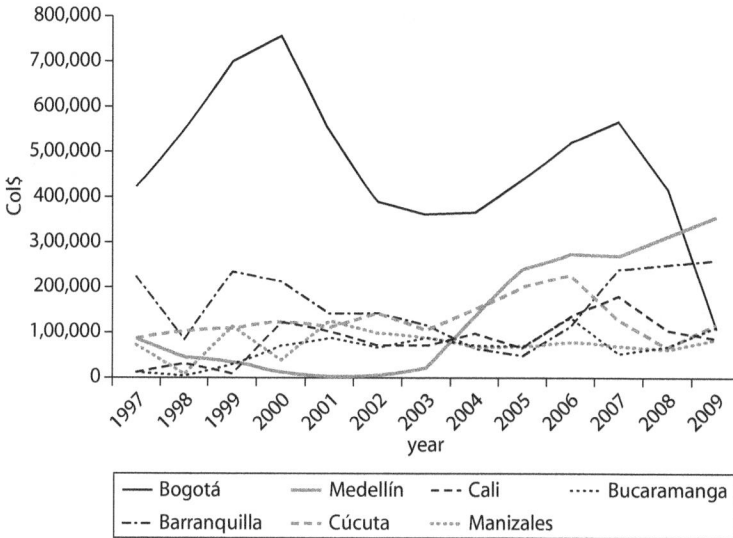

Chart with y-axis labeled "Col$" ranging from 0 to 800,000, and x-axis labeled "year" from 1997 to 2009.

Legend:
—— Bogotá   —— Medellín   – – – Cali   ····· Bucaramanga
–·– Barranquilla   –··– Cúcuta   ····· Manizales

Source: SICEP.

Multilateral banks can play a role in coordinating funds to this sector into a structured flow to address short-term comprehensive investment and business modernization plans.

Traditionally, credit from multilateral banks was concentrated in large cities, while credit for a wider geographical area was provided through national agencies. This can be seen in table 5.3. Policy reform undertaken since 2004 has allowed for sector indebtedness to be produced regionally (with the endorsement and guarantee of the nation). As a result, the World Bank and Corporación Andina de Fomento (CAF) were able to structure credit operations to finance water and sanitation departmental plans in a number of departments. It should be noted, however, that evidence points to a relationship between increases in SGP transfers and reduced credit, suggesting that they incent credit substitution (Andres, Sislen, and Marin 2011).

Transportation. Levels of direct municipal investment in transportation were low but relatively stable in absolute terms from 2002–09, averaging the equivalent of 0.6 percent of the GDP. As figure 5.10 highlights, Bogotá and Medellín invest considerably more than other large cities. However, while investment rates are declining in the capital, Medellín has

Figure 5.10   Large Cities' Investment and Sources of Funds

a. Large cities' investment in transportation

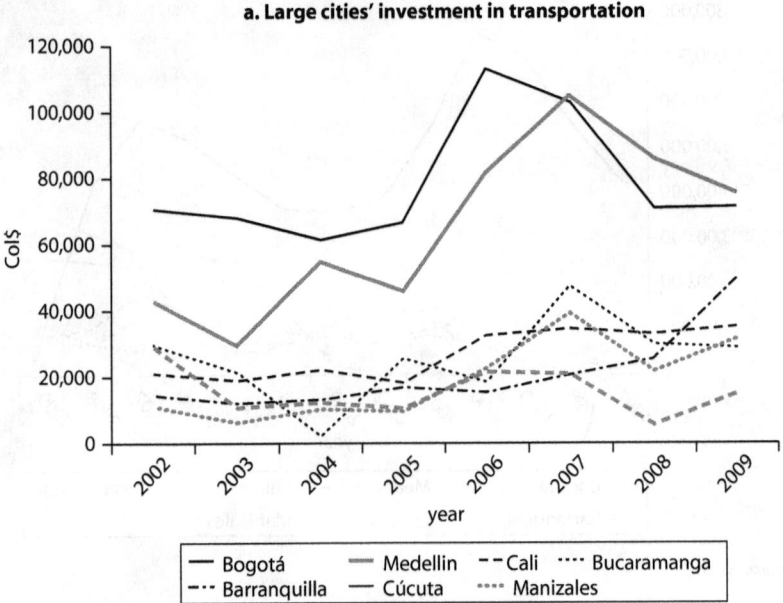

b. Source of funds (all municipalities, average 1995–2009)

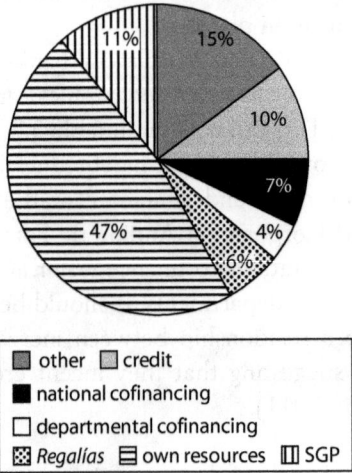

Source: SICEP.

expanded its investment in this sector over the past years. Overall, municipal investment in transportation remains a small portion of municipal expenditure, accounting for less than 15 percent of Special Category investment in 2009 and closer to 10 percent of investment for most other municipal categories.

Direct municipal transportation investment can be disaggregated into: (1) construction and maintenance of roads; and (2) infrastructure and urban transportation. Investment in the construction of roads as a percentage of the total investment is both the greatest and the most volatile in Special Category municipalities. Between 1999 and 2009, it fluctuated from approaching 18 percent of the total investment to less than 8 percent. Investment in the maintenance of roads has seen a general decline over this period. The downward trend is particularly pronounced in all municipal categories as of 2006.

The greatest investment source in this sector is own resources, which averaged 43 percent over this period and peaked at 64 percent in 2006. The average composition of sources of funds of investment in this sector can be seen in figure 5.10. The national government has played an important role in incentivizing investment through cofinancing arrangements in this sector. This is explored further in box 5.1.

Housing. Colombia currently suffers from a housing deficit of 1.2 million units, according to the 2005 Census. In addition, more than 2.4 million Colombian households suffer from inadequate housing related to substandard structures and inadequate access to basic services.

Municipal investment in the housing sector demonstrates a downward trend across all municipal categories between 1996 and 2002 and stabilizes to fairly constant levels after that. As figure 5.11 indicates, the proportion of municipal investment dedicated to housing investment declined for all municipal categories between 1996 and 2002. There have also been general declines in absolute and per capita terms in investment in municipal housing across the different municipal categories. Investment in the largest cities (Special Category), for example, decreased from 3.6 percent of the total investment in 1996 to 2.2 percent in 2009, although these municipalities continued to invest the largest amounts in this sector in absolute terms. This declining expenditure contrasts with the rising housing deficit in the country, which includes a qualitative deficit of 1.2 million households with substandard structures and inadequate access to basic services.[10]

The most important source of funding for municipal investment in housing is own resources, which accounted for an average of 45 percent

Box 5.1

National Government–Supported Investment Programs: The Case of Urban Mass Transit

A number of cases of national government support for sector investment and reform programs has created sound policy and incentive frameworks to encourage significant increases in capital investment—often in the context of mobilizing specialized private operators under concession or related contract structures. Outcomes in the sectors have been transformational and the models provide an important example of how the national government can effectively support urban infrastructure finance through sound policy frameworks and output-based cofinancing arrangements.

The case of urban mass transit is particularly interesting because it reflects a positive evolution in the use of national cofinancing as a framework to incentivize sound investment. The first major case of Government of Colombia (GoC) involvement in urban transportation projects was the Medellin Metro, in which the government guaranteed the city's debt to build the infrastructure. This project was successful in that the metro transports an estimated 500,000 passengers per day, but it was also beset by 12 years of financial and legal costs and is estimated to have incurred a total investment cost of US$3 billion. In response to these difficulties, the model for national cofinancing has evolved, and in 1998 when the GoC entered into an agreement with the city of Bogotá to cofinance a Bus Rapid Transit (BRT) system the long-term agreement was structured to encompasses total investment plans of about US$1.2 billion through 2016. The completion of the first phase of investments of about US$400 million included US$100 million of private financing, and within three years, the BRT system was servicing a daily demand of 700,000 passengers, or 15 percent of the total public transportation trips in the city.

Building on the success of TransMilenio in Bogotá, the GoC renegotiated a prior agreement to fund a rail-based system in Cali and defined the GoC's financial commitments at about US$241 million through 2007 to develop the first phase of Mio, the BRT system in Cali. Two National Economic and Social Policy Council (CONPES) documents, which were approved in 2002 and 2003, define a framework for subsidiary agreements that define the scope of the intervention, the financial structure, and the obligations of the respective parties. These agreements are signed by the GoC, through the Ministry of Finance, the selected municipality, the preconstituted BRT agency, and the participating city.

(continued next page)

Box 5.1 *(continued)*

Through this model, the GoC (1) creates an incentive for the municipalities to implement the program by securing future GoC and municipal budget support and eliminating the risk of a potential change in GoC or municipal policy; (2) transfers execution of the program to participating cities; and (3) provides an incentive for municipalities to focus on sound and longer-term policy and related investments. In addition, the GoC disbursements are undertaken against executed civil works with accounting reconciliations every three months to ensure an appropriate and transparent link between disbursements and completed works.

The financial contributions from each participating city depend on specific project characteristics and the fiscal situation. The main source of funding for the cities is the gasoline surtax, mostly paid by automobile users. This surtax provides approximately 34 percent of the total NUTP cost and, most important, provides the municipalities with a source of funding that can be matched against GoC contributions for the implementation of the projects. The World Bank, Inter-American Development Bank (IDB), the Andean Finance Corporation (CAF), and the Organization of Petroleum Exporting Countries (OPEC) also supported and financed the implementation of the NUTP under independent parallel arrangements.

The Colombian experience with national transport programs suggest that there is a role for national government leadership in the implementation of urban transport reforms. In particular, sector reforms usually require a large scale of investments accompanied by technical decisions. The national government's participation and strong political commitment is crucial to promote reforms at the municipal level since cities often lack financial and technical resources. In a similar context, the regulatory framework is the key to implement long-term reform. The implementation of the NUTP demonstrates important synergies that were created because of the simultaneous implementation of projects in participating cities. This has resulted in a continuous flow and exchange of best practices and knowhow among participating cities, benefiting from these informal knowledge-sharing arrangements to strengthen the implementation and institutional capacity of the new midsized cities that will begin implementation under this operation.

of the investment in this sector over the 1995–2009 period. SGP transfers are also an important source of funding, providing an equivalent of 23 percent of the resources for investment over this period. *Regalías* and credit each funded less than 10 percent of the investment between 1996 and 2009. More interestingly, in per capita terms, all municipalities, independent of their size and urbanization levels, seem to be

Figure 5.11   Municipal Investment in Housing

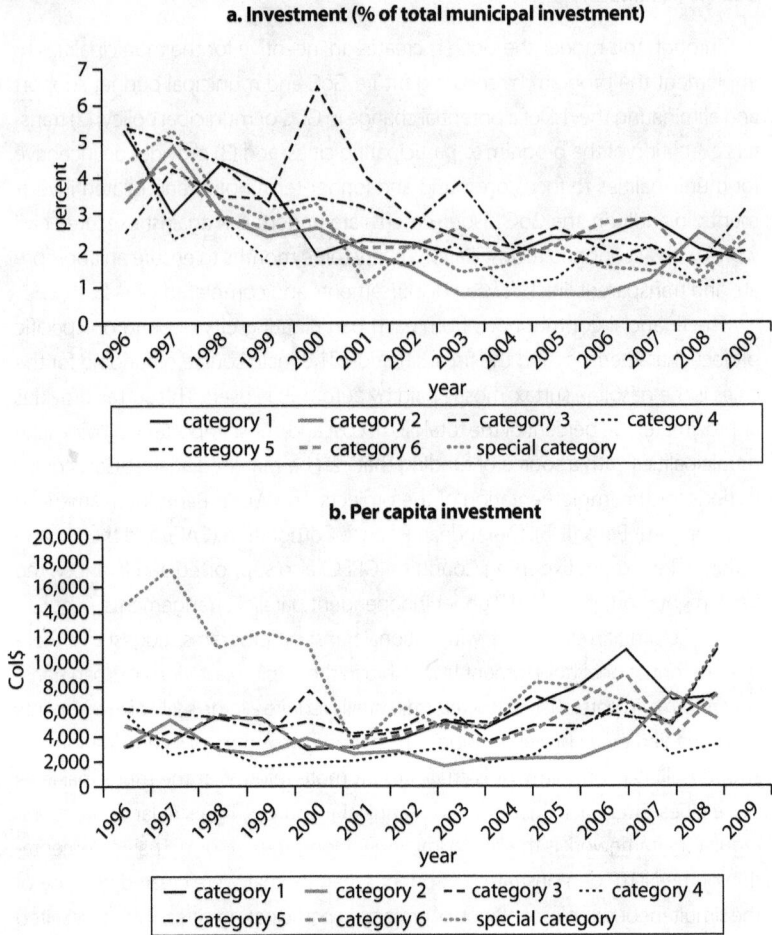

a. Investment (% of total municipal investment)

b. Per capita investment

Source: SICEP.

spending similar sums on housing, with the exception of Category 5 municipalities, which spent more in per capita terms than larger municipalities in 2009.

Education and health. Education accounts for one of the largest portions of investment by municipalities, primarily because of the large percentage of the SGP resources dedicated to the sector. Education accounts for more than 40 percent of investment by municipalities in categories 1 through 3.

Figure 5.12   Education Spending as a Percentage of Municipal Spending

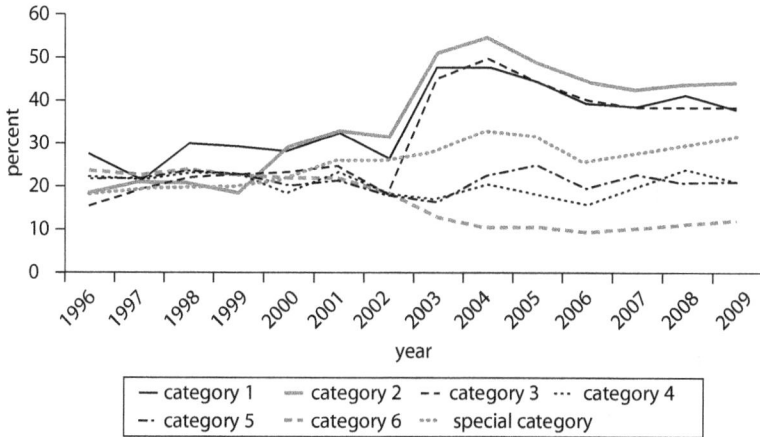

Source: SICEP.

This figure falls for municipalities in categories 4, 5, and 6, as shown in figure 5.12. Special category municipalities have seen the greatest growth in their education investment trends, perhaps due to a declining dependence on transfers for education spending. SGP as a source of education funding declined over this period from close to 50 percent in 2001 to 30 percent in 2007, before rising again in 2008 and 2009.

In per capita terms, the levels of investment are relatively consistent across municipality types, with Category 5 municipalities investing the most at 36,000 per capita in 2009. Categories 4, 5, and 6 spend the most per capita on education. This may be tied to the earmarking of SGP funds, which as figure 5.13 highlights, accounted for more than 50 percent of spending in this sector over the period 1995–2009. It may also be tied to the high costs of providing education services in areas with highly disperse populations.

Payroll expenses account for the largest share of municipal spending on education. As figure 5.14 illustrates, payroll expenses are the single-largest expenditure and demonstrate strong growth trends. They accounted for an average of 43 percent of resources between 1996 and 2001 and rose to 62 percent between 2002 and 2009. Infrastructure investment, in contrast, accounted for 15 percent and 18 percent of resources over the same periods.

Health investment has increased in all municipal categories, but amounts vary by municipal category. Health expenditure per capita is highest for the smallest municipalities. Municipal expenditure per capita

Figure 5.13   Per Capita Education Investment and Sources of Funds

**a. Per capita spending by municipal type
(education infrastructure)**

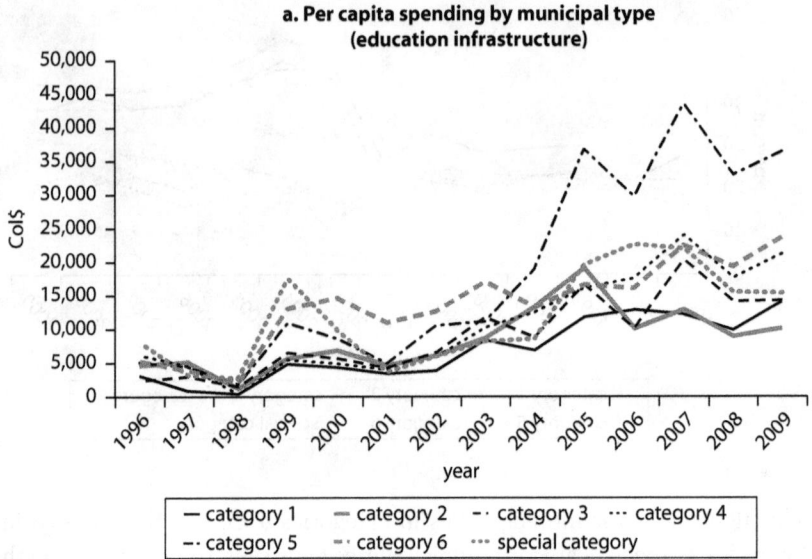

y-axis: Col$ — 0; 5,000; 10,000; 15,000; 20,000; 25,000; 30,000; 35,000; 40,000; 45,000; 50,000

x-axis: year — 1996, 1997, 1998, 1999, 2000, 2001, 2002, 2003, 2004, 2005, 2006, 2007, 2008, 2009

— category 1   — category 2   -· category 3   ··· category 4
-· category 5   -· category 6   ··· special category

**b. Source of funds (1995–2009 average for
all municipality types)**

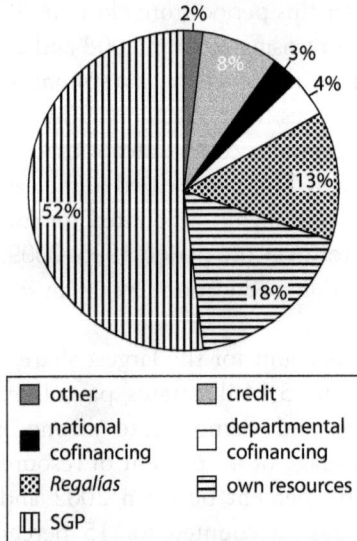

2%
8%
3%
4%
13%
52%
18%

▨ other	▨ credit
■ national cofinancing	☐ departmental cofinancing
▨ *Regalías*	▤ own resources
▥ SGP	

Source: SICEP.

Figure 5.14   Municipal Spending on Education by Expenditure Type

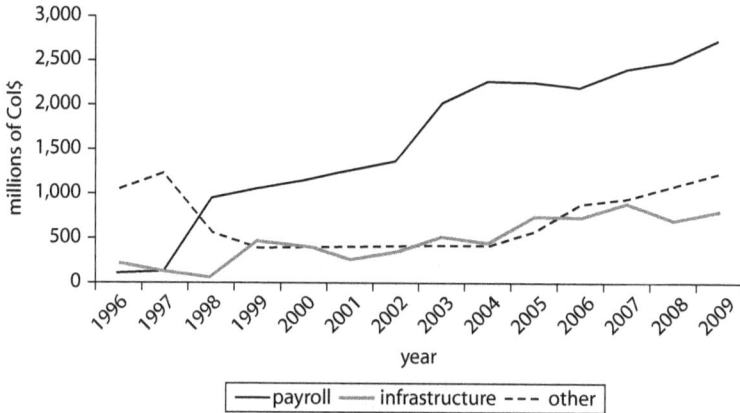

Source: SICEP.

for categories 6, 5, 4, and 3 is the greatest and has demonstrated the strongest growth trends (figure 5.15). Health investment also forms a larger portion of the investment expenditure of these categories.

SGP is the single-largest source of municipal funds for health investment, although these funds have declined as a portion of municipal investment sources since 2002. This decline is particularly marked for Category 6 municipalities, which experienced a reduction in the proportion of funds that came from SGP funds—from 80 percent in 1995 to 54 percent in 2009. National cofinancing has increased in importance as a municipal investment source, particularly because the Territorial Company for Health (ETESA) fund and the Guarantee and Solidarity Fund (FOSYGA) have grown. Since 2003, these funding sources account for 26 percent and 16 percent of Special Category and category 6 municipality funds, respectively.

Moving Ahead: Thinking About Differentiated Policies for Infrastructure Financing

The Role of the Central Government: Improving the Efficiency of Transfers through the Introduction of Performance-Based Infrastructure Financing

The dependence of smaller cities and municipalities on national transfers for infrastructure financing opens an important door for the central government to promote universal access and improved quality of

Figure 5.15   Municipal Investment in Health

a. Health expenditures by source

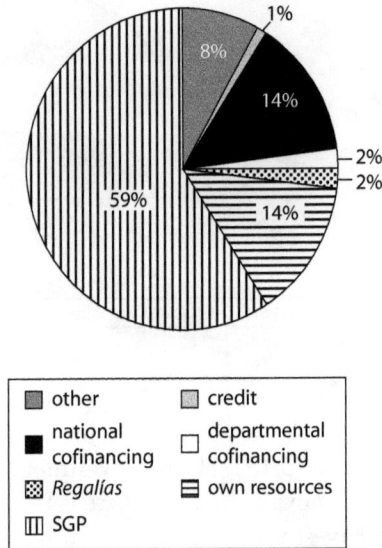

■ other	■ credit
■ national cofinancing	□ departmental cofinancing
▨ *Regalías*	⊟ own resources
⊞ SGP	

b. Per capita investment

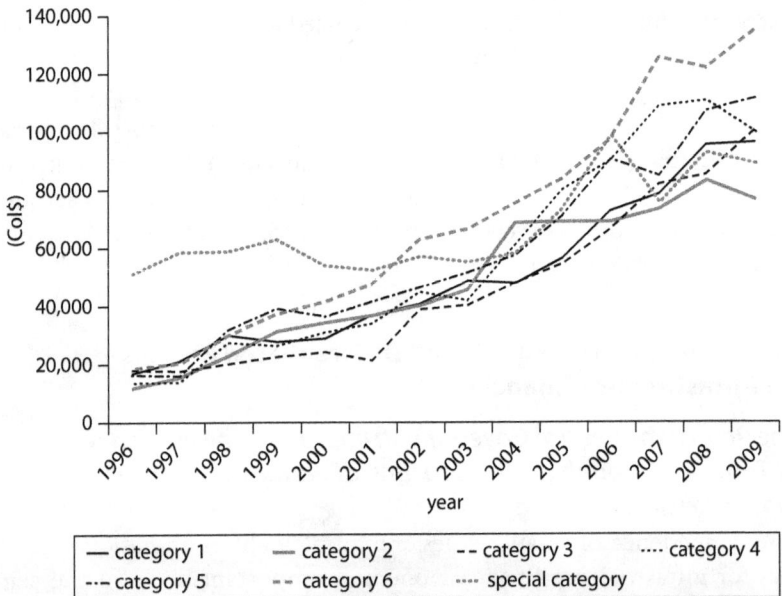

— category 1	— category 2
- - category 3	···· category 4
-··- category 5	-- category 6
····· special category	

Source: SICEP.

basic and social services in these areas. However, caution must be exercised as national transfers have been associated with reduced accountability and efficiency of investment. As discussed in the preceding section, transfers can be assigned without reference to the absorptive capacity of local governments, and they may be spent with relatively little oversight and accountability. Integrating sector performance targets into existing fiscal transfer programs may incentivize more efficient investment.

Performance-based fiscal transfers for infrastructure financing can provide financial incentives to promote coordination across different municipalities. Such systems can also be used to address specific development issues facing individual regions or municipalities such as transportation planning, lack of infrastructure quality, and the need to improve service standards. Incentive structures can be effective tools to address the current limitations of the national fiscal transfer system.

A growing trend in infrastructure finance links disbursement to measurable outputs or performance targets. Performance-based or output-based infrastructure financing provides incentives for improvement by linking a local government's performance in predetermined areas with both access to and a specific amount of funding. The trend reflects a move away from the tight *ex ante* control of the local government toward strong performance-based incentives and *ex post* monitoring and assessments. It differs from conventional financing mechanisms in that the performance-based financing is paid once the agreed performance indicator or output is delivered and verified, rather than up-front disbursement tied to individual expenditures or contracts (see figure 5.16).

Performance-based grants have been applied for infrastructure financing across the world. Many countries, including some Organisation for Economic Co-operation and Development (OECD) countries, have introduced incentive structures and conditionality into their intergovernmental fiscal transfers and infrastructure financing. The case of Indonesia is highlighted in box 5.2. Another example is China which has employed a performance-based grant system for many years and is planning new initiatives with a broader focus. Current schemes include a system designed to reduce fiscal deficits at the county and township levels by allocating a fiscal "reward" that is calculated using a coefficient of local government performance. Other pertinent examples are the use of incentives to encourage administrative mergers, which aim to foster economies of scale in service provision (Steffensen 2010).

Figure 5.16 Traditional and Output-Based Approaches to Service Delivery

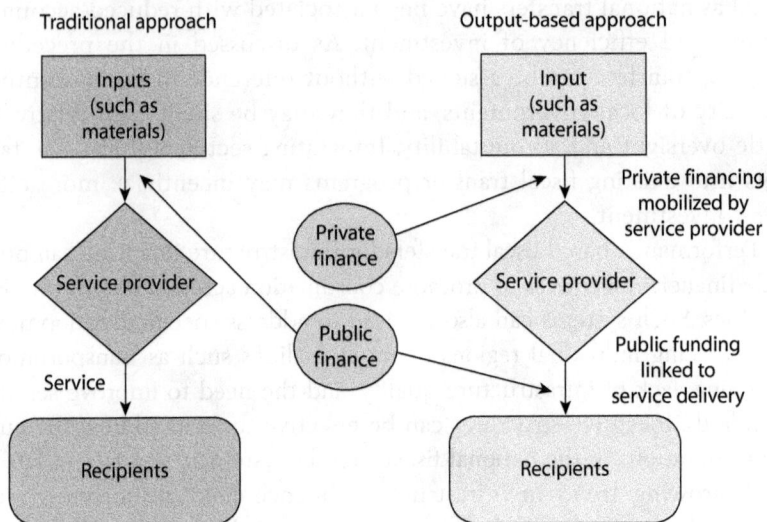

Traditional approach

Output-based approach

Inputs
(such as
materials)

Input
(such as
materials)

Private
finance

Public
finance

Private financing
mobilized by
service provider

Service provider

Service provider

Public funding
linked to
service delivery

Service

Recipients

Recipients

Source: Brook and Petrie 2001.

Box 5.2

Strengthening Fiscal Transfers in Indonesia Using an Output-Based Approach

In 2001, Indonesia was one of the world's most centralized countries, in administrative, fiscal, and political terms. Today, it is one of the most decentralized countries in the world. The process of decentralization led local governments to assume new responsibilities, manage new financial resources, and undertake more than 50 percent of all public investments. Although some of the resources to cover this expenditure are generated at the local level, the bulk is transferred by the central government to local authorities. The Government of Indonesia designed an output-based disbursement system to incentivise efficient use of these transferred funds at the local level, with the support of the World Bank.

A World Bank loan of US$220 million is funding the further design and implementation of an output-based disbursement to help improve the planning, budgeting, and investment execution of transfer funds, as well as monitoring and evaluation of

(continued next page)

Box 5.2 *(continued)*

results. The focus of the program is Specific Purpose Grants (Dana Alokasi Khusus, DAK). DAK are designed to finance investment expenditures, accounting for 7 percent of all national transfers in 2010. The output-based disbursement is currently being piloted in four DAK-financed infrastructure subsectors—irrigation, roads, sanitation, and water. The central concept of the system being piloted is that service providers will be reimbursed for physical outputs delivered. These outputs are pre-agreed and independently verified.

The key characteristics of output-based DAK programs can be summarized as follows:

- *Reference unit costs.* Reference unit costs for eligible program outputs are calculated by the Ministry of Public Works based on existing (competitively priced) contracts, before the annual DAK cycle begins. These reference unit costs take into account relevant differences between regions, including variation in the construction cost index.
- *Central government pre-financing.* The limited capacity of local governments to pre-finance investments is a major challenge in implementing output-based disbursements. In addition, the DAK framework limits the degree to which operational and investments risks can be transferred to local government. In the pilot scheme designed, the national government performs the pre-financing role through the DAK allocations, which are used by local governments to engage private contractors for output delivery work. If the agreed output is not delivered according to the scheme, the central government retains the power to withhold future fiscal transfers to local government. This incentivizes local governments to complete projects within reasonable budget and time constraints, both by delivering outputs on time and by complying with financial and technical reporting.
- *Additional incentives and rewards.* The DAK program further rewards local governments for successfully delivering outputs by reimbursing the 10 percent local counterpart funding that is a prerequisite for participation in the DAK program. The reimbursed funding is not earmarked for infrastructure expenditures.
- *Technical assistance.* The central government also provides a support for investment planning, budgeting, and reporting, with the aim of facilitating greater local government participation in the program, and avoiding possible problems.

Source: Ellis, Mandri-Perrott, and Tineo 2011.

International experience suggests that the design of incentive mechanisms is key to guaranteeing the success of performance-based instruments. Examples from around the world indicate that—if well-designed—performance-based transfer systems can result in improved local government performance in the key areas of planning, budgeting, financial management, transparency, and social inclusion (World Bank 2005). While experiences vary across countries and institutional and legal contexts, there are a few key issues to consider when designing performance-based infrastructure financing:

- *Clearly Defined Performance Target or Output.* A key design element of performance-based infrastructure financing is to clearly define the performance indicators or outputs against which the financing will be made. Objective, transparent, and easy-to-measure performance targets and indicators are critical to the design of successful performance-based infrastructure financing. In some cases, it is easy to identify discrete indicators, for example, the number of water connections or school enrollment. Performance indicators become much more difficult where the performance target is associated with quality improvement or qualitative indicators that can be subject to different interpretations.

- *Parallel Capacity-Building Program.* International experiences suggest that performance-based financing becomes more effective if it is accompanied by well-designed capacity-building programs to address capacity bottlenecks in municipalities and to support the preparation of appropriate capital-investment projects (Steffensen 2010). A capacity-building program can be organized through a grant scheme embedded in the overall performance-based transfer scheme. It is important to establish demand-driven capacity-building programs so that municipalities can adjust the programs to their local needs and their own capacity-building priorities.

- *Monitoring and Verification Process.* The mechanism by which the agreed performance is assessed is of vital importance for the functioning of performance-based financing. Keeping the performance-verification process neutral, shielded from conflicts of interest, and independent from the administration of the transfer system are key factors to making it successful. In many cases, monitoring and verification tasks are delegated to existing regulators, independent institutes, nongovernment organizations, private firms, and local community organizations.

Expanding Alternative Infrastructure Financing Sources for All City Sizes: Strengthening Financial Intermediaries

The diagnostics on municipality financing sources point to the need for Colombian cities and municipalities of all sizes to explore alternative financing sources. Innovative instruments can foster market access for municipalities and help increase the flows of private funding for local governments. There is a wide range of instruments that municipal and central governments in Colombia could consider in applying to expand financing options for infrastructure investments. These include deepening municipal bond and credit markets, restructuring existing municipal development funds, establishing specialized financial intermediaries, fostering PPPs, and developing existing land-based financing instruments (box 5.3). Examples from Peru are outlined in box 5.4.

Box 5.3

Lessons from International Experiences: Municipal Development Funds and Development Banks

Municipal Development Funds: In several countries, the central government has supported local governments by creating Municipal Development Funds (MDFs). The World Bank has also supported a number of projects by financing MDFs. While there is no comprehensive evaluation of World Bank experience in MDFs to date, results from a number of reviews into the investment components of MDFs indicate positive results in terms of achieving physical targets, municipal infrastructure capacity, and support for local governments in building a credit record. MDFs have not, however, achieved the same success in terms of institutional development and local administration and technical capacity building. Reviews suggest that, despite some successes, MDFs have not led to resource mobilization beyond transfers, and are often associated with government subsidies or guarantees, directed or inefficient allocation of credit, and in some cases, political patronage.

The experience of MDFs suggests that future operations should focus on the role they can play in encouraging the transition to market-based municipal credit systems, including self-sustaining financial intermediaries for local government investments. In order to support this objective it is important that the necessary policy conditions for local government borrowing are established, and that the steps by which existing MDFs could be transformed into market-based operations are detailed.

(continued next page)

Box 5.3 *(continued)*

Municipal Banks: Local governments use municipal development banks extensively to finance local investment projects. In principle, municipal banks can provide support to local municipalities while the local governments step up to become credit-worthy and participate in the credit market. In this context, development banks not only provide central government subsidized rate loans to municipalities, but they also provide capacity building technical assistance through, for example, the preparation of project documentations, financing plans, etc. Similar to MDFs, municipal banks often obtain preferential access to sources of long-term savings, and are dependent on government subsidies. As a result of this preferential access there is the risk that municipal banks may crowd out competition from other private financial institutions. Many municipal banks were challenged by financial sector deregulation reform during the 1990s.

Source: El Daher 2000.

Box 5.4

Tapping into the Capital Markets—The Case of the Municipality of Lima, Peru

In 2002, a new law set in motion a process of cautious political and fiscal decentralization in Peru. The Decentralization Framework Law established the foundation for greater decentralization in what was one of the most centralized countries in Latin America. Under decentralization local governments have become increasingly responsible for operating costs and capital expenditures for service delivery. Subnational governments are heavily dependent on transfers from the central government to meet these costs, with funds that are largely provided by mining royalties. Indeed, regional governments, who do not have the authority to levy taxes, finance less than 5 percent of their total public investments with own resources. Even municipalities—who can levy taxes including property tax, real estate transaction tax, and other fees, but who do not have authority to set taxation rates—depend on transfers for a large portion of capital expenditures.

Local governments have begun exploring alternative financing options to meet large infrastructure investment needs. At present, only 1 percent of this

(continued next page)

Box 5.4 *(continued)*

investment is covered by borrowing, a large share of which is by the municipality of Lima. Private sector activity in this sector is limited; commercial banks only provide working capital for a small number of local governments. The only subnational bond issuance to date securitized Lima's toll road revenues.

In 2008, the World Bank provided technical assistance supported by the PPI-AF's (Public-Private Infrastructure Advisory Facility) Sub-National Technical Assistance (SNTA) program to facilitate subnational access to financing from commercial banks and capital markets. The program aimed to diversify funding sources, lengthen the maturity of available commercial bank financing, create and strengthen credit histories, and introduce financial discipline to subnational investment financing. Specifically, the project worked with eleven subnational governments to prepare infrastructure projects for commercial financing.

A second SNTA grant was designed to support the Municipality of Lima in obtaining a credit rating from an international credit rating agency, identify potential new sources of finance, and evaluate means to replace existing short-term debt with sustainable longer-term financing. This work enabled Lima to comply with the subnational fiscal responsibility framework and helped the city make a significant contribution to the Metropolitano Bus Rapid Transit Corridor Project, also supported by the World Bank and the Inter-American Development Bank. The technical assistance contributed to the successful facilitation of a US$70 million commercial bank loan to the Municipality of Lima by BBVA Banco Continental, in April 2010, backed by a US$32 million International Finance Corporation guarantee. This loan was significantly larger than any other subnational transaction in Peru, and had twice the maturity of previous municipal debt. The program also led to tangible fiscal management improvements, such as consolidation of the accounts of the Municipality of Lima and the public companies it controls.

Source: PPIAF Impact Stories 2011.

Large cities in Colombia still face challenges in implementing PPPs in midsized and small municipalities. Colombia has pioneered sophisticated instruments for infrastructure financing and is often cited for its good track record with PPPs, ranging from the case of TransMilenio and the BRT system in Bogotá, to water concessions. However, there are fewer examples in midsized cities and small municipalities, where the potential of these instruments is still untapped.

Market-based local government financial intermediaries. One way to foster market access and bridge the funding gap in the medium term for small and midsized cities is to consider market-based local government financial intermediaries (MLGFIs). MLGFIs can independently mobilize long-term debt on private markets for on-lending, with priority for local infrastructure investments. For a majority of the small and midsized cities, direct access to long-term credit markets is not feasible in the foreseeable future, since long-term efforts are needed to develop the necessary financial infrastructure. As an alternative to the municipal bond market, a number of cities have relied on the pooling capacities of financial institutions to set up workable MLGFIs and to reduce the transaction costs of accessing the credit market. Many European countries have established financial intermediaries—including Finland, France, Spain, and Sweden—while provincial municipal financial corporations predominate in Canada and state-level municipal bond banks operate in the United States.

A successful example of an MLGFI in Colombia is Financiadora del Desarrollo Territorial S.A. (FINDETER), a government company created in 1989 to finance regional urban infrastructure projects. The national government owns 92.53 percent of the company and the departments own 7.47 percent. FINDETER provides resources to financial intermediaries who assign them to regional authorities. FINDETER has received funds from multilateral banks and has consistently received very high credit ratings. According to the most recent data in 2011, FINDETER has over 1,500 projects disbursed among over 140 municipalities in 28 departments.

MLGFIs pool financial arrangements for local infrastructure investments and provide smaller local government borrowers with access to long-term debt markets. Lending products leverage the intermediary's equity funds through bond issuance. MLGFIs may also offer nonlending products to local governments, including fee-based financial advisory services, although these tend to be directed toward larger local administrations. As the intermediary's portfolio is diversified among a large number of local government borrowers, it provides good security for, and strength to, the credit quality of its debt issues.

MLGFIs and municipal bond markets can provide complementary approaches to improving local government access to long-term credit for capital investments. Efficient municipal bond markets can provide an important source of funding for larger local governments, and can thereby help to reduce their claims on scarce national budgetary resources. This might, in turn, release additional fiscal space for smaller local governments with no capability to access private credit. Municipal bond markets are also a source of long-term funding for MLGFIs and, indirectly, local governments.

The ownership structure of MLGFIs can be private, public, or joint private/public, although private ownership structures are generally considered preferable. Best practice indicates that under all ownership structures it is important to ensure that MLGFIs (1) do not have a monopoly on local government finance and (2) are regulated and operated under the same rules as other private financial institutions involved in the sector. It should also be noted that, in the case of public ownership, where public equity funds are leveraged in private credit markets, government guarantees to back the intermediaries' debt issues ought to be priced accordingly and structured to reduce the likelihood of its being called upon. Should intermediaries handle budgetary transfers/grants from the central government, this should be done on an off-balance basis and against a fee.

There are three main inherent risks that MLGFIs must effectively manage in their lending business. These are as follows:[11]

1. *Interest rate and off-balance sheet risks.* MLGFIs need long-term resources to match the long-term loans they issue for long-dated assets. They must manage any interest rate or duration risk that may arise from maturity mismatches between their resources and applications. In particular, they must have the capability to manage off-balance sheet exposure and other contingent liabilities, and this should be reflected in the cost of capital in MLGFI transactions.
2. *Credit risk.* MLGFIs must be creditworthy to be able to mobilize long-term debt on private markets. Creditworthiness is dependent on asset quality—that is, the quality of the portfolio of local government loans—which can be improved through diversification. A diversified portfolio in terms of subsectors and borrowers can (1) strengthen the credit quality of MLGFI-issued debt and thereby provide good security to creditors and (2) allow the use of credit-enhancement structures. MLGFIs can, therefore, use guarantees, derivatives, and securitization to increase market acceptance or lower the cost of interest.
3. *Foreign exchange risk.* MLGFIs can have difficulty hedging foreign currency exposure. This risk may be passed on to borrowers or assumed by government. As local governments may not generate any foreign currency resources, the national government may decide to assume this risk. The national government is well placed to hedge and manage foreign currency risk given that they control monetary policies and foreign

exchange reserves; however, if the national government assumes this risk, a duly priced fee should be levied from either the intermediary or beneficiaries to cover the exposure.

Additional Funding Sources for the Largest Cities

As urbanization advances, cities face additional pressures on their infrastructure and must find new and additional financing sources to support urban expansion and redevelopment. Land-based financing instruments can be used as part of an overall portfolio of investments. Land-based financing instruments may include property taxes, exaction and development impact fees, and land sales or leases.

Land-based instruments provide cities with an opportunity to enhance urban efficiency by intensifying the use of land and managing densities, while sharing the cost of infrastructure provision with private landowners and developers. Land-based financing tools can be combined with planning instruments to manage densities and enhance the efficiency of the city. Planning instruments include the floor space index (FSI), zoning and use controls, height and bulk limits, and requirements for public spaces and right of ways. An example is the case of TDR, where the sale of exchange of additional density limits are used to finance specific infrastructure and urban development. Other innovative instruments which involve private sector participation include the TIF instrument.

Land instruments can be effective instruments to accommodate growth and finance infrastructure when they are applied in the context of an overarching policy framework; they may have unintended consequences when used in isolation. At early stages of urbanization, policies that facilitate rural-urban land-use conversion are critical to support urban expansion. Strong institutions can help to minimize transaction costs and information asymmetries to enhance the fluidity of incipient land markets. As urbanization advances and reaches intermediate levels, population pressures in cities increase and policies that promote the coordination of land-use management, infrastructure development, and densification gain importance. Well-designed policies may allow cities to grow vertically, accommodate higher-value economic activities, and support more people. While the core land institutions mentioned above remain important, city and neighborhood level zoning, building codes, and FSIs gain importance. Finally, as demand for urban built space increases with incomes, cities spread out (sprawl), and individual cities become part of a larger metropolitan area. Policies that promote coordinated and consolidated management of metropolitan areas will gain importance in the land-policy portfolio for middle-income countries and cities at mature stages of urbanization. Land-based financing instruments can be used to support land policies and urban infrastructure expansion if considered under this overarching framework.

Innovation in land-based financing instruments is already underway in Colombia's largest cities, and there is much to learn from these cases. In fact, some of the land-based instruments used in Colombia are cited as innovative and successful in the international arena. However, in many cases, the application and implementation of these instruments has been beset by methodological ambiguity, unclear institutional roles and responsibilities, and a myriad of legal issues. Cities such as Bogotá, Cali, and Medellín have learned from their own experiences and adopted instruments that reflect their local context and experiences. However, the lessons from these experiences have not been widely or systematically shared across cities in Colombia.

The value of refining existing instruments based on lessons learned and experience on the ground is high. In this context, the central government should consider taking up a more-active role in catalyzing knowledge sharing and providing a platform to exchange experiences with various financing instruments for urban development in the country. As an example, the case of Medellín's *Impuesto de Construcción en el Poblado* is exemplary and yet, it is not well known among cities in the rest of the country. This could be particularly beneficial for smaller cities with less capacity that are trying to expand their financing tools beyond more-traditional sources of fiscal transfer and local revenue.

An overview of four land-based financing instruments is provided in the following section. The first two have been used in several Colombian cities and have been considered good practices worldwide: betterment fees (*valorización*) and land-value capture (*plusvalía*) (table 5.2). Strengthening these tools in large cities, as well as extending their use to midsized cities, is a first step toward further exploiting the use of land-based financing in Colombia. This section highlights the main characteristics of these tools as well as their key limitations. This section also provides an overview of instruments that have not been implemented in Colombia, but are being explored as financing mechanisms in the largest cities: TIF and TDR. A review of international experiences is provided to highlight the challenges that Colombian cities may face as they consider implementing these tools in the near future.

Table 5.2   Financing Instrument under Act 388

Typology	Method
Distribution of charges and benefits	Compensation, benefits and costs: increase the benefits of urban space vs. user charges
	Transfer of construction and development rights (environmental, heritage, and public space)
Instruments for intervention in the legal structure for public and private urban management	Land adjustments
	Real estate integration
	Cooperation between participants
Instruments for public entities to intervene in property and land markets	Voluntary alienation
	Judicial expropriation
	Administrative expropriation
	Right of preference
	Real estate banks
	Project announcement
	Development declaration, priority construction, and forced alienation
Finance instruments	Plusvalía
	Sale of construction rights (direct or in financial markets)
	Betterment levies
	Real property tax
	Public service charges
	Environmental charges

Betterment levy (valorización). Colombia has a long history of using "betterment fees" or "valorización" to finance public infrastructure and urban development. This instrument has been used as an important source of local financing in Colombia since the 1920s. It has financed about 50 percent of road networks in Bogotá and has constituted up to 32 percent of the municipal income of Cali during its peak in the 1980s. In Bogotá alone, more than US$1.0 billion was collected from 1997 to 2007 to finance city streets and bridge improvement programs.

Colombia's betterment levies follow two methodologies, one based on Bogotá's model and one on Medellín's. The Bogotá model relies on calculating the benefit of an infrastructure project and charging commensurate levies (box 5.5). The Medellín model, which has also been used in cities such as Manizales and Bucaramanga, uses a dual-appraisal approach, which relies on preassessment and post-assessment values to determine the value capture increment. In this model, the betterment plan is enacted first. This involves defining the financial and

Box 5.5

Case Study of *Valorización* in Bogotá, Colombia: Agreement 180 of 2005

Agreement 180 was the most-ambitious public works plan financed by *valorización* in Colombia. It levied a tax on real properties within the city boundaries that benefited from the implementation of public sector works. The agreement specified (1) a levy collection timeline; (2) a work plan for the public works that would be financed through the levy; and (3) related costs, including technical studies and designs, properties or lots needed to be acquired, and construction and administrative costs. This agreement also made clear that the source of such payments would be private properties inside the boundaries of the city that benefit from public works of general interest.

The most controversial aspects of the agreement were establishing the "zone of influence" and the methodology for calculating contributions. The zone of influence was determined as the area that would benefit from the works, taking into account factors such as (1) the socioeconomic conditions of the owners and (2) the physical characteristics and land uses of the properties or lots.[a] The radius of influence was established at 2.0 kilometers for metropolitan works, 1.0 kilometer for zonal works, and 0.5 kilometer for local parks.

The payments or contributions for all properties subject to *valorización* were determined by an algorithm that incorporated plot size, the social strata (1–6) of residential units, the number of floors of the buildings, the land use or zoning, as well as distance from the works, among others. For example, in the case of sidewalk construction, a distribution of benefits is measured according to the size or front/facade of the buildings using a conversion factor ratio per meter of works. For works such as water and sewerage, which will have a uniform effect per meter of land in any point of the zone of influence, the conversion factor is obtained by dividing the total cost of the work by the number of square meters of area benefited. A "combined method" was also used, where the total cost of the work is distributed in proportion to 50 percent fronts and 50 percent in proportion to the areas of the properties benefited.

Agreement 180 is worth more than US$1.13 billion. This amount is defined by Agreement 389 of 2009 that modified Agreement 180. Of this amount, US$1.09 billion correspond to infrastructure works and the remaining US$35.0 million in public space investment. The investment includes construction of 137 public works including pathways, intersections, pedestrian bridges, sidewalks, and parks. Specifically, the city

(continued next page)

Box 5.5 *(continued)*

will invest in 45 roads, 26 intersections (road bridges, tunnels, level crossings, or roundabouts), 31 pedestrian bridges, 19 sidewalks, and 16 new parks. Nearly 80 percent of the *valorización* was levied on residential properties, 13 percent on commercial properties, and less than one percent on industrial property.[b] Contributions were collected locally, and depending on the amount to be paid, taxpayers could use several months to pay the entire cost.

Agreement 180 was to be collected in four phases and cover four large groups of investments. In two-year phases starting in 2007, the collection process had been largely a success. However, the pace of construction had not been equivalent. Construction in many cases started two years after payments were made and some projects had been caught in the middle of corruption scandals involving politicians and developers. The *valorización* process had been legally challenged many times and some works have been revised or canceled. As a result of these issues, the government had to pay back taxpayers, with interest, for all works that were not completed. Most of the Agreement 180 works are located in high-income areas. These residents, with the ability to pay, have benefited mainly along the corridor between downtown and the city's north. However, it is in the south that public investment is most needed. Local *valorización* is highly effective in areas of high income, emphasizing the social inequality existing in the city between poor families in the south and the rich in the north.

a. These factors include the natural environment (rivers, mountains, or wetlands), as well as built infrastructure and legal limitations (economic zones and cadastral classification).
b. US dollars are calculated at 1,800 pesos rate.

construction plan, identifying the properties that will benefit from the betterment and will be subject to levy and, finally, assessing these properties. To identify the properties that benefit from the infrastructure project, authorities look at proximity and accessibility to the project. Properties in a comparable area are also assessed to provide the hypothetical increase in values. These estimated changes in value are then used to create a map of changes in prices in the area of influence that is then used to distribute the betterment levy. To estimate the benefits of the project, a multidisciplinary team works together. Economic, transport road network, urban, and real estate studies are developed jointly to determine benefits in specific areas. Finally, the method of dividing the amount of levy to be paid by each party is determined.

Different jurisdictions have used alternative methods (Andres, Sislen, and Marin 2011).

While *valorización* continues to be an important tool to finance public works in an environment where public resources are limited, reliance on the instrument has declined since the 1990s to the point that, in some cases, it became an insignificant contributor to municipal finance. Between 1968 and 1978, municipal revenue from *valorización* declined by almost 50 percent in real terms. Between 1980 and 1990, municipal revenue from *valorización* fell from 15 percent of total municipal revenues to 5 percent. As shown in table 5.3, the importance of the betterment levy as a source of revenue in Bogotá and Cali fell even more precipitously.

One reason for the declining use of *valorización* can be attributed to the difficulties faced during actual implementation. In recent years, the implementation processes in Bogotá of Agreement 180, the largest *valorización* package ever structured, has been plagued by implementation delays and accusations of a lack of transparency. Delays have been caused by a series of legal challenges to the a priori formulae used to estimate land-value gains from public investment, which often produced results at odds with actual market values. There has also been a large time gap between resource mobilization and actual implementation, where private landowners have paid far in advance for works that took too long to start. Similarly, there have been serious problems with its planning and construction, coupled with a lack of the appropriate documentation and socialization needed to initiate construction in residential areas. Finally, *valorización* was initially designed to be used for large infrastructure, such as parks or roads. Instead, the instrument has in many cases been used to pay for sidewalks in high-income parts of the city.

The use of *valorización* has also become less frequent as municipalities have gained access to alternative financial sources. With the new Constitution of 1990, resources and transfers from the central government,

Table 5.3   Share of *Valorización* as a Percentage of Municipal Revenues in Bogotá and Cali, Colombia, 1980–90

Year	Bogotá	Cali
1980	5.1	31.7
1983	13.5	18.0
1990	1.4	8.9

Source: Peterson 2009.

from SGP or *Regalías*, come earmarked for specific social infrastructure projects for municipalities, in areas such as health and education. On the one hand, cities and especially small towns have more resources available for selected local infrastructure, such as roads and parks, because their social needs are covered by the central government. As a result, the incentive to mobilize additional resources through instruments such as *valorización*, which are considered rather difficult to implement, has diminished. On the other hand, cities have increased property tax revenues through the improvements in the management of cadastral, integrated property tax valuation and collection, and property registration systems.

To maximize the economic potential of the *valorización* instrument, it is necessary to further refine its methodology. In particular, the methodology to calculate the distribution of benefits and anticipated land-value increases from infrastructure investment should be refined. In addition, the associated calculations for contributions should include an evaluation of relevant geographic, socioeconomic, and political aspects. Finally, transparency and citizen engagement is important for successful application of *valorización*.

The national government could also promote, regulate, and support the process of *valorización* in large and midsized cities requiring an update of Decree 1604 of 1966. Regulations such as the Statute of *Valorización* of Bogotá could serve as a useful guideline. It would also require strengthening the institutions, as strong institutions are a prerequisite for successful implementation of land-based financing instruments. Specifically, capacity to clearly define property rights, guarantee standardized and objective methods of land valuation, and support and oversee the process of land management, land sales, and tax collection will need to be built.

Further, as *valorización* tends to benefit middle- and high-income families over low-income families, the use of indirect *valorización* could be explored. Indirect *valorización* is based on the principle that improvements in the quality of life in lower-income areas positively impact the entire city. In practice, indirect *valorización* is structured under a progressive fee structure with an implicit cross-subsidy from higher- to lower-income segments. Amounts charged to low-income families could be incremental as the construction of the first set of works will increase the value of local properties and, accordingly, leverage the subsequent rounds of construction. Contributions from low-income residents may encourage local ownership, promoting greater maintenance and care of local roads and parks by residents. Low-income areas in Colombia have a long history of social organization and co-payment of small and communal infrastructure by local groups.

Value capture contribution (plusvalía). Value capture contribution (*plusvalía*) is based on capturing land value increases derived from land-use changes linked to the introduction or updating of land-use norms or government-led investment. Unlike property tax, land-value capture tends to be more dynamic and linked to urban and social changes. Seventy percent of revenues from *plusvalía* is earmarked for social housing (*vivienda de interes prioritario tipo I*), and the remaining 30 percent is earmarked to support recreation, parks, public space and environmental protection.

While land-value capture in Colombia is often cited as an international example of success, the use of this instrument has been limited to Bogotá and Pereira. Further, table 5.4 shows that the impact and overall revenue in Bogotá from this instrument has been marginal in relation to the size of the investment projects underway in the city. Additionally, the transaction costs associated with collecting *plusvalía* is high, often exceeding the actual revenues obtained.

Successful implementation of *plusvalía* has been undermined by methodological limitations and complex regulatory norms. As is the case with betterment levies, *plusvalía* suffers from the lack of a precise methodology for measuring changes in property prices. Currently, it is determined by actual norms (such as floor area ratio, number of floors, or zoning) in place when the property or the land was last acquired, as opposed to the real-time market value. Measuring *plusvalía* based on market price is not a difficult task for many Colombian cities where such information is available. Many city cadastral offices and other public offices have now accumulated historical records of land markets with the information needed to construct these values. Unfortunately, these cities have not used this information to adopt a new methodology and

Table 5.4   Value Capture in Bogotá

Year	Pesos ($ millions)	Growth rate (%)
2004	1.203	
2005	10.796	797.42
2006	11.453	6.09
2007	12.819	11.93
2008	15.269	19.11
2009	25.100	64.39
2010	13.278	−47.10
Total	89.918	

Source: Dirección de Economía Urbana, Secretaría Distrital de Planeación (Division of Urban Economy, Bogotá Secretary of Planning).

are missing an opportunity to further exploit the instrument. In terms of the second limiting factor, a large number of decrees, laws, and legal instruments apply to land use in Colombia. This regulatory complexity makes it difficult for homeowners and contractors to understand and can result in subjective interpretation and application of *plusvalía*.

Improving Land-Based Financing Instruments in the Largest Cities and Extending Best Practices to Midsized Cities

Tax increment financing. Larger Colombian cities have recently shown interest in utilizing TIF in the context of urban renovation to capture future value increases of land within specific geographic or renovation areas. TIFs may be a useful instrument to finance infrastructure investment in Colombia, as they provide financing for public investment projects by leveraging their anticipated impact on future tax revenues. Specifically, TIFs finance projects by issuing debt against the expected tax flow "increment" associated with the project. For example, public infrastructure investment can cause surrounding real estate values and property tax revenues to increase. TIFs leverage this relationship and fund the initial investment by issuing debt against the anticipated tax increment. It is consequently a "value capture" financing instrument, designed to unlock future revenues to finance specific current expenditures.

TIF is a tool to foster development in specific geographically defined areas that would not otherwise receive investment. TIF projects tend to focus on providing public goods or removing obstacles to market-driven investment in "blighted" areas. Examples include upgrading inadequate infrastructure, remediating brownfield sites, organizing land assembly, or rehabilitating historic buildings or public spaces. TIFs are also often used to leverage private sector investment to pursue a range of secondary urban planning objectives, such as the stimulation of more-optimal land use, reduction of a city's carbon footprint, and provision of low-income housing. In this light, TIF is a local development tool that allows designated jurisdictions to pursue broader urban planning objectives.

TIF responds to an identified financing gap, which is an obstacle to investment in a defined area. As figure 5.17, panel a, indicates, the TIF investment: (1) causes tax revenues to rise without levying any new taxes; (2) does not compete with current taxation expenditures because it is not funded from the existing tax base; and (3) leads to an augmented tax base for the entire district once it expires. However, as figure 5.17, panel b, highlights, a TIF investment would act as an unwarranted subsidy to

Figure 5.17   TIF Investment and Unwarranted Subsidies

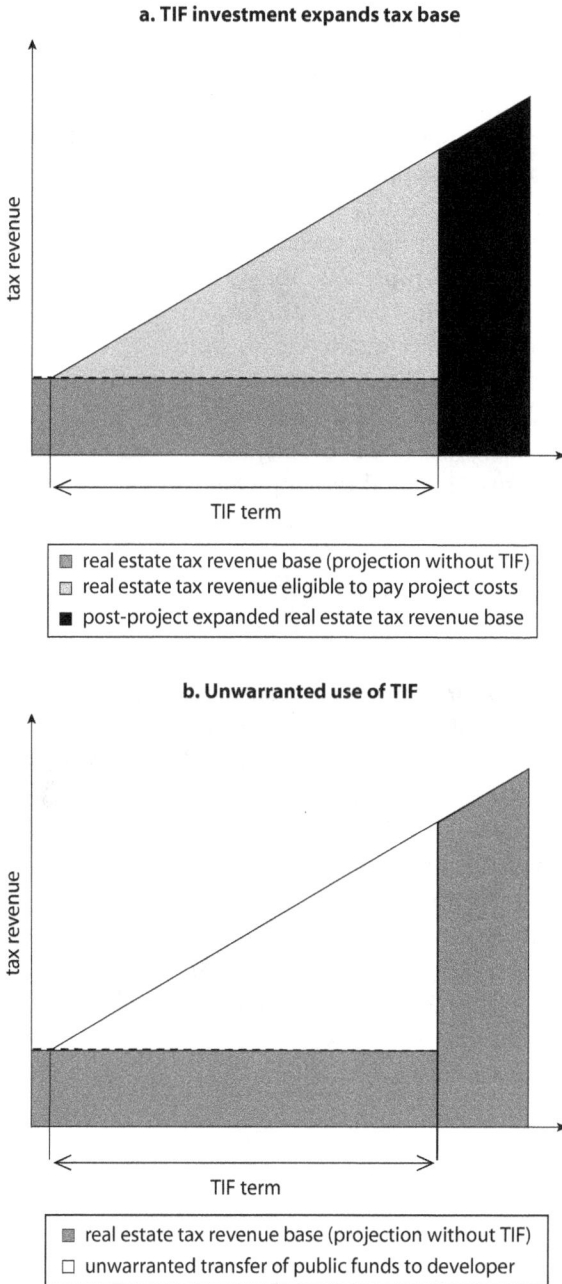

a. TIF investment expands tax base

▨	real estate tax revenue base (projection without TIF)
▢	real estate tax revenue eligible to pay project costs
■	post-project expanded real estate tax revenue base

b. Unwarranted use of TIF

▨	real estate tax revenue base (projection without TIF)
▢	unwarranted transfer of public funds to developer

developers in the absence of a financing gap. If the investment would have occurred in the absence of a TIF, the effect of the TIF is simply to transfer taxation revenue away from other recipients to private developers without stimulating any new revenue gains. As a result, almost every TIF statute in the United States, for example, requires that proposed TIFs meet the standards set by a measure indicating that the investment stimulated would not occur in the absence of a TIF.

TIF has been most widely used in the United States where it was developed in the 1950s as a means of providing matching funds for federal urban renewal programs. Today, it is estimated that there are more than 3,000 TIF districts in the country (Hummel 2010). TIF is used to finance projects as diverse as industrial expansions in rural Leominster, Massachusetts, to the International Spy Museum in Washington, D.C. (Weber and Goddeeris 2007). TIF is also used in retail development, mixed-use development, housing projects, transportation and transit-orientated development, brownfield redevelopment, development of schools and complexes, community development, and economic development (box 5.6).

A review of best practice in the application of TIFs indicate that community buy-in is vital to the success of the investment. That TIFs have a "special" regulatory status can open room for regulatory capture. The legal mechanisms for TIF oversight and accountability can be obscure, and the decision-making process within TIF districts can be highly subjective. It is, consequently, important that (1) key stakeholders and their specific interests are identified and (2) public policies are clearly explained and applied. Generally, TIF stakeholders include governmental jurisdictions, neighborhood groups, and business leaders. It should also be noted that some analysts warn that TIF eligibility criteria can be eroded over time. In the United States, for example, the state of Virginia deleted the word "blight" from its TIF statute in 1990 to broaden the application of TIFs to areas that are not specifically suffering from lack of investment because of blight-associated market failures. These criteria are important to ensure that TIF does not act as an unwarranted subsidy to developers.

TIF structuring should also account for potential "hidden costs" for public services that can be associated with TIF investments. Specifically, successful TIF investments are likely to increase demand for public services, such as education, policing, and health. These costs—along with any "natural"[12] or inflationary increments—should be taken into account when determining the allocation of public expenditure during the TIF

Box 5.6

TIF Case Studies: Use of TIF for Brownfield Rehabilitation and Greenfield Development

There are a number of examples of the successful application of TIF for brownfield rehabilitation, including the 2001 Atlantic Station in Atlanta, Georgia.[a] Brownfield rehabilitation projects can be complex to structure, as base property tax values do not always reflect the impact of site contamination on the market value of the land. In the case of Atlantic Station, the 138-acre site had been environmentally contaminated by the production of fertilizer under previous industrial use. The high costs associated with rehabilitating this land dissuaded investor involvement in the absence of a TIF, despite its location as a "gateway" to the city of Atlanta. The project was created by enabling legislation in 1999 and launched in 2001. The TIF was set to develop 2 million square feet of retail establishments, nearly 3,700 residential units, 1,250 hotel rooms, and 5 million square feet of office space over a 15-year period, subject to market conditions. The project also fostered economic growth and a more energy efficient urban development: "smart growth" principles were used to foster business growth, facilitate walkability, and secure public transportation access.

The financial structure of the Atlantic Station TIF required regulatory innovation. First, in April 2001, Georgia's Redevelopment Powers Act had to be amended to allow interest capitalization on the bonds to be increased from 18 months to up to 42 months. Second, to mitigate the risk of lower-than-projected incremental tax revenues, the city created—by separate legal authority—a special district coterminous with the tax-allocation bond district and agreed to levy a tax on all special district taxpayers if pledged incremental tax revenues were ever insufficient to pay bond debt service. This "generally applicable tax" provided a means to enhance creditworthiness without jeopardizing the federal tax exempt status of bond interests, as would have been the case if private developer guarantees had been used. The bonds were sold exclusively to nine high-yield mutual funds on a nonrated basis.

The TIF-funded rehabilitation of the Atlantic Station land and promotion of the project transformed the property tax revenues from the site from US$300,000 annually to approximately US$8 million in 2005 and US$25 million in 2010.[b] The success of the project is also attributed to the structuring of community input and cooperation. In particular, analysts point to local school board engagement, adjacent landowner cooperation, and third-party dissemination agents to facilitate stakeholder engagement.[c]

(continued next page)

Box 5.6 *(continued)*

Mesa del Sol in Albuquerque, New Mexico, is an example of using TIF for greenfield development. It is a mixed use development project involving 37,500 residential units and 18 million square feet of commercial space to be built over a 35- to 50-year time frame. Specific revision of state TIF legislation was required for Mesa del Sol. The project required revitalization and revision of the TIF laws to (1) include greenfield development and (2) capture a share of state, city, and country gross receipts tax (GRT), which is a broad-based business activity tax that provides a significant share of local and state revenues. Five Tax Increment Development Districts (TIDDs) have been applied for to pay for the infrastructure, with a 67 percent share of GRT; US$500 million in TIDD bonds were backed by the state GRT share alone. A large portion (38 percent) of the projected tax increment is anticipated from retail sales.[d]

There is active debate on whether TIF should be used in the case of greenfield development. The absence of significant market barriers caused by factors such as blight or contamination raise questions about whether or not this development would not have occurred in the absence of the subsidy. In the case of Mesa del Sol, the TIF is subject to an annual test to demonstrate that it does not contribute any other expense to the city. Nonetheless, the location of the greenfield has led detractors to caution that the TIF could encourage urban sprawl.[e] The TIF has, as a result, been the subject of extensive debate, including a vote in the Albuquerque City Council to amend the TIDD ordinance to prohibit greenfield development, which was ultimately vetoed by the mayor. This reiterates the importance of integrating TIF with development planning objectives and ensuring that the case for TIF financing is well articulated.

a. http://www.atlanticstation.com/.
b. Rachel Weber and Laura Goddeeris, Lincoln Institute of Land Policy (2007).
c. Council of Development Finance Agencies and International Council of Shopping Centers Tax Increment Finance Best Practices Reference Guide, 2007.
d. http://www.mesadelsolnm.com/.
e. 1000 Friends group, as quoted by Council of Development Finance Agencies and International Council of Shopping Centers Tax Increment Finance Best Practices Reference Guide, 2007.

term. However, this element of TIF structuring can be problematic when TIF districts fall in overlapping municipal jurisdictions and the cost of additional services required by an emerging TIF district are met at a governmental level that does not receive any additional taxation revenue from the development. The regulatory framework for the TIF will determine the nature of the relationship between overlapping jurisdictions. In the United States, for example, county and school districts can sometimes be compelled by the local government to participate in the TIF project; in most cases, however, these districts will determine their involvement independently and dictate terms.

It is important that TIF investments are coordinated with broader development objectives. For example, evidence from Minnesota[13] found that TIFs that encouraged the relocation of firms into TIF districts contributed to urban sprawl. Of 86 deals involving 8,200 jobs in the Twin Cities metro area, 22 firms moved more than 10 miles out of the center area to areas that had: (1) higher growth rates, as measured by property wealth tax; (2) lower racial diversity; (3) greater household income; and (4) less poverty than the center. Additionally, 60 companies moved to locations that were inaccessible by public transport, even though 24 of these 60 previously benefited from public transport accessibility.[14] This case highlights the importance of coordinating TIF with integrated urban planning to avoid unintended negative externalities and ensure that the TIF supports established urban development objectives. In terms of municipal finances, poorly conceived and executed TIFs that fail to meet developmental and revenue goals can necessitate a municipal bailout for the TIF-linked bond payouts. Such a bailout can impact municipal finances directly, as well as indirectly, through the impact on municipal credit ratings. Table 5.5 summarizes some of the benefits and potential difficulties that should be considered when structuring TIF.

Transfer of development rights. Transfer of development rights (TDR) is an additional development instrument that many local governments, especially in the United States, have used extensively (Hanly-Forde et al.). TDRs are a market-based planning tool used to preserve open space, agriculture, historic buildings, or housing, or to increase the density of development in the areas. TDRs provide a means for communities to preserve specific areas of land—such as farm land—while compensating landowners who lose development rights. Specifically, TDRs allow developer rights to be "severed" from properties that lie in government-designated protected (and low-density) areas, permitting the landowners to sell them as developer rights in high-density designated areas. This can often make TDRs a politically palatable yet equitable method for preservation.

From a local government's perspective, TDR programs offer several advantages. Unlike purchase development rights (PDR), TDRs do not

Table 5.5   Summary of Arguments in Favor of and Against TIF

Pros	Cons
• TIFs can "unlock" funding for investments with high positive externalities that would otherwise not have taken place. They act as an important funding gap bridge.	• TIF revenues can have hidden costs for municipalities, as follows: (1) service costs rise with economic development, and (2) municipalities may have to bail out TIFs in the event of commercially unsuccessful projects. TIF allows local authorities to circumvent borrowing restrictions and due process for committing tax revenues. This is negative because: (1) it could curtail the rights of residents of TIF areas; (2) there may be reduced public scrutiny and accountability; and (3) it could lead to poor urban planning at the regional level.
• It is a source of funding that (1) does not increase taxes; (2) is not subject to municipal borrowing restrictions and is not included in a city's general debt obligations; (3) does not require explicit electoral approval; and (4) attracts additional private financing.	
• It improves project design and implementation because it: (1) requires financial rigor to attract bond investors; (2) encourages a long-term view in local planning; (3) can work well with the zoning of districts; and (4) gives local authorities sources to implement local development plans and pursue secondary local development objectives.	• Funds can be unjustly apportioned by absorbing all tax increments at the expense of other beneficiaries (for example, schools) and regardless of the origin of the revenue growth.
• TIFs have a catalytic impact on economic development and enhance tax flows once the TIF bonds are retired.	

use local government funds for land purchase; TDRs link developers and landowners to achieve development objectives (for example, preserving land or increasing density). It is estimated that preserving 48,000 acres of land in Montgomery County, Maryland (see box 5.7), for example, would have cost the county about US$68 million if it had been done by purchasing development rights (PDR). Second, it is an easier way to implement zoning, as it is likely to encounter less political resistance. If well designed, the TDR program can also reduce variance in zoning as developers can use the market—rather than connections—to secure the number of development rights they would

Box 5.7

TDRs in the United States

An interesting TDR case study is that of Montgomery County—a prosperous county in the suburbs of Washington, D.C. In 1980, Montgomery county implemented a TDR program with the aim of preserving 90,000 acres in the northwest of the county. The TDR program was combined with initiatives to promote high-density and transit-oriented development along the metro-rail corridor. Under this program the land designated for protection was "down-zoned" from 1 house on 5 acres to 1 house on 25 acres. In terms of acreage preserved, this TDR program is considered one of the most successful in the USA.

Several key factors can be identified in the success of the Montgomery County TDR program. First, the county played an important role as a "market maker." The county actively engaged with landowners and developers to provide information about the program and facilitate the communication and information exchange between landowners and developers. It has also closely monitored the market and provided an oversight role to ensure that the market is working. In addition, long-term political commitment and leadership to keep the growth of the county along the transit-oriented corridor, while maintaining fiscal sustainability, contributed to the success of the TDR program in the county. The case also highlights the importance of a well-functioning land and housing market and a master plan directly connected to zoning.

Source: Walls and McConnell 2007.

like. This can make the development more predictable and transparent. TDR programs have the potential to compensate landowners for down-zoning or other restrictions on their land. TDRs provide landowners with a means to recapture some of the economic value that a property can lose from changes in zoning. In particular, they can mitigate the economic impact of "down-grading" in land-use regulations that occur when land zoning is changed from residential use to agricultural use, for example.

There is significant variation in program design of TDRs. For example, the use of TDRs in São Paulo in detailed in box 5.8. Within the United States, the design of the approximately 140 TDR programs varies considerably. The outcomes of these programs also differ greatly, and the results

Box 5.8

TDRs in São Paulo

Urban Operations (UOs) are regions in which additional construction rights can be sold based on adjustments to plotting indexes such as floor ratios to create a municipal revenue stream that must be invested within the specific geographic area of the corresponding adjustment. These investments are intended to improve the urban transport and environmental infrastructure, as well as increase access to public transport and public space in the context of an integrated urban redevelopment investment. At present, 11 UOs are under development in São Paulo, each requiring varying degrees of public-sector engagement. They can be placed in three broad categories: (1) market-led operations, which offer attractive locations for middle- to high-end commercial and residential real estate development, with relatively modest structural public infrastructure investment requirements (Água Espraiada and Faria Lima); (2) UOs with a "mix" of potentially highly attractive areas or pockets for commercial and residential real estate development and other areas that are more suited for middle- and lower-income residential uses, which may require greater incentives for private engagement (Vila Leopoldina, Vila Sonia, Carandiru-Vila Maria, Celso Garcia, Anhangabaú-Centro, the Greater Lapa-Brás UO [Agua Branca and Diagonal Norte], and Mooca-Carioca/ Diagonal Sul); and (3) UOs focused on lagging regions in which there is a need for significant public investment, such as the Rio Verde-Jacu UO. A key financing instrument for UOs are Certificates of Additional Building Potential (CEPACs). CEPACs are municipal bonds that are sold in stock market auctions through a municipal urban development company or in a private placement.[a] The CEPAC provides the buyer with the right to build at higher indexes than had previously been permitted within a geographically defined OU area. A key characteristic of CEPACs is that they are tradable development rights—they are not linked to specific lots or parcels of land within the operation, and they can be converted across residential and commercial uses. This innovation increases the revenue-generating potential from developer rights as it opens the window for a wide range of investors to enter the CEPAC market alongside developers with specific project interests. The advantages of this innovation have not yet been fully realized in practice: most CEPACs issued by São Paulo to date have been purchased directly by real estate developers with specific project interests and there has been only nominal trading or sales of CEPACs in the secondary market post-auction. CEPACs have also only been used in two UOs—Água Espraiada and Faria Lima—because of

(continued next page)

Box 5.8 *(continued)*

administrative and legal complications in their implementation.[b] Nonetheless, the introduction of CEPACs to UOs has allowed the city of São Paulo to raise an estimated US$1.7 billion in off-budget revenue over seven years. This revenue has been used to finance affordable housing, transportation, and urban infrastructure.

a. Private placement of CEPACs was used primarily as an option for paying suppliers or defraying compensation payments for expropriated properties.
b. CEPACs are inherently complex, requiring detailed financial engineering to balance the objectives of the UO with the demands of capital markets. Issuance revenues must also be matched with an investment program, as stipulated by bond issuance laws in São Paulo.

have varied from virtually no transfers at all (and, consequently, no land protected from development) to preservation of 49,000 acres.

There are several important design features that city governments need to consider when setting up TDR programs: (1) the baseline zoning and designation of the sending and receiving areas, as the more restrictive the zoning the less lucrative the development option will be vis-à-vis preservation; (2) the TDR allocation rate, which is the number of TDRs that landowners in the sending area are permitted to sell, which is a determining factor in the relative value of preserving the land; (3) the additional density that will be allowed above the baseline with TDRs (usually expressed as dwelling units per acre); and (4) the number of TDRs required for an additional dwelling unit.

TDR program and government regulations and programs interact with local housing and land-market conditions. Features that affect the functioning of a TDR program can include the demand for and supply of land for different uses, the demand for residential density, and the extent to which density limits established in the zoning code constrain the local housing market. As a result, it is important that local governments have a good understanding of the local housing and land market in order to be able to accurately assess the actual demand for TDRs (box 5.7).

It is important to highlight that the administration of TDR programs can be costly, particularly when compared to traditional zoning. Successful administration of TDRs requires that local governments act as a "market maker" by facilitating information between the demand and supply side, by collecting, updating, and maintaining transaction records and data, as well as monitoring program implementation. The local government can also provide important technical assistance for the preparation of legal documents to ensure the market works effectively. In addition, the local government may require the ability to intervene in the market if it is adversely effected by housing market cycles; for example, helping to stabilize the price in swings by purchasing TDRs when prices are low. Furthermore, education and outreach play an important role in successful TDR programs, as they ensure that the mechanisms and objectives of the TDR program are well understood. In the case of Montgomery County, both mailings and public meetings were used to communicate with landowners in sending areas, potential developers, and the residents of receiving areas.

Summary of Policies for Different City Sizes

Despite improvements in basic infrastructure and service access in Colombia, the capacity of cities to plan infrastructure investment, mobilize financing instruments, and implement an investment project varies considerably with size and urbanization level, as highlighted throughout this chapter. There is a clear need to improve the effectiveness and accountability of investment funded by transfers in all municipalities.

Policy priorities to address the challenges facing Colombian cities must necessarily reflect differences in capacity and context found across the system of cities. In particular, large cities can mobilize their own sources of funding through private sector participation, municipal bond issuance, and access to other sources of funding. The key priority for these cities is to refine the financial instruments they have already developed, to function more effectively. Additional innovative instruments, such as TIFs and TDRs, should also be explored. Small and midsized cities, in contrast, are heavily reliant on fiscal transfers to finance most of their public infrastructure programs. This may have serious implications for the efficiency of infrastructure investments, given the associated risks of fiscal laziness and lack of accountability in spending. These cities should broadly focus on improving their sources of own revenue by applying innovative infrastructure financing tools that have been pioneered in Colombia. Finally, the priority for the smaller municipalities is to improve the effectiveness of their infrastructure investment and quality of services. The central government has an important role to play in providing appropriate incentives to improve accountability and efficiency in the spending of transfers, as well as the provision of technical assistance. Table 5.6 provides a summary of these policy priorities.

Table 5.6   Summary of Key Policy Issues and Potential Interventions, by City Type

City categories	Key policy issues identified	Possible policy interventions at the central government level
All cities	Need to improve monitoring and evaluation of the use of fiscal transfer and public infrastructure investment Lack inter-jurisdictional coordination in public investment	Strengthen the monitoring and evaluation of the use of public funds in infrastructure investment, particularly related to quality enhancement. Introduce performance-based fiscal transfer/infrastructure facility. Align better land-use planning, financing, and implementation.
Large and midsized cities	Need to refine existing infrastructure investment Should explore innovative instruments based on local needs (for example, TIFs and TDRs)	Act as a knowledge platform to share the lessons and experiences learned from infrastructure financing, including new innovative instruments. Provide assistance to municipalities to facilitate credit ratings and implement financial assessment and coaching, supporting transaction preparations so that municipalities can tap into the financial market.
Small cities and rural municipalities	Heavy reliance on fiscal transfer for infrastructure financing Lack of capacity in planning, financing, and implementing infrastructure investment and other social investment Need to expand sources of infrastructure financing, such as land-based financing and access to the credit market	Introduce performance-based fiscal transfer/infrastructure facility. Strengthen existing technical assistance to local government on municipal finance, infrastructure investment planning, implementation, and financing instruments. Consider market-based local government financial intermediaries and technical assistance to strengthen creditworthiness.

Notes

1. World Bank, Infrastructure in Latin America and the Caribbean Region, 2007.

2. The main national cofinancing funds are the Fondo de Cofinanciación para la Inversión Social (FIS), the Instituto Colombiano para el Desarrollo Rural (INCODER), and the Fondo de Cofinanciación para la Infraestructura Vial y Urbana.

3. Law 2132 of 1992.

4. As of 2010, Special Category municipalities are Bogotá, Medellín, Bello, Envigado, Bucaramanga, and Cali.

5. Article 116 specifies the following: (1) recovering the navigable channel and flood readiness of the lower Magdalena, through Cormagdalena and the respective regional entities; (2) preventing and readying for natural disasters or large-scale calamities on the national level, and especially so for the La Mojana region; (3) an educational component focused on expanding coverage to the poor; and (4) recovering the *Macizo Colombiano* watershed.

6. Both subnational levels also establish vehicle tax rates. Vehicle ownership tax is collected at the departmental level, but 20 percent is shared with municipalities.

7. This study applied a methodology to measure the efficiency of subnational governments based on the Data Envelopment Analysis (DEA) technique, which estimates the efficiency of the subnational government by comparing its performance with that of the "best-practice" entity chosen from its peers, in the education and health sectors. See Annex 6, World Bank (2009), *Colombia Decentralization: Options and Incentives for Efficiency*.

8. Fiscal laziness refers to the case where fiscal transfers reduce the incentives of local authorities to raise own-source revenues, such as taxes.

9. While some studies have found empirical evidence to support the hypothesis that national transfers tend to reduce fiscal efforts (Bird and Slack 1983; Chaparro, Smart, and Zapata 2005), others do not find conclusive evidence to support the hypothesis of fiscal laziness (Sanchez and Gutierrez 1994; Sanchez, Sourdis, and Parra 1995; World Bank 1996; DNP 2002). Some studies in turn stress the great differences among municipalities (Acosta and Bird 2003). See World Bank (2009), *Colombia Decentralization: Options and Incentives for Efficiency*.

10. World Bank estimate based on 2005 census data.

11. See El Daher (2000).

12. From small developments that may have occurred in the absence of the TIF.

13. Minnesota's economic development disclosure law of 2000 requires localities to report any incentives given for corporate relocation.

14. International Council of Shopping Centers and Council of Development Finance Agencies (2007).

Bibliography

Acosta, O. L., and R. M. Bird. 2003. "The Dilemma of Decentralization in Colombia." No. 404, International Tax Program Papers from International Tax Program, Institute for International Business, Joseph L. Rotman School of Management, University of Toronto.

Acosta Restrepo, P. 2010. "Instrumentos De Financiación Del Desarrollo Urbano En Colombia: La Contribución Por Valorización Y La Participación En Plusvalías. Lecciones Y Reflexiones." *En Desafíos* 22 (1): 15–53.

Andres, L. A., D. Sislen, and P. Marin, eds. 2011. *Charting a New Course: Structural Reforms in Colombia's Water Supply and Sanitation Sector.* Bogotá: PPIAF/ World Bank.

Benavides, J., M. Olivesa, O. Arboleda, and C. P. Quintero. 2011. "Financiación de intraestructura y el desarollo urbano." Background report for the *Colombia Urbanization Review.*

Bird, R., and E. Slack. 1983. *Urban Public Finance in Canada.* Toronto: Butterworths.

Bogotá Secretary of Planning. 2010

Brook, P. J., and M. Petrie. 2001. "Output-Based Aid: Precedents, Promises and Challenges." In *Contracting for Public Services: Output-Based Aid and Its Application,* ed. P. J. Brook and S. Smith, 3–14. Washington, DC: World Bank.

Caballero, A., Monica Torrado Parra, Karen Ortiz Becerra, and Maria Retana de la Peza. 2011. "Innovation and Employment: Evidence from Colombian Manufacturing Firms." Research project funded by the Diagnostic Facility for Shared Growth at the World Bank and also a collaborative work with team of the project KCP-RG 1164 Innovation and Employment at the Inter-American Development Bank, June.

Calderón, C., and L. Servén. 2003. "The Output Cost of Latin America's Infrastructure Gap." In *The Limits of Stabilization: Infrastructure, Public Deficits and Growth in Latin America,* ed. W. Easterly and L. Servén, 95–118. Palo Alto, CA: Stanford University Press; Washington, DC: World Bank.

Chaparro, J. C., M. Smart, and J. G. Zapata. 2005. "Intergovernmental Transfers and Municipal Finance in Colombia." In *Fiscal Reform in Colombia: Problems and Prospects,* ed. R. M. Bird, J. M. Poterba, and J. Slemrod, 287–318. Cambridge, MA: MIT Press.

El Daher, S. 2000. "Specialized Financial Intermediaries for Local Governments: A Market-based Tool for Local Infrastructure Finance." Infrastructure Notes, Municipal Finance Urban FM-8d, World Bank, Washington, DC. http://www.worldbank.org/urban/publicat/publicat.htm.

Ellis, P., C. Mandri-Perrott, and L. Tineo. 2011. "Strengthening Fiscal Transfers in Indonesia Using Output-Based Approach." OBA Approaches Note 40, Global Partnership on Output-Based Aid. http://www.gpoba.org/gpoba/node/562.

Fay, M., and M. Morrison. 2007. *Infrastructure in Latin America and the Caribbean: Recent Developments and Key Challenges*. Washington, DC: World Bank.

Hanly-Forde, J., G. Homsy, K. Lieberknecht, and R. Stone. "Transfer of Development Rights Programs Using the Market for Compensation and Preservation." http://government.cce.cornell.edu.

Hummel, G. 2010. "Presentation: Tax Increment Finance Seminar Understanding Your TIF Statute; Inside Financing—TIF Bond Issuance and Structure." Case Studies, Bryan Cave LLP. May 5. Accessed April 4, 2011.

The Integrated Mass Transit Systems Project. 2004. May 14. http://documents .worldbank.org/curated/en/2009/07/10836986/colombia-second-additional-loan-integrated-mass-transit-systems-project.

International Council of Shopping Centers, and Council of Development Finance Agencies. 2007. "Tax Increment Finance Best Practices Reference Guide." http://www.icsc.org/government/CDFA.pdf.

Kalmanovitz, S., and L. E. Enrique. 2006. *La agricultura colombiana en el siglo XX*. Bogotá: Fondo de Cultura Económica.

Ochoa, O. B., E. D. Oscar, J. Hernández, and M. Montaña. 2011. "Evaluating the Practice of Betterment Levies in Colombia: The Experience of Bogotá and Manizales." Working Paper, Lincoln Institute of Land Policy, Cambridge, MA.

Ochoa, O. B., and E. D. Trujillo. 2010. *Effects of Land Policy on the Price of Undeveloped Urban Land in Colombia: The Cases of Bogotá, Medellín and Pereira*. Cambridge, MA: Lincoln Institute of Land Policy.

Perry, G., and M. Olivera. 2009. "El impacto del petróleo y la minería en el desarrollo regional y local en Colombia." CAF Working Papers 2009/06, Corporación Andina de Fomento, Caracas.

Peterson, G. E. 2009. "Unlocking Land Values to Finance Urban Infrastructure." Trends and Policy Options 7, World Bank, Washington, DC.

PPIAF (Public-Private Infrastructure Advisory Facility) Impact Stories. 2011. "PPIAF helps Peruvian Sub-Nationals Tap Financial Markets." November. http://www.ppiaf.org/ppiaf/sites/ppiaf.org/files/publication/PPIAF-Impact-Stories-Peru-SNTA_0.pdf.

Sanchez, F., and C. Gutierrez. 1994. *La Descentralización Fiscal en América Latina: Problemas y Perspectivas. El Caso de Colombia.* Washington, DC: Banco Interamericano de Desarrollo.

Sanchez F., C. Gutierrez Sourdis, and J. C. Parra. 1995. "Transferencias Intergubernamentales y Comportamiento Fiscal de Los entes Territoriales. Una Aproximación Economotrica." *Coyuntura Economica* 24: 89–109.

Steffensen, J. 2010. *Performance-Based Grant Systems, Concept and International Experience.* New York: UN Capital Development Fund.

Support to the National Urban Transit Program Project. 2011. June. http://documents.worldbank.org/curated/en/2011/06/15639500/colombia-support-national-urban-transport-program-project-colombia-proyecto-de-apoyo-al-programa-nacional-de-transporte-urbano.

Uribe, M. C. 2009. "Bogota's Betterment Levy PLANEACIÓN—Secretaría Distrital de Planeación Presentation." Bangalore, September 14. http://indiausp.org/brookings/Bogota-Betterment-Levy.pdf.

Walls, M., and V. McConnell. 2007. *Transfer of Development Rights in U.S. Communities Evaluating Program Design, Implementation, and Outcomes.* Washington, DC: Resources for the Future.

Weber, R. N., and L. Goddeeris. 2007. *Tax Increment Financing: Process and Planning Issues.* Cambridge, MA: Lincoln Institute of Land Policy.

World Bank. 2004. *Recent Economic Developments in Infrastructure (REDI).* Washington, DC: World Bank.

———. 2005. "Output-based Aid: Supporting Infrastructure Delivery Through Explicit and Performance-based Subsidies." OBA Working Paper Series 4, World Bank, Washington, DC. March.

———. 2008a. *Infraestructura Logística y de Calidad para la Competitividad de Colombia.* Washington, DC: World Bank.

———. 2008b. *Colombia: Inputs for Sub-Regional Competitiveness Policies.* Washington, DC: World Bank, PREM-LAC.

———. 2009. *Colombia Decentralization: Options and Incentives for Efficiency.* Washington, DC: World Bank.